"Allison has written a con   ...1
Gulf War. Students of Histo.   v
welcome its thorough explora
President George H.W. Bush':   ...ational
coalition."

—**Spencer** ...   ...ia *Military Institute, USA*

In August 1990, Saddam Hussein's Iraqi forces boldly invaded and occupied neighboring Kuwait. It was a move that shocked the world and threatened the interests of those countries, such as the USA and the nations of Europe, that were dependent on oil from the Middle East. The ensuing Gulf War signaled, for many, a new dawn in warfare: one based upon lethal technology, low casualties, and quick, decisive victory.

Incorporating the latest scholarship, William Thomas Allison provides a concise overview of the origins, key events, and legacy of the first Gulf War as well as of the major issues and debates. He also examines the relevance of this war to other twentieth-century conflicts and to the ongoing situation in the region. .

William Thomas Allison is Professor of Military History at Georgia Southern University, USA. His previous publications include *Military Justice in Vietnam* (2006).

TWENTIETH-CENTURY WARS

General Editor: Jeremy Black

Published titles

Gerard DeGroot	*The First World War*
Francisco J. Romero Salvadó	*The Spanish Civil War*
Spencer C. Tucker	*The Second World War*
Peter Lowe	*The Korean War*
David L. Anderson	*The Vietnam War*
D. George Boyce	*The Falklands War*
William Maley	*The Afghanistan Wars* (2nd ed)
Robert Johnson	*The Iran-Iraq War*
William Thomas Allison	*The Gulf War, 1990–91*

Twentieth-Century Wars
Series Standing Order
ISBN 978–0–333–94629–9 hardback
ISBN 978–0–333–77101–3 paperback
(*outside North America only*)

You can receive future titles in this series as they are published by placing a standing order. Please contact your bookseller or, in case of difficulty, write to us at the address below with your name and address, the title of the series and the ISBN quoted above.

Customer Services Department, Macmillan Distribution Ltd, Houndmills, Basingstoke, Hampshire RG21 6XS, England

THE GULF WAR, 1990–91

William Thomas Allison

First published 2012 by
PALGRAVE MACMILLAN

Palgrave Macmillan in the UK is an imprint of Macmillan Publishers Limited, registered in England, company number 785998, of Houndmills, Basingstoke, Hampshire RG21 6XS.

Palgrave Macmillan in the US is a division of St Martin's Press LLC, 175 Fifth Avenue, New York, NY 10010.

Palgrave Macmillan is the global academic imprint of the above companies and has companies and representatives throughout the world.

Palgrave® and Macmillan® are registered trademarks in the United States, the United Kingdom, Europe and other countries.

ISBN 978–0–230–20264–1 hardback
ISBN 978–0–230–20265–8 paperback

This book is printed on paper suitable for recycling and made from fully managed and sustained forest sources. Logging, pulping and manufacturing processes are expected to conform to the environmental regulations of the country of origin.

A catalogue record for this book is available from the British Library.

A catalog record for this book is available from the Library of Congress.

10   9   8   7   6   5   4   3   2   1
21   20   19   18   17   16   15   14   13   12

Printed in China

Contents

Maps and Figures

Maps

Figures

Every effort has been made to trace the copyright holders of maps and figures, but if any have been inadvertently overlooked, the Publisher will be pleased to make the necessary arrangement at the first opportunity.

Preface

On August 2, 1990, Iraqi forces invaded and occupied Iraq's small but immensely wealthy Persian Gulf neighbor, Kuwait. While few anticipated the actual Iraqi attack, still fewer greeted images of Iraqi tanks rolling through the streets of Kuwait City with complete surprise. The invasion and subsequent war to liberate Kuwait, known as the Persian Gulf War of 1990–91 or simply the Gulf War, came at a unique moment in the twentieth century.[1] In the waning days of the Cold War, tensions between the United States and the Soviet Union had eased enough to signal what many hoped would be the dawn of a new world order. The Wilsonian ideal of nations acting collectively to right the wrongs of an evil transgressor fit perfectly in this utopian realignment of world politics. Realists, however, also had their day in the sun. The coalition of countries joining the United States in taking military action against Iraq did so for more than a Wilsonian ideal; they did so to protect their own respective national interests, not the least of which included oil, the life blood of the world economy.

Wars do not occur in a vacuum. Unique circumstances converge to persuade a nation-state to war on another in the hope of achieving a crucial political objective that leaders determine they cannot obtain by other means. Ideally, war ought to be the policy choice of last resort after exhausting all other options, and, as counterintuitive as it may seem, nations ought to undertake war rationally. History, however, offers countless examples of peoples and nations embarking on wars of choice with reckless impatience, often based upon faulty assumptions, to fight irrationally in pursuit of superfluous or unreachable objectives. As the great military theorists across history such as Sun Tzu and Carl von Clausewitz frequently warned, being the most extreme human activity war is fraught with unknown twists and turns, as well as unintended consequences. In this sense, the Gulf War differed from no other.

Nevertheless, the Gulf War had its unique moments. Seldom had there been such a diverse and unusual coalition of nations supporting a war in so many ways, as dozens of countries contributed troops, material, and money to oust Iraqi troops from Kuwait. Never had so much of the world watched a war unfold live on television through the advent of twenty-four-hour news channels born in the cable television revolution of the 1980s. Seldom had airpower played such a prominent if not decisive role, one that reignited the vociferous voices of airpower advocates and critics alike. Never before had environmental warfare been so maliciously applied, as Saddam Hussein did in ordering hundreds of oil wellheads set alight to bring on an acrid night in the desert sun while commanding his troops to open major pipeline valves at full flow to spill hundreds of thousands of barrels of crude oil into the Persian Gulf. And rarely had a national leader committed the fate of his nation through such a grave strategic miscalculation as Saddam Hussein did in deciding to invade and occupy Kuwait. These and other points indeed lead to some controversy when discussing the Gulf War, which may best be described as a war that marked the transition from the collapse of the international system of the Cold War to the much-hoped-for new world order of the post-Cold War world.

The Gulf War also highlighted the enormous potential of what many considered a revolution in warfare, one that announced the lethal marriage of information and technology on the battlefield. The Gulf War energized debate over the future of warfare and US military supremacy in the new world order. The technological wizardry and video game-like imagery displayed to television viewers throughout the war captured the popular imagination and delighted the defense establishment. The Gulf War had introduced a lexicon that was familiar to the military but that was mostly new to American popular culture. Terms like "stealth," "surgical strike," "Hummer," and "collateral damage" found their way into everyday usage.

Despite a second war initiated in 2003 by the American-led invasion of Iraq and the trial and execution of Saddam Hussein in 2006, for many Americans the Gulf War of 1990–91 may have replaced the Korean War of 1950–53 as the "forgotten war." Indeed, an entire generation of Americans now has no living memory of the conflict. Should the Gulf War be viewed as a crucial turning point in twentieth-century world history and modern military affairs? Or, should the conflict be seen as an aberration, a "one-off" that will likely not be repeated? With the departure of US forces from Iraq in 2011, following the 2003 United Nations (UN)-sanctioned invasion to topple Saddam Hussein, it is worthwhile to revisit the Gulf War, examine its origins, how it was fought, and its effects on the world today and beyond.

This book intends to do just that while providing readers with a general overview of the conflict. It begins with a review of the history of modern Iraq since its inception after World War I. It then examines the rise to power of Saddam Hussein and his subsequent decision to invade and occupy the Emirate of Kuwait in August 1990. Various chapters detail the US-led international response to the Iraqi invasion, the advent of DESERT SHIELD, and the failure of diplomacy to resolve the crisis. Then follow chapters describing the stunning DESERT STORM war to liberate Kuwait and the short- and long-term impact of the conflict. Maps and illustrations are included to give the reader context along with a chronology and glossary of terms. A list of suggested readings offers guidance for further inquiry.

Many generous people provided invaluable assistance in the conception, writing, and production of this book. I am most grateful to Jeremy Black, the editor of Palgrave Macmillan's *Twentieth Century Wars* series, for asking me to tackle this volume. He and the readers he arranged for the volume were constructive, professional, and wise in their guidance and advice. The wonderful and patient people at Palgrave Macmillan, especially Sonya Barker and Felicity Noble, offered direction, perspective, and gentle encouragement at just the right moments. My friends and colleagues gave praise, criticism, leads to sources, and ideas. Among the many who helped me, I am especially appreciative of Professor Vernon Egger at Georgia Southern University, Joe Frechette at the US Army Center of Military History, and Professor Tom Hughes at the US Air Force School for Air and Space Studies for their assistance and advice. My 2010–2011 year as a visiting professor at the School for Advanced Air and Space Studies, Maxwell Air Force Base, Alabama, greatly facilitated the researching and writing of this volume. My colleagues there, especially Professors Jim Forsyth, James Kiras, Mike Pavelec, Jim Tucci, John Sheldon, Hal Winton, Rich Muller, Kevin Holzimmer, Ev Dolman, Steve Wright, Derrick Frazier, and Steve Chiabotti, and the serving officers on the faculty, especially Colonel Mike Kometer, Lieutenant Colonel Ian Bryan, Colonel Jeff Kubiak, Colonel Suzanne Buono, Lieutenant Colonel John Davis, Colonel Ed Redman, and Commandant Colonel Tim Shultz, were of more help than they know in providing informal support, suggestions, and gracious collegiality during what was for me the best professional development opportunity of my career. I am also indebted to the fine staff at the Air University Library at Maxwell Air Force Base for their generous assistance. Finally, to my wife Jennifer, a special thank you for letting me be away for a year and for untold and unselfish support.

This is not the final word on the Gulf War, nor is it intended to be so. The Gulf War, though a short conflict in regard to time compared to most other American wars, was nonetheless a complex, uncertain, and dangerous war. Despite its apparent decisiveness, it was an imperfect war – one that should be studied, not forgotten.

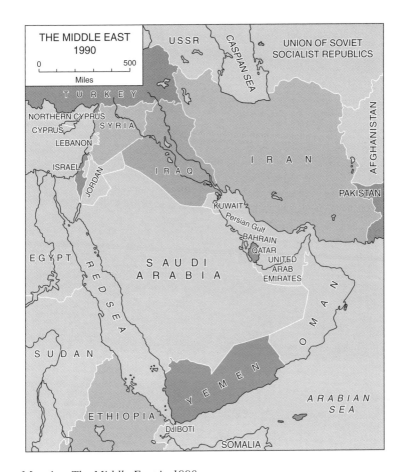

Map 1   *The Middle East in 1990.*
Source: United States Army Center of Military History.

1

Inventing the Middle East and Iraq

In the twentieth century, few regions of the world rivaled the Middle East in volatility and complexity. The intense diversity of culture, religion, geopolitics, and economics in the region made long-term stability difficult, as forces for progress routinely clashed with those resistant to change while those who craved power struggled to take it from those who ruled. The imperial designs of Western powers, the existence since 1947 of Israel as a Jewish state in a sea of Arab countries, the strategic interests (crude oil) of the United States and the Soviet Union during the Cold War and Arab nationalism compounded these tensions, and continue to do so in the early twenty-first century. Many hoped the end of the Cold War would bring opportunities finally to establish lasting peace in this volatile region. The predominant faith of the Middle East, Islam, in reality served only as a superficial unifier for the region; even the teachings of Muhammad provided inadequate common ground to resolve troubled relations between secular and non-secular states, state borders that defied traditional tribal and ethnic areas, and historical tensions between Sunni and Shia Muslims.

The Sunni and the Shia

The historical tensions between Sunni and Shia run deep indeed, dating back to the Prophet Muhammad's death in 632 CE. In the years following Muhammad's death, two major and divergent groups of his followers vied for the position of legitimate political successor to Muhammad as well as for the Prophet's religious legacy. Sunni followers of Muhammad believed in personal spiritual discovery of God's will through reading and following the Qur'an and other relevant Islamic texts. The

1

name Sunni originated from the Arabic word *as-sunnah*, loosely meaning "path" or "tradition." Those that followed the *sunnah* or "path" of Muhammad by living the Prophet's teachings and practices would find enlightenment. The early Sunnis had no use for an ecclesiastic class of priests or holy men and established their own mosques led by what was in essence a lay clergy of scholars who held positions through consensus rather than through any sort of formal appointing process. Sunnis also rejected the idea of an Imam who served as both religious and political leader of the Muslim world. Imams to Sunnis simply led prayers at the local mosque or served as caliph but were not the ultimate authorities on religious matters. Over time, Sunni scholars developed rituals and practices for the Sunni faithful to follow that became the Shari'a, which remains the principal handbook of laws for Sunni Muslims.

Shias gravitated to a more clerical if not dogmatic brand of Islam that unlike the more popular Sunni variant embraced a hierarchy of clergy whom the faithful relied upon to issue spiritual edicts and other pronouncements. Their Imams must also have divine authority, a direct link with God. While they share many Islamic practices with Sunnis, their belief in divine authority is a significant difference from that of the Sunnis, who take a more egalitarian approach to practicing their faith. Shias have remained a minority in Islam.

As the majority in this nascent but rapidly growing religion, Sunnis chose Muhammad's father-in-law Abu Bakr to succeed Muhammad as the first caliph, or leader, of the emerging Muslim world. Because Muhammad left no clear instructions as to his successor, Sunnis believed that the caliph should be elected by the Muslim community. Abu Bakr died in 634 CE to be succeeded by two other Sunni caliphs who led the Islamic conquest of what is today Syria, Egypt, and Iraq, achieved mainly under the caliphate of Umar ibn al-Khattab, who was assassinated in 644 CE. Umar's successor, Uthman ibn al-Affan, also met a violent end. Uthman's excessive practice of nepotism and overt favoritism toward Islamic elites in Mecca at the expense of the many converts to the new faith in recently conquered lands created many enemies. In 656 CE, violent protesters against Uthman's policies broke into his home to murder the caliph.

Uthman's successor, Ali ibn Abi Talib, would be the first Shia caliph. Common Muslims held Ali in high regard as well for his piety and loyalty to Muhammad as his skill and success as a warrior. His sometimes outspoken criticism of Uthman's policies and practices also endeared him to many Islamic faithful, especially the insurgents who ultimately deposed Uthman. Ali had been very close to Muhammad and was himself a cousin and son-in-law of the Prophet—Ali had married Muhammad's daughter Fatima. Despite his background and relationship to Muhammad, Ali's ascension to the caliphate caused dissension in the Muslim community. His popularity threatened the old guard of Sunnis and their position in Islamic society. Some alleged Ali had been complicit in Uthman's death. Those supporting Ali believed him to be the rightful successor to the Prophet who should have been the first caliph upon Muhammad's death in 632 CE.

Ali's followers became known as Shias or Shia, a term referring to partisans or supporters of one side or another in some dispute. Shi'ism eventually evolved to describe those who favored Ali and a variant of Islam different from that of the Sunnis. The Shias have also held firm to their belief that their religious leaders should be descendants of Ali. Ali's caliphate was short but eventful. An extended civil war broke out between Ali and Sunni supporters of Uthman, including Muhammad's youngest wife A'isha, and this then expanded to include one of Uthman's relatives, Mu'awiya of Syria, who, like Uthman, was of the Umayyad clan. In 661 CE, Ali was assassinated, opening the door for Mu'awiya to become caliph. Now martyred, Ali was interred in Najaf, which soon joined Medina and Mecca as the third holiest site in the Shia world. Ali, in the view of many Shias, had given his life for God. Such sacrifice, for many Muslims, revealed martyrdom as the path to heaven. Ali's youngest son, Husayn bin Ali, fought Mu'awiya's son and successor Yazid in a great battle near Karbala in 680 CE, where Husayn and his followers were slaughtered. For Shias, Karbala now became a most holy site, and it remains so today. Along with Karbala, Najaf too became a Shia holy site and education center, drawing Shia pilgrims from throughout the Muslim world. By the nineteenth century, Shias dominated this region that would become southern Iraq, as they do today.

The succession of the caliphs as well as the legitimacy of religious leaders dominated much of the conflict in the Muslim world. The Sunnis for the most part tolerated the dynastic rule of the Umayyad caliphs, believing that such toleration was preferable to the violence and upheaval of revolting against a corrupt Umayyad caliph. If familial lineage was the best determinant of legitimacy, then the Hashemites had an advantage because Muhammad himself had been of the Hashemite clan (Hashemites may hold the title "sharif" as a direct descendant of Muhammad). The Abbasids, who deposed the Umayyads in 750 CE, traced their Hashemite lineage to one of Muhammad's uncles, Abbas ibn Abd al-Muttalib. The Fatimids, too, claimed a blood tie, through Ali's wife Fatima.

Shias often found themselves under threat by the Sunni caliph, who brutally put down any challenge to their authority. The Abbasids, for example, assassinated numerous Shia Imams whom they considered threats against Abbasid rule. The last of these Imams, the Eleventh, was murdered in 874 CE. Those Shias who believe these eleven Imams to be the true carriers of Muhammad's message are known as the Twelvers—they believe that the son of the Eleventh Imam, the Hidden or Twelfth Imam, will return as a the messiah-like Mahdi who will sit in judgment of humankind, much like the return of Jesus Christ in Christian doctrine. The Twelvers remain the potent religious if not political force among Shias. The current Iraqi Shia leader Muqtada al-Sadr, for example, derives his lineage from the original eleven Imams and his direct lineage from Muhammad's family.

Thus began decades followed by centuries of tense rule in the Muslim world. Umayyad caliphs fell to Abbasids, and so on, while through conquest Islam spread throughout the Middle East, North Africa, and ultimately into parts of southern Europe. The expanse of territory falling under Islamic rule contributed to the political and religious decentralization of the Muslim world, as caliphs ruled from Cordoba, Cairo, Baghdad, and other cities. The Abbasids, for example, held either political or religious authority from roughly 750 CE through 1258 CE, during which many of the cultural, scientific, and literary contributions of the Muslim world occurred, leading scholars to consider this period as the Golden Age of Islam.

Such aggressive and dramatic expansion of this relative newcomer to the Western religious world threatened the spiritual hegemony of Catholic Europe. By the end of the seventh century, the Holy Land lay under Muslim rule, though in their tolerance of Christianity Muslim leaders generously allowed Christian pilgrims to travel unhindered to Jerusalem and other sites. Spain and the Byzantine Empire appeared under threat by advancing Muslim forces. Alarmed, in 1095 CE Pope Urban II declared that the Christian kings of Europe must return the Holy Land to Christian rule. Thus began the First Crusade, which restored Christian sovereignty over the Holy Land for almost fifty years. For the next 150 years, crusading armies of Christian knights battled with Muslim armies for control of the Holy Land. The barbarity with which the Christians fought and ruled during their Crusades to destroy Islam left among Muslims a permanent scar of hatred of the West.

As the dynamic of conflict between Christians and Muslims became entrenched, so too did conflict between Sunnis and Shias within the Muslim world. In 1453, Constantinople fell to the Ottoman Turks, thus

finally putting to rest the Christian Byzantine Empire, which had survived the fifth-century collapse of the western half of the Roman Empire.
The Ottomans established a Sunni empire that stretched from Istanbul
(their new name for Constantinople), to Mesopotamia (much of modern Iraq), to North Africa. Conflict with Shias, now ensconced in Persia
(modern Iran), raged for three centuries, as Sunni Ottomans tried to
invade Shia Persia while Shia Persians attempted to conquer Sunni-
dominated Mesopotamia. Sunni Ottomans desecrated Shia shrines in
Karbala and Najaf, while Shia Persians executed thousands of Sunnis
in Baghdad. In 1733, Shia Persians laid siege to Baghdad, during which
over 100,000 Sunni inhabitants starved to death. In the nineteenth century, Ottomans assaulted Karbala, where they allegedly slaughtered over
30,000 Persian Shias. The memory and oral tradition of these massacres
long outlived those who witnessed them, regardless on which side one
may have been.

As the Ottoman Empire became less dogmatic and more bureau-
cratic by the mid-nineteenth century, Ottoman leaders found it more
beneficial to the empire to maintain internal stability than to let the
Sunni–Shia blood feud continue unabated, as it had by this point for
centuries. Without question Sunnis continued to dominate government
positions throughout the empire, but the Ottomans made efforts to separate ethnic groups as much as possible to maintain order and stability.
In what is today Iraq, the Ottoman Turks established provinces centered
around Mosul, Baghdad, and Basra for the Kurds, Sunnis, and Shias,
respectively.[1]

The Imperial Powers

During the nineteenth century, the region returned to prominence for
European powers, which finally began taking full advantage of the area
as a natural conduit to imperial possessions in Africa and the Far East.
The British-built Suez Canal, followed later in the twentieth century by
railroads across what is today Jordan, Syria, and Iraq, provided commercial access to the Middle East and beyond, but only if Western powers
secured the area from often ambitious and warring tribes through milita-
rized imperial rule. The Ottoman Empire, too, stood in the way of these
grand schemes. Great Britain, France, and to a lesser extent Germany,
invested varying degrees of blood and treasure in the region, as they vied
for influence in the area, even within the Ottoman Empire. For these
imperial players, trade and empire, then later oil, drove the "great game"

in this increasingly important part of the world. In the early twentieth century, bureaucrats in European foreign offices developed the idea of the Middle East as a distinct part of the world to differentiate the area from the Far East (China) and the Near East (the Ottoman Empire, then later Turkey). US Naval Captain Alfred Thayer Mahan may have coined the term in 1902, but some scholars suggest that "Middle East" had found its way into common usage in the West before that time. In its original form, this Eurocentric notion of a "Middle East" generally included the mostly arid region from Morocco in the west, across Mesopotamia and Persia, all the way to Afghanistan in the east.[2]

So important had the Middle East become that during World War I the region became a significant theater of the war. In part because the Ottoman Empire allied with Germany but more so because of competing imperial interests in the region, Great Britain and France used the outbreak of war as an excuse to drive the Ottomans out of the Middle East. The Ottomans, quite naturally, relished the opportunity to do the same to the British and French for the purpose of retaining control of the region. While the scale of fighting in the Middle East during the war nowhere near approached that of the Western Front in Europe, the belligerents expended significant resources and personnel in these difficult and complex desert campaigns.

British and French post-war plans for the Middle East ran counter to Arab desires for independence and freedom from Western imperialism. The still present suspicion of the West among many peoples of the Middle East is understandable considering the ambitious game of empire played by the Western powers and their near-constant meddling in Middle Eastern affairs through much of the twentieth century and beyond. Great Britain in particular had definite plans for the area after the defeat of the Ottoman Empire. An interdepartmental working group, established by Prime Minister H. H. Asquith in 1915, outlined for the British government its goals for the region. Known as the de Bunsen Committee, the group included Sir Mark Sykes, a member of the House of Commons and a frequent traveler to the Middle East, and General H. H. Kitchener's special representative on the committee. As the only member of the de Bunsen Committee with personal experience in the region, Sykes held sway over the group and became one of the British government's principal Middle East hands. He had earlier been one of the strongest supporters of the Ottoman Empire within the British government, but under Kitchener's influence, Sykes abandoned that position completely to become the principal proponent of a British-dominated Middle East. The committee's report, delivered to Asquith in June 1915, proposed that the Ottoman Empire be divided with little regard to Ottoman administrative boundaries into five provinces: Syria, Palestine, Armenia, Anatolia, and Jazirah-Iraq. The committee also proposed a road built from Haifa on the Mediterranean to Iraq and possible linking with the port at Basra (which the British occupied in 1915), along with British oversight of these five semi-autonomous provinces, which would give Britain unfettered control of the region and along with the Suez Canal unhindered access to India.[3]

To facilitate the political side of these plans, the British government established an Arab Bureau based in Cairo upon which Sykes would exercise great influence. With the failure of the British Dardanelles campaign in 1916, Sykes, Kitchener, and representatives of the British Foreign Office had to seek another military means to defeat the Ottomans. With defense of the Suez Canal occupying a significant part of Britain's limited forces in the region, the British sought allies to join their fight against the Ottoman Turks. Early in the war, Great Britain made assurances to Hussein bin Ali, the Hashemite Sharif of Mecca who claimed direct lineage from the Prophet Muhammad, of the creation of an independent Arab state existing amid British and French-controlled territories. Correspondence between the British High Commissioner in Cairo, Sir Edward McMahon, and Hussein indicated British support for an Arab state that would include parts of Syria, including Damascus. McMahon recognized such a state would anger the French but was willing to accept such a risk for greater British objectives in the region. Still, McMahon cleverly left vague British commitments that might conflict with French interests, suggesting that the Arabs would have to be content with a territory in the Hejaz known simply as "Arabia." Hussein, too, recognized the potential conflict with French interests and went so far as to warn McMahon that if necessary his forces would fight France for control of Damascus. In exchange for British support, Hussein promised to lead an Arab revolt against the Ottomans, who reportedly planned to depose Hussein at the end of the war. Hussein, perhaps, had nothing to lose in his dealings with McMahon, which became known as the controversial McMahon–Hussein Correspondence.[4]

The idea of an Arab revolt was nevertheless not new, nor was the concept of some sort of Arab state. The Arabs as a whole, however, were not unified in their own objectives, nor were they all behind the idea of an Arab state ruled by Hussein. An independent Arab kingdom may have been wanted by Hussein, but many in Syria wanted their own autonomy and were extremely wary of French and British intentions. The Arabs in Iraq, too, wanted independence and feared possible annexation by India.

Despite these divisions, however, the Arab Bureau remained convinced that an Arab revolt would best serve British purposes.[5]

French interests in the region centered on Syria. An odd alliance of French political, commercial, and religious interests kept the concept of a French presence in the Middle East at the forefront of French politics. The face of this "Syria Party" in the French Senate was Pierre-Etienne Flandin, a young and ambitious politician who believed France had both a historic and cultural mandate in Syria that dated back to the Crusades. Claiming France had been instrumental in developing the "France of the Near East" for centuries, Flandin and his supporters proposed a single French-controlled state consisting of both Syria and Palestine. The "Syria Party" claimed the region held great potential economic wealth, so much so that France could ill afford to let Great Britain gain control of it. Moreover, controlling Damascus, one of the holiest cities in the Islamic world, would also give France a significant strategic edge in the region, so argued Flandin and his adherents. Flandin and the "Syria Party" found their champion in the French government in François Georges Picot, a staunch colonialist in the French Foreign Ministry.

For British and French forces on the one side, and Ottoman forces on the other, the various tribes across the region were the key components of their war strategies. Money, in the form of gold, proved most crucial in buying tribal allegiance to one side or the other. While building an actual army of various Arab tribes ultimately fell short of British and French expectations, using bands of Arab fighters as guerrillas to destroy railroads and attack enemy outposts proved especially effective against the Ottoman Turks. For example, a unique British officer, T.E. Lawrence, made famous by reporter and promoter Lowell Thomas as "Lawrence of Arabia," proved particularly successful at organizing Arab guerrilla raids against Turkish outposts along the Hejaz railway during the last year and a half of the war. For Great Britain and France, organizing and arming the Arabs came at more than a financial cost. Bucking British and French imperialism and the harsh rule of the Ottoman Turks, a variety of Arab nationalist movements gained momentum during the war. Organizing Arab forces to fight the Turks now involved the risk of having to fight those same forces later. Both Great Britain and France offered Arab tribes veiled pledges of pseudo-independence and dangled promises to powerful Arab families to enthrone them as the new royal families of post-war Arabia, all in exchange for revolting against Turkish rule. While militarily effective from the Allied viewpoint, the so-called Arab Revolt of 1916 revealed the deep fissures among the Arab tribes, leading many

Social-Darwinist Westerners to conclude that the peoples of the Middle East had little capacity for self-governance.[6]

The Sykes–Picot Agreement of 1916, however, undercut Arab aspirations and took the "great game" to an entirely new level from that of the de Bunsen report and the McMahon–Hussein Correspondence. Negotiated by Mark Sykes and François Georges Picot without Arab input and publically unknown until released by the Bolsheviks in Russia in late 1917, the document divided the Middle East between France and Great Britain, with some concessions to the then Imperial Russia. An embarrassing revelation for both the British and French governments, the agreement gave France direct control over an area covering Beirut to the south and Adana to the north while ensuring French influence over a large swath of territory from Damascus in the south, Aleppo to the north, and Mosul to the east. Great Britain would gain direct control over much of modern Iraq, including Baghdad and Basra, and modern Kuwait, while maintaining a sphere of influence from the Egyptian border to the west, north to Amman, then south and east toward Baghdad and the Persian Gulf. Both France and Great Britain acknowledged the possibility of an independent Arab state existing within their designated areas of influence though not in their zones of direct control.

Negotiating the agreement had been an extremely sensitive process. In London, the well-established Picot and experienced Arthur Nicolson, who was soon replaced by the inexperienced Sykes, began their delicate talks in November 1915. Picot went to London intent on gaining French control of as much Mediterranean coastline of the Ottoman Empire as possible and a Lebanon expanded beyond its current 1915 conception. As for Syria, Picot realized directly that ruling such a vast swath of territory would quickly exhaust French resources if not patience. Instead, Picot favored indirect French rule through Arab puppet governments. To achieve his intentions, Picot tried to convince his British counterparts that he wanted direct control over all of Syria. Through faint compromise, he could "settle" for his true objectives.

For the British, Sykes, working under the direction of Kitchener, wanted the French to indeed have direct control over all of Syria. The British rightly feared the expansionist tendencies of the then Imperial Russia, which would certainly gain some territory from the partition of the Ottoman Empire. Having France control a line of territory from the Mediterranean east to Mesopotamia would establish a French buffer zone between the British and Russian spheres of influence in the Middle East. Sykes was even prepared to sacrifice British claims on Mosul to get this French protective belt into the final agreement. The British also wanted the French to support an Egyptian offensive and an invasion of the Ottoman Empire through the port of Alexandretta. For his part, Sykes sincerely believed British demands were in sync with Arab hopes for an independent state. In reality, Kitchener and the British used their support of Arab interests to promote their own.

The final 1916 Sykes–Picot Agreement reflected what both Sykes and Picot actually wanted. The British desire for a *cordon sanitaire* synchronized perfectly with French desires to have influence over Syria. On the military end, Kitchener had to settle for Acre and Haifa in place of Alexandretta to use as ports for his campaign against the Turks. Thus, neither France nor Great Britain controlled the area they loosely called Palestine. For the Arab nationalists, the Sykes–Picot Agreement left little doubt that Great Britain and France intended to solidify if not expand their imperial hold on the Middle East.[7]

The Balfour Declaration of November 2, 1917 complicated matters further by openly promising British support of a Jewish homeland in Palestine, a concept which irritated both the French and the Arabs. The brainchild of British Foreign Minister Arthur Balfour, the document (actually a letter from Balfour to leading Zionist Lionel Walter Rothschild) gave a dramatic boost to the Zionist movement both in Europe and in the United States, even though it called for a "national home" rather than an actual independent state in Palestine for the Jewish people. American Zionists such as Louis Brandeis had pressured President Woodrow Wilson to be more outspoken in his support of the movement. In a meeting with Wilson in Washington in April 1917, on the heels of the US declaration of war against Germany, Balfour broached the idea of the United States administering Palestine rather than the international oversight of the territory called for in the Sykes–Picot agreement. Wilson, along with his erstwhile advisor "Colonel" Edward House, demurred, not wanting to get involved in what both men feared would be a fertile place for war among imperial powers. Wilson, however, did support Balfour's idea of support for a Jewish state, and publically said so in September 1918. Those against the declaration, such as William Yale, warned that a Jewish state could only be established through war and if successfully created would then have to survive amid a people violently opposed to its existence.[8]

The Birth of Modern Iraq

Both the Sykes–Picot Agreement and the Balfour Declaration, the former intended to be a secret division of spoils and the latter a public statement of policy supporting the Zionist movement, gave Arab peoples plenty of cause to question British and French intentions and doubt their promises of independence and self-rule. Ultimately, the collapse of the Ottoman Empire and post-war settlements decided the fate of the peoples in the region. These and other settlements created much of the modern Middle East, including the modern state of Iraq. By the early 1920s, only Iran (formerly Persia), the Kingdom of Hejaz (consolidated in 1932 under a monarchy ruled by the House of Saud to become Saudi Arabia), and Yemen obtained true independence. The remaining states, owing their borders to the arbitrary actions of distant British and French bureaucrats drawing maps to reflect their nations' respective interests, fell under either the new League of Nations mandate system or direct British or French colonial administration as established by various agreements concluded following the war to deal with the demise of the Ottoman Empire. Negotiated separately from the Versailles settlement of 1919, in these talks Great Britain, France, Italy, sometimes Japan, and the Ottoman Empire and its successor spent much of 1920 through 1923 deciding the fate of the Turks while pursuing their own imperialist ambitions in the region. First in London, then San Remo, then, so it seemed at the time, finally at Sèvres, the Western powers filled their plates at the Ottoman buffet. The San Remo agreement of April 1920 implemented much of what Sykes and Picot had agreed to in 1916. The Treaty of Sèvres, concluded in August 1920 to carve up what remained of Anatolia, recognized the Kingdom of Hejaz and the creation of an independent Armenia, turned over control of the Ottoman Empire's finances to the Western signatories, and confirmed the "zone of influence" for France over Syria while declaring Kurdistan's fate would be decided by referendum. Great Britain's "zone of influence" had been largely determined by the San Remo agreement in April 1920. While Oman and Kuwait fell under direct British rule, Palestine, Trans-Jordan, and Iraq became British mandates under the League of Nations mandate system.[9]

Outside of Egypt, Iraq became the principal focus of British attention in the Middle East. British forces first entered Baghdad in 1917, remaining there for the duration of the war and then beyond. British bureaucrats replaced Sunni bureaucrats, breeding resentment toward the British among the Sunnis due to the resulting increased unemployment. Having expected liberation after the collapse of the Ottoman Empire, the people of Baghdad found themselves again lorded over by another foreign imperial power. This time however, in the new state of Iraq, the British established a constitutional monarchy in 1921 under the son of Sharif Hussein, Prince Faisal, whom the French had ousted as king

of Syria in 1920. At a March 1921 conference in Cairo, British Colonial Secretary Winston Churchill, with the approving nod of Faisal's
friend and comrade-in-arms T.E. Lawrence, handpicked Faisal to be
King of Iraq, believing correctly that Faisal's pro-British sympathies
and Hashemite roots both served British interests and assuming incor-
rectly that this gave Faisal legitimacy among the diverse peoples in Iraq.
Because he was an outsider, Faisal was proclaimed king through a clearly
rigged referendum that gave him 96 percent of the votes. Now king,
Faisal had to govern, under the watchful eye of a British high commissioner, a new mandate state whose borders included Kurds, Shia
Muslims, and Sunni Muslims.[10]

Oil had much to do with the way Great Britain chose to administer
Palestine, Trans-Jordan, and Iraq. In the 1910s, the British Royal Navy
converted from coal to oil to fuel its mighty fleet. Coal had been plentiful
for the Royal Navy, as Great Britain, like the United States, had a seemingly endless supply of coal within its own shores. The shift to more
efficient oil, however, presented a potentially debilitating problem—
Great Britain, unlike the United States, had no oil. From oil fields in Iran,
and now Iraq, Great Britain needed secure pipelines and transportation
routes to the Persian Gulf, the Red Sea, and across to the Mediterranean
to provide fuel for the Royal Navy, the backbone of the British Empire.
To the British, constitutional monarchies under their tutelage provided
the best chance for security and stability.[11]

The concept of an independent Kurdish state had fallen by the way-
side in the rush of mandates and monarchies following the World
War I settlements. The 1923 Treaty of Lausanne formally ended the
Ottoman Empire and replaced the now defunct Treaty of Sèvres. In the
Lausanne agreement, however, the new Turkish government largely
confirmed the stipulations the Ottomans had agreed to in the Treaty
of Sèvres. When drawing the borders of the new Iraq, Great Britain
included much of the Kurdish region in the new state because of the
immense oil reserves near Mosul. This, however, left the Kurdish people divided among Turkey, Iraq, and Iran. Kurdish nationalists, bridled
under Ottoman, then British, and now Hashemite rule, understandably
clamored for self-determination, so much so that the Iraqi government
maintained only nominal control of the Kurdish region of northern Iraq,
sometimes referred to as Kurdistan. Open rebellion by the Kurds often
required the Iraqi army to use brute force with the occasional help of
British forces, especially the Royal Air Force. Such regional and ethnic nationalism as that of the Kurds made unifying a national Iraq quite
difficult.[12]

Under Ottoman rule, Kuwait had been part of the Basra administrative district governing much of the southern region of what was now the new Kingdom of Iraq. Under the local rule of the al Sabah family since the 1700s, the port of Kuwait had been only nominally under Ottoman control. The al Sabahs courted British protection in the 1890s, when a proposed railway from Berlin to Baghdad exposed further German influence on the Ottoman Empire and German desires in the region.[13] Not trusting Ottoman assurances, the al Sabahs sought protection elsewhere. Ever eager to extend influence in the region to maintain the link between the Suez Canal and India, the British eagerly concluded an agreement with the al Sabah emir in 1899. In 1913, Kuwait City and its strategically located port gained mutual recognition as a semiautonomous enclave through an agreement with both Great Britain and the Ottoman Empire, but when hostilities erupted between the Western powers and the Ottoman Empire in 1915, the British quickly brought Kuwait under its sole protection.

The borders of Kuwait that evolved out of the post-war agreements can be attributed to Gertrude Bell, an expert on the region akin to if not greater than T.E. Lawrence. Working with Percy Cox as "oriental secretary" in Baghdad following the war, Bell helped draw the borders for Iraq. To maintain Kuwaiti autonomy under British influence, Bell expanded the tiny emirate at the expense of Iraqi access to the Persian Gulf. Bell gave much of the coastline to Kuwait, leaving Iraq with access to the gulf from Basra via the Shatt al-Arab waterway, which would play a prominent role in the Iran–Iraq War in the 1980s. Bell had in essence created a buffer zone between Iraq and the new Kingdom of Saudi Arabia, drawing boundaries based upon known and suspected oil reserves rather than any concern for tribal territories or religious (Sunni or Shia) differences. Religion entered British calculations only in that Bell and others believed Sunnis to be more reasonable than the often emotional and erratic Shias, and to be more reliable to govern under British supervision and to maintain control over the immense oil reserves in the region. Once part of the Ottoman province of Basra, Kuwait under the al Sabah emirs now stood apart under British rule, not gaining independence until 1961.[14]

In Trans-Jordan, Great Britain established Faisal's brother Abdullah as king. Iraq remained a British protectorate until 1932, when Great Britain gave Iraq nominal independence through a constitutional monarchy under King Faisal. Meanwhile, new oil discoveries across the region, including in Kuwait, Iran, and Saudi Arabia, enhanced the Middle East's strategic importance to the West, especially Great Britain and increasingly the United States, which though at the time the largest oil producer in the world nonetheless had several oil companies with interests in the Middle East.

Iraq's independence in 1932 initiated decades of political instability for this artificial state created to serve British interests. King Faisal worked to incorporate Shia and Kurdish participation across the Iraqi government to unify Iraq, but tribal tensions and the increasingly stratified class structure of this developing country stifled progress. The National Assembly became the protector of propertied interests, while the Iraqi army devolved into a haven for Pan-Arabists and ideologues. Faisal's successors instituted policies that further alienated the propertyless classes, while the expected boom from oil revenues failed to materialize until decades later—both exacerbated tensions among Sunnis, Shias, and Kurds, and widened the prosperity gap between the few elites and the great masses.[15]

These heated tensions often boiled over into violence and frequent coups. The British-trained and equipped Iraqi army, for example, quickly and brutally put down an uprising by Assyrian Christians in Mosul in 1933. King Ghazi, crowned upon Faisal's death in 1933, suffered repeated coup attempts against his governments throughout his six-year reign. The most serious uprising occurred in October 1936, when reformers demanding land redistribution and broader Shia political participation overthrew the government of Prime Minister Yasin al-Hashimi. A new government under the leadership of Hikmat Suleiman and General Bakr Sidqi attempted to implement reforms but lasted only through 1937, when Suleiman resigned after reactionary factions in the army murdered Sidqi.

By 1941, the Iraqi army, in particular the officer corps, had become a key force in Iraqi politics. Many in the army espoused Pan-Arabism and Arab nationalist ideologies and envisioned Iraq as the historic if not natural leader of the Arab world. Supporters of Pan-Arabism hoped to politically unify all Arab countries, an idea that dated back to the Arab Revolt. Similarly, Arab nationalists considered all Arab peoples as a single nation and encouraged Arab history, culture, and language. Both were largely anti-Western and sought a new golden age of Arab culture and Islamic religion. Recognizing the percolating influence of Pan-Arabism and Arab nationalism, no Iraqi politician dared undertake radical action, especially a coup, without the support of the Iraqi army. The army forced the government of Jamil al-Madfai to resign in 1938, which brought in a new government under the experienced Nuri al-Said, whom many officers in the army believed shared their Pan-Arab vision.

A consummate politician, al-Said became sovereign in all but name upon King Ghazi's death in an automobile accident in 1939. Prince Abdullah acted as regent for the new child king, Faisal II, relying greatly on al-Said for political guidance. Interestingly, before his death, King Ghazi had approved plans for annexing Kuwait, whose exclusion from Iraq by British politicians and cartographers had never been fully recognized by the Iraqi government.[16]

World War II further complicated Iraqi politics. Great Britain naturally expected Iraq to give its full support to the Allies, but al-Said's government proclaimed neutrality in the conflict while its actions made it appear pro-German. With al-Said's electoral defeat in March 1940, the new government of Rashid Ali al-Gailani came to power with hopes of taking advantage of the war in Europe to oust the British finally from Iraq. The British, however, recognized Iraq's strategic value and could ill afford to allow the region to fall into German hands. British pressure on al-Gailani initiated a revolt against British interference in April 1941. With the support of Pan-Arabist zealots in the army, led by a small group of officers known as the Golden Square, al-Gailani forced Prince Abdullah and the young King Faisal II, both of whom many Iraqis considered simple stooges of the British, out of Iraq. The British responded with military intervention, landing troops originally destined for Malaya, near Basra, in late April 1941. After fighting their way through Ramadi, Fallujah, and other places that would become so familiar to Americans in the early 2000s, British forces took control of Baghdad on May 31, 1941. With King Faisal II and al-Said restored to power, the British secured a mostly symbolic Iraqi declaration of war against Germany and Italy. The British army maintained a sizable occupation force in Iraq to ensure oil transport and movement of supplies to the southern parts of the Soviet Union and to preserve a presence in Great Britain's former mandate. Al-Said's government tried and executed the leaders of the Golden Square. Al-Gailani, however, escaped to Germany.[17]

The end of World War II did not end British influence in Iraq. Great Britain tried to enhance its power over the Iraqi government through a new treaty, signed in 1948 by al-Said, giving the British until 1973 to withdraw their military forces from Iraq. Though negotiated in secret, the Treaty of Portsmouth sparked violent protests across Iraq, especially in the capital city of Baghdad. Pan-Arabists and an increasingly strong Iraqi nationalist movement bristled at the prospect of imperial domination, while prolonged poor economic conditions among the vast masses of Iraqis provided explosive fuel for rebellion. Al-Said responded with brutal tactics, using the Iraqi army and British assistance to put down the

so-called Wathba Rebellion. Ever the politician, al-Said offered compromise to the nationalists by denouncing the Treaty of Portsmouth, an act
that bought him time with his detractors and signaled the weakening
British influence in Iraq. Al-Said's increasingly dictatorial and secre-
tive rule, however, only deepened resentment both among rural folk and
nationalist elites, and adversely affected his relationship with the army.[18]

Crisis after crisis erupted in the Middle East, making more difficult
the already daunting set of domestic problems with which al-Said and
King Faisal II had to contend. Support for Arab nationalism drove much
of Iraq's response to regional issues. The Arab-Israeli War of 1948, for
example, gave Iraq its first real opportunity to perform on the regional
stage. Allied with forces from Syria, Jordan, Lebanon, and other Arab
states, Iraq contributed 18,000 troops to the Arab fight to destroy the
Israeli state after the Israelis declared independence on May 14, 1948, in
anticipation of the expiration of the British mandate over Palestine. Iraqi
forces faced the Israelis in May 1948 at Zefat, north of the Sea of Galilee,
and then at Gesher, near the Jordan River, but they were beaten back by
stiff Israeli resistance in both instances. Just weeks later, the Iraqis held
the city of Janin for several days in the face of an Israeli offensive. The
Israelis took the city but lost it to a combined force of Iraqis and troops
of the Arab Legion. Iraqi casualties were substantial, but their sacrifice
gave Jordon control of Janin, which it maintained until the Israelis retook
the city in the 1967 Six Day War. While Israel survived the brief but
intense 1948–49 war, Iraqi forces had made a mixed contribution to the
Arab cause. They had fought well when attacked and in the broader picture had facilitated Jordan's occupation of the West Bank of Palestine,
but critics charged that the Iraqis lacked initiative and fighting spirit, to
which ground commanders responded that without clear guidance from
their superiors in Baghdad, they often simply stayed put in static positions. Poor discipline, lack of tactical skill, and careless maintenance of
weapons and equipments gave the Iraqi high command plenty to improve
upon after the war.[19]

Because of the war emergency, the Iraqi government declared martial law, which helped as well to curtail the remaining Wathba protests
against the Treaty of Portsmouth. The war also gave several within the
Iraqi government the excuse to carry out a pogrom against Jews in Iraq.
In addition to curbing civil rights and deporting hundreds of Jews, Iraqi
officials, notably Minister of Defense Sadiq al-Bassam, ordered the torture and execution of untold numbers of Jews suspected of organizing
aid and other support for the new state of Israel. International outcry
against these acts and the Israeli defeat of Arab forces compelled Prince

Abdullah, as regent, to form a new government, once again relying upon Nuri al-Said to act as a "strongman" to bring both Iraqi politics and Iraq's diverse population under control through what amounted to authoritarian rule. Such tendencies became the norm for whoever governed Iraq.[20]

Enter the United States

As the Cold War intensified in the 1950s, Iraq sought security in multilateral defense pacts. While the Arab League provided some assurances and had been the umbrella organization for fighting Israel in 1948, it existed under politically fragile circumstances. Established in 1945, the Arab League consisted of Lebanon, Jordan, Syria, Iraq, Saudi Arabia, Egypt, and Yemen. Its member states looked to the Arab League basically as a collective security organization and as a forum to resolve disputes between Arab countries. The more idealistic among Arab leaders viewed the League as a means to unify the Arab world, to coordinate policies, and to build regional economic strength. As a new organization of states that had the dichotomous distinction of having little history as independent countries while having long histories of tribal and ethnic division, the Arab League had Israel to thank for its temporary unity in the late 1940s. Still, the Arab League had inherent frailties, as its member states vied against one another to be the leader of the Arab world. On the one hand, the United States and Great Britain saw the Arab League as a bulwark against Soviet expansion in the Middle East, which to some Arabs made the Arab League appear as the tool of imperialist foreigners. On the other, many Pan-Arabists viewed the organization as the spear point for the creation of a single Arab nation. Several member states, especially Iraq, feared such lofty visions would come at the expense of their own national and regional interests.[21]

Collective security for Iraq came to fruition, albeit briefly, in the 1955 Baghdad Pact. Formally known as the Pact of Mutual Cooperation between Iraq and Turkey, the defense agreement culminated several years of discussions to establish a NATO-like defense alliance for the region. From the Iraqi standpoint, such an alliance would likely involve Turkey, and therefore the West; otherwise, according to one Iraqi official, collective security "was meaningless."[22] A collective security arrangement for the region also fit nicely with US Secretary of State John Foster Dulles' vision of a "northern tier" security cordon to deter Soviet encroachment into the Middle East. For Eisenhower and Dulles, the Middle East became an important region in the overall US strategy of containing the Soviet Union. Dulles, however, found on his 1953 tour of the region many Arab states, especially Egypt, less than impressed with the Soviet threat and still less enthusiastic about any Western-supported regional security arrangement. Arab focus on Israel and the region's historical tension with British and French imperialism, Dulles worried, distracted Arab leaders from what for the US secretary of state was the true threat to regional stability—Soviet communism. Dulles did find more sympathy in Turkey, Iraq, and Iran, and realized as well that these "northern tier" countries offered a more effective geostrategic barrier to Soviet expansion than an arrangement based around the Suez Canal. Dulles' "northern tier" threatened both Britain and Egypt's position in the Middle East precisely for the same reason—under the US framework the Suez Canal would no longer be the linchpin to regional security and Western influence.[23]

Building upon the Turkey–Pakistan defense agreement of 1954, Iraq and Turkey concluded a defense treaty in February 1955 with the blessing of Great Britain and the United States. Pakistan and Iran joined the multilateral arrangement later that same year. While the United States did not formally join the pact, the Eisenhower administration strongly supported the arrangement with funding and military aid. Wanting to maintain some influence in the region, especially Iraq, Great Britain also in 1955 became a signatory to the Baghdad Pact, much to the delight of Dulles, who hoped to use Great Britain as a surrogate in the region, despite British concerns about Egypt and the Suez Canal. Iraq also made economic overtures to Syria and Jordan, raising eyebrows among leaders in Egypt and Saudi Arabia over Iraq's growing influence, in particular its strong support of Arab nationalism.[24]

The clash between Cold War priorities and nationalism in the Middle East, in Egypt in particular, would soon unleash a wave of volatility not seen in the region since World War I. In Egypt, the Free Officer movement within the Egyptian army provided fertile ground for rebellion. Gamal Abdul Nasser, a dynamic Egyptian military officer, along with Muhammad Najuib, led a successful coup against Egypt's King Farouk in 1952. Nasser and Najuib quickly tangled over several issues, but at base was the simple fact that the egos of neither man could allow sharing power with the other. Nasser prevailed and quickly established himself as the self-styled leader of the Arab world, and just as quickly gained the blessing of the United States at the expense of Great Britain, which evacuated its troops from Egypt in 1954. Dulles played a large role in helping Nasser convince the British to withdraw from Egypt. For Dulles, Nasser represented a new type of Arab leader, one that could facilitate the end of the British and French colonial presence as well as transition to independence, and also stand firm against Soviet forays into the region. Each of these suited US interests in the region quite well, so thought Dulles, who initially believed Nasser could be the foundation for a NATO-like Middle East Defense Organization (MEDO). Nasser, however, refused to play stooge for the United States in the Middle East. He balked at joining any US-backed regional defense alliance, refused peace negotiations with Israel, protested the establishment of the Baghdad Pact, and befriended communist states, notably China, all the while enhancing Egypt's position as an unaligned regional hegemon, much like Jawaharlal Nehru's India.[25]

In 1955, Dulles authorized one of his many schemes to exercise US influence in the Middle East, in this case a covert plan to weaken Egypt's, and therefore Nasser's, influence by subsidizing pro-US governments in Lebanon and Jordan, perhaps even Syria, and by making the Saudi King a sort of "Islamic pope" of the Middle East. After the Egyptian leader's rejection of Dulles' offer to mediate tensions between Egypt and Israel over lost territories in the 1948–49 war, the US secretary of state now had no use for Nasser and even withdrew promised US financial support for Egypt's Aswan Dam project. Nasser, however, remained unmoved in his dreams of Arab glory, as Dulles' meddling in the region floundered. In retaliation for the withdrawal of US support for the dam, in 1956 an emboldened Nasser nationalized the Suez Canal, alarming Great Britain and France, which likened Nasser's audacity to that of Hitler's brazen geopolitical expansion in Europe from 1936 through the beginning of World War II in 1939. Nasser went further still, accepting timely assistance from the Soviet Union to continue the Aswan project.

The United States tried to stay out of the crisis, not wanting to overtly support Nasser's nationalism nor provide additional life support for British and French imperialism in the region. Dulles seemed content to let the British and French resolve the Suez Crisis, but hostilities escalated and threatened to get out of control. With French support, in October Israel attacked Egyptian forces near the canal, while the British and French air forces bombed Egyptian airfields. Focused on the uprising in Hungary, from Washington President Eisenhower and Dulles watched in alarm as Israeli paratroopers clashed with Egyptian forces near Sinai's Mitla Pass while Israeli tanks dashed toward Gaza. In a rare act of Cold War cooperation, the United States and the Soviet Union co-sponsored a resolution in the UN General Assembly that condemned the British and French-backed Israeli attacks on Egypt and called for UN peacekeeping forces to occupy the Suez Canal. In early November, British and French expeditionary forces landed in Egypt in an attempt to secure the canal.

Not wanting World War III to begin in the Middle East (or in Hungary), the United States put economic heat on Great Britain and France while the Soviet Union threatened military intervention to stop the fighting. US and Soviet pressure, combined with stiff Egyptian military resistance, forced the Anglo-French forces to withdraw from the Suez Canal. Israel, too, felt the sting of US pressure and withdrew from Gaza and Sinai. The blunder cost Great Britain and France whatever little clout both declining imperial powers had in the region. The Soviet Union gained new popularity among Arabs for its firm stand against British and French colonialism. Historian Michael B. Oren succinctly assessed the end of the Suez Crisis for the United States: "Spurred by romantic notions of Middle Eastern nationalism and an anti-colonialist creed, the United States had banded with its perennial Soviet enemy against its European friends and saved an Egyptian dictator whom Dulles had plotted to depose." For all its effort, according to Oren, the United States "earned contempt from the Soviet Union, acrimony from the British and the French, and antagonism from many Arabs." For the United States, the crisis exposed Dulles' flawed strategy of simultaneously supporting Israel while promoting Arab nationalism. Nasser emerged triumphant, having thumbed his nose at the West, denied any thanks to the United States for saving his regime, and firmly established himself as the leader, in as much as one person could be, of the Arab world.[26]

Before tangling with Nasser and Egypt, in 1953 Dulles had successfully co-opted the Nasser-like brief regime of Iranian Prime Minister Mohammad Mossadegh, who had served the young and US-backed Shah of Iran, Mohammad Reza, as prime minister, during which time Mossadegh had nationalized the Anglo-Iranian Oil Company. The dramatic act, of course, triggered an intense crisis with the British, who initiated a blockade on Iranian oil exports. Popular with urban conservatives while detested by many in rural Iran, Mossadegh resigned as prime minister in July 1952 after postponing elections that would have assuredly ousted him from power. The Shah's replacement as prime minister proved ineffectual, as Mossadegh's supporters held rallies, staged strikes, and caused general unrest in Tehran and other cities. A panicked Shah begged Mossadegh to return, promising him near complete political and military power. Mossadegh exercised his emergency powers to institute land reform, nationalize industries, and curb the powers of the Shah, while courting the support of the communist Tudeh Party in Iran. He also cut diplomatic ties with Great Britain.

With the US-supported Shah all but deposed, Dulles feared Mossadegh's regime would cause a domino-like effect to spread nationalist and anti-Western ideals throughout the Persian Gulf at the expense of US security interests (oil) and to the benefit of Soviet influence in the region. Dulles adamantly sought to return the Shah to power and with the help of Great Britain's MI-5, Dulles and the US Central Intelligence Agency (CIA) orchestrated Operation AJAX to overthrow Mossadegh. The plot worked, though not without some difficulty in convincing the rather spineless Shah to go along with the plan. Kermit Roosevelt, the CIA's man in Tehran, organized demonstrations and riots against Mossadegh, whose enemies now flocked to CIA contacts to oust the controversial prime minister. Ultimately, in August 1953 Mossadegh was arrested, tried in an Iranian court, and convicted of treason. His death sentence was later reduced to house arrest for the rest of his life. The Shah returned from exile in Rome to Tehran, where his men embarked on a brutal crackdown against Mossadegh's supporters, executing and imprisoning hundreds.

The CIA-sponsored overthrow of Mossadegh ended Iran's brief flirtation with democracy and returned Iran to dictatorship under the Shah. The United States had for the first time overthrown a head of state in the Middle East, a fact that may have inspired Dulles to move against Nasser when the Egyptian leader's anti-US intentions became more clear and that certainly emboldened similar US plans in places such as Guatemala. For Iranians, the restoration of the Shah by the United States was unforgivable and seared a deep hatred and suspicion of that country, which strongly supported the Shah through to his overthrow by Iranian Islamic revolutionaries in 1979. The CIA also attempted a coup in Syria in 1956, but failed when Syrian officers recruited by the US Embassy reported the planned attempt to their superiors.[27]

US efforts to simultaneously build Arab support for its Cold War policies and support Israel's right to exist ended in predictable frustration. Each instance had its own negative impact for US interests in the region. Collectively, however, the damage was much greater, as the negative perception of the United States among Arabs became a natural state of being. For many Arabs, the United States replaced Great Britain and France as the imperious outsider. For many Arab nations, distrust of the United States made it all the more easy for them to seek relations with the Soviet Union and China and to pursue a nonaligned, regional foreign policy. Events in Iraq would only add to US disappointment, as a coup finally ousted the Iraqi monarchy from power.[28]

2

Republican Iraq and the Rise of Saddam Hussein

Like the United States, Iraq, too, had difficulty navigating the treacherous waters between Arab nationalism and Western interests. Al-Said and King Faisal II feared Nasser's growing influence in the Middle East and desired to remain on friendly terms with the West, especially with the United States. For al-Said, little could be worse for Iraq than a Pan-Arab union ruled by the messianic Nasser. Even Arab nationalists in Iraq abhorred such a possibility. In early 1958, Nasser established the United Arab Republic (UAR), consisting of Egypt and Syria. In response, al-Said convinced Jordan to join Iraq in a union governed by a single constitution, with al-Said, not surprisingly, as prime minister. Al-Said hoped this new entity, called the Arab Union, would deter further expansion by Nasser.[1]

The End of the Kingdom of Iraq

Facing possible isolation, al-Said endeavored to save the pro-Western regime of Lebanese President Camille Chamoun from pro-Nasser Arab nationalists. In 1958, al-Said funneled Iraqi money and arms to Chamoun and ultimately attempted to move elements of the Iraqi army to Jordan under the guise of the Arab Union to prevent Syrian intervention in Lebanon's civil war. Meanwhile, officers in the Iraqi army plotted to overthrow both the Iraqi government and the monarchy. Weary of al-Said's increasingly authoritarian rule and his overt support of the West, forces led by Brigadier General Abdul Karim Qassim and Colonel Abdul Salaam Arif moved into Baghdad on July 14, 1958. Originally headed for Jordan, Qassim and his forces instead entered the capital city and quickly seized control of key government buildings, then seized King Faisal II in his palace. There, Qassim's men killed Faisal and later captured al-Said as he tried to flee the city. Purportedly caught dressed as a woman to disguise his attempted escape, al-Said, too, lost his life at the hands of Qassim's men. Crowds dragged al-Said's corpse through Baghdad's streets, mutilating it to the point that it became unrecognizable. Thus began the Republic of Iraq.

The United States reacted with great caution. US Marines had just landed in Lebanon to restore order in Beirut and shore up pro-American factions there. With 14,000 Marines ashore, Eisenhower considered invading Iraq to restore the Iraqi monarchy, but resisted the temptation. Eisenhower realized that the presence of such a large non-Arab force on Middle Eastern soil was already feeding Nasser's propaganda mills, which portrayed the United States not inaccurately as an opponent of Arab nationalism and only interested in maintaining American access to oil. Ironically, while the American interest in oil certainly resonated with those suspicious of American intentions, so too did Arab interest in keeping that oil flowing to the United States and other paying customers.[2]

Qassim ruled Iraq through a Revolutionary Council, with himself serving as prime minister. Although not a communist, Qassim quickly moved to formalize relationships with the Soviet Union and China and courted the support of the Iraq Communist Party (ICP). Despite abolishing the Arab Union with Jordan, Qassim shied from enthusiastically supporting Nasser's UAR. And despite their unified beginning, Qassim and Arif soon found themselves on opposing sides of two key issues. Wary of submission to Nasser's *wahda* (union), Qassim instead wanted to bring Sunnis, Shias, and Kurds together in a truly national Iraq, while Arif strongly supported joining Egypt at the expense of Iraqi nationalism. Communism also divided the two leaders of the new Iraqi republic. Qassim recognized the practical benefits of Soviet support and tolerated the expansion of the ICP. Arif, however, abhorred communism and instead fully embraced Nasser's brand of pan-Arabism. The wedge between the two men came to a head before the year's end. After implicating Arif as the instigator of several uprisings against the new Iraqi government, Qassim had Arif imprisoned.[3]

In 1959, Qassim withdrew Iraq from the Baghdad Pact, which subsequently adopted the Central Treaty Organization (CENTO) as its new moniker. A new alliance with the Soviet Union erased any remnants of pro-Western attitudes in Iraq, while Qassim's rejection of Nasser irritated Iraqis who supported a more flexible attitude toward the UAR. Uprisings of all sorts exploded across Iraq. A major revolt occurred in Mosul in March 1959, for example, where Pan-Arabist supporters in the army garrison there attempted to take control of the city. In many instances, pan-Arab sentiments proved superficial, as the ensuing chaos allowed old tensions to rise to the surface. Clan fought clan, faith fought faith, and ethnic group fought ethnic group. It took Iraqi forces loyal to Qassim several days to restore order. An equally bloody revolt took place in Kirkuk in July that same year, while demonstrations in Baghdad occurred with increasing regularity. Qassim issued swift retribution to the leaders of these revolts, publically executing dozens of officers and other leaders. Purging enemies, both perceived and real, in brutal crackdowns became a way of life in republican Iraq.

Amid this instability, the Iraqi Ba'ath Party emerged as a potent force. Founded in Syria in the 1940s, Ba'athist doctrine advocated Arab unity, socialism, and rejection of imperial rule. Ba'ath in Arabic means "rebirth" or "insurrection," and was a fitting name for this pro-Arab, anti-Western party. While the Syrian variant promoted a regional focus (coming to power in Syria in 1963), the Ba'ath Party in Iraq grew into a militant force for Iraqi nationalism. In the 1950s, the Iraqi Ba'ath Party appealed to young elites, especially Sunnis. At the time of the overthrow of the monarchy in 1958, Iraqi Ba'athists had radicalized their message of Arab unity and opposition to communism and Western influences. Sensing Qassim's vulnerability after the Mosul and Kirkuk uprisings, Ba'ath leaders took action. A gang of Ba'athists attempted to assassinate Qassim on October 7, 1959, in Baghdad, but only wounded him. The assailants included a young Sunni from Tikrit named Saddam Hussein, who although wounded in the assault fled to Syria to escape Qassim's vengeance on those involved in the attempt on his life.[4]

Born in 1937 in the small village of al-Quja near Tikrit, Saddam probably never knew his father, who either died or abandoned his family around the time of Saddam's birth. His name in Arabic means "one who confronts." Deep tribal and familial politics dominated the heavily Sunni culture of Tikrit and its surrounding impoverished farming villages. For a young Saddam, poverty was a way of life, as was violence and loyalty to family and tribe. His mother's brother, an Iraqi army officer, took baby Saddam into his home; but a few years later when his mother remarried, Saddam returned to his mother's household. His new stepfather treated him as an outcast, as did many in their village, including other children, who mercilessly teased and abused young Saddam. His stepfather's frequent beatings served only to heighten Saddam's sense of isolation in his family and community. This formative period in Saddam's life perhaps set him on the path to becoming one of the most brutal dictators of the twentieth century.

Like many officers in the Iraqi Army during World War II, Saddam's uncle had supported Nazi Germany in the hope that German forces could remove once and for all the British imperial stranglehold over Iraq. Having participated in the failed 1941 rebellion against the British-dominated Iraqi royal family during the war, Saddam's uncle had luckily received only a short prison sentence, a fortunate outcome, considering many Iraqi army officers found themselves in front of firing squads or at the end of a hangman's rope. Unluckily, Saddam found himself again under the bullying abuse of his stepfather.

His uncle's release from prison in 1947 saved Saddam from his stepfather's harsh treatment. At ten years of age, Saddam escaped this sadistic existence to live with his uncle, who gave the boy a strict disciplined upbringing, to which Saddam seemed to have responded favorably as a young fatherless child. The trauma surrounding his uncle's participation in the rebellion and subsequent imprisonment also deeply affected Saddam. His uncle instilled in the boy a deep belief in Arab nationalism as well as an intense hatred of Western imperialism and its puppet kings in Iraq and the Middle East. The return of his uncle, however, gave Saddam some light in an otherwise very dim existence. With his uncle's family, Saddam moved to Baghdad as the young boy reached his teenage years. In Baghdad, Saddam attended law school and applied for admission to the Baghdad Military Academy. Poor performance in his entrance exams, however, barred Saddam from admission and from becoming an officer like his uncle.

While his motivation for becoming politically active will never be fully understood, the sense of community and belonging that a political organization afforded must have attracted Saddam. He had been brought up in a cutthroat, deeply political culture that rewarded blind loyalty and that espoused intense hatred of Jews, Iranians, and of course Western imperialism. Many political parties in Iraq catered to these feelings, adding Iraqi nationalism and Pan-Arabism to the mix. As a young man, Saddam joined the Ba'athists, perhaps because his uncle's Tikriti cousin held a high position in the party. Family ties, even somewhat removed, and hometown connections influenced Saddam's world. Saddam was initiated into the world of political killings when he murdered a Tikriti communist politician.[5]

Soon after his first political assassination, Saddam joined the Ba'athist Party as a low-level thug to lead an intimidation gang of like-minded Iraqi youths. In 1959 he attempted to assassinate Qassim, who had attempted to tighten his tenuous control over Iraq through a diametrically opposed program of terror and reform. While censoring the press and restricting political parties through a licensing process, Qassim offered limited land reform to Iraqi peasants and gained modest concessions from the Iraq Petroleum Company (IPC), hoping these and other reforms would buy some longer-term support from the disparate groups that dotted the Iraqi political landscape. He improved rights for women and appointed women to important government positions, including one as head of a government ministry. He cut Iraq's currency away from the British sterling system. He improved public education, increased salaries for government bureaucrats, established a social security system, and put government resources into improving medical care as well as building hospitals. Secularism was Qassim's watchword, as many of his reforms and initiatives challenged traditional Islamic values.[6]

Qassim again went after the IPC, this time dramatically increasing the tax on oil revenues and taking back much of the IPC's oil rights to vast swaths of Iraqi territory. Iraq had heretofore recouped only 5 percent of oil revenues generated by the IPC. Qassim boldly insisted that half of IPC's revenue go to Iraq's coffers and that the IPC hire only Iraqis rather than the foreign labor it currently employed. With strategic foresight, Qassim also demanded 90 percent of all undrilled IPC concessions in Iraq. Qassim's Public Law 80 implemented many of these measures directed at the mostly Western-owned oil industry and nationalized the IPC in all but name. While the comprehensive assault on the Iraqi oil industry actually had little short-term impact, it found popular appeal among Iraqis as a strike against imperialism and laid the foundation for Iraqi control of its petroleum reserves and oil revenues.[7]

To increase both his and Iraq's stature in the Persian Gulf and the Arab world, Qassim also moved to incorporate Kuwait into Iraq. Indeed, many in Qassim's inner circle viewed the Persian Gulf as the obvious alternative goal for Iraqi hegemony to Nasser's UAR—Qassim's government even renamed the area the Arabian Gulf in an overt sop to Arab nationalists. A large Soviet loan helped Iraq build a new port at Um Qasr to improve Iraqi access to the Persian Gulf, signaling to both Kuwait and Iran that Qassim's regime intended to flex its presence in the region. Perhaps looking for a foreign affairs success to distract his domestic detractors, Qassim stepped up his claim that Kuwait belonged to Iraq. In June 1961, Great Britain ended its protectorate over Kuwait, granting the tiny kingdom its independence as well as concluding a defense agreement to safeguard its former protectorate. With blustery language, Qassim lambasted the continued presence of British imperialism in an area that to Qassim rightfully belonged to Iraq. Just days after Kuwait gained its independence, Qassim declared Kuwait part of the Basra district, even going so far as to name the ruler of Kuwait a sort of county commissioner subservient to the governor of Basra. Kuwait, Great Britain, Saudi Arabia, and the Arab League protested the Iraqi claim in the strongest terms. British troops, replaced later by forces from Arab League member-states, reinforced the small Kuwaiti army, while Qassim responded by recalling Iraq's ambassador to the Arab League. Unwilling to risk war with other Arab nations and further antagonize Iran, Qassim decided to back down. A new Kurdish rebellion in northern Iraq could have helped persuade Qassim to rethink his gambit against Kuwait, as he needed every available soldier in what became a long grinding conflict against the Kurds. While many Iraqis supported annexing Kuwait, they also believed Iraq had lost face among its Arab neighbors because of Qassim's poor handling of the crisis.[8]

Despite Qassim's assault on the IPC, his Kuwait debacle, harsh rule, and tacit support of the ICP, along with the violent revolts among the Kurds in northern Iraq, meant he had become a liability to powerful Iraqis and a concern for the Kennedy administration, which feared Qassim might move Iraq closer to the Soviet Union. With support from the CIA, the Ba'ath Party railed against Qassim's bumpy rule. In 1963, nationalist Iraqi Army officers in league with Ba'ath supporters successfully overthrew Qassim, killing him and many supporters of his regime, as well as leaders of the ICP. Qassim was captured alive, put before a kangaroo court, convicted, then executed, all in less than an hour. State television showed Qassim's bloodied corpse to prove to the Iraqi people that he was dead and gone.[9]

The Ba'athists installed Qassim's comrade-in-rebellion from 1958, Abdul Salam Arif, as president and established a powerful National Council of the Revolutionary Command (NCRC) to govern Iraq. The Ba'ath Party, however, soon lost control of the loose coalition that made up the NCRC and violence broke out as the Ba'athist National Guard bullied opposition parties. Ultimately, Arif formed his own paramilitary force, the Republican Guard, and with the help of the Iraqi army eradicated the National Guard. By the end of 1963, Arif had brought together a still fragile coalition of militant Ba'ath Party members (many from Tikrit) and Arab nationalists, including many Nasserites, under a new ruling National Revolutionary Council (NRC).

Arif nationalized Iraqi banks and much of Iraq's growing industrial base, a move that discouraged both domestic and foreign investment in Iraqi industry, and also gained more concessions from the IPC, but Iraq still remained an underdeveloped country of predominately poorly educated peasants and day laborers. Arif died in a helicopter crash in 1966, a tragedy that brought his younger brother, Abdul al-Rahman Arif, into the presidency. Al-Rahman Arif, who had been head of the Iraqi army, quickly discovered how little support he actually had from the army. Embittered over deep cuts in the defense budget and al-Rahman Arif's meddling in the army's campaigns against Kurdish rebels in northern Iraq, army officers also feared for their lucrative patronage networks. Moreover, for al-Rahman Arif, communist uprisings in southern Iraq further complicated matters. Also, many officers viewed Iraq's nominal participation in the 1967 Six Day War with Israel with embarrassment. The swiftness and decisiveness of the Israeli attacks had caught the Iraqis completely unprepared to contribute in any meaningful way to the Arab response. Iraqi armored units were caught with over one-third of their tanks in disrepair; and once the Iraqis did get mobilized to move to the front, they were held short by Israeli aircraft unleashing lethal firepower upon the exposed Iraqis. Israeli airstrikes also pummeled the Iraqi air force, leaving Iraqi planes burning while they were still parked on its airfields. Some gallant Iraqi pilots managed to get their fighters into the air and shoot down at least three Israeli aircraft. The loss of over twenty Iraqi aircraft in the process, however, obviously left the tally strongly in favor of the Israelis. Still, compared to Egypt, Jordan, and Syria, Iraq came out of the brief but intense war unscathed and territorially intact. Israel had given the Arab world a stinging defeat and gained the Sinai, Jerusalem, the West Bank, and the Golan Heights. In Iraq, al-Rahman Arif and his tenuous regime drew fire as the local scapegoat for the Arab disaster.[10]

Saddam Comes to Power

By 1968, Iraqi officers had had enough of al-Rahman Arif, as had the Ba'ath Party. Together with the so-called Arab Revolutionary Movement, General Ahmad Hassan al-Bakr and Colonel Abd al-Razzaq al-Nayif, an officer in the Republican Guard, staged a bloodless coup on July 17, 1968, taking control of the government and exiling al-Rahman Arif. Al-Bakr, the principal Ba'ath Party leader, took over as the president of the Republic of Iraq on the day of the coup. Within only a few weeks, he solidified his control over the new Revolutionary Command Council (RCC), named himself head of the Iraqi army, and placed Ba'ath Party members in important positions across the Iraqi government. In short order, Iraq became a one-party state, with Ba'ath Party membership all but required to hold any significant government position, even at the regional level. Tribal kinship also played a crucial role, as al-Bakr surrounded himself with appointees and officers from his native Tikrit—these included Saddam Hussein.[11]

Upon his return from Syria and Egypt in 1963, Saddam, though still a junior member of the Ba'ath Party, managed to work his way into al-Bakr's inner circle and remained so through al-Bakr's falling out with Arif in 1963. Because of his close association with the now jailed al-Bakr, Saddam frequently found himself trying to avoid arrest by Arif's security police, but his luck ran out in 1964 when police finally caught up with him. Along with two other prisoners, Saddam escaped to become one of the Ba'ath Party's primary underground leaders while al-Bakr remained imprisoned. When al-Bakr became president after the 1968 coup, he gave Saddam a golden opportunity to prove his loyalty, if not his capacity for brutality. Not long after the coup, al-Bakr decided to rid himself of al-Nayif, who now served as prime minister. Having ensured his complete control over the Republican Guard, al-Bakr left al-Nayif alone with Saddam following a brief meeting at the presidential palace. Saddam pistol-whipped al-Nayif mercilessly, but did not kill him. Al-Bakr exiled al-Nayif to Morocco, but Saddam had the final word on al-Nayif's fate, having his agents murder the former officer ten years later in London. Al-Bakr quickly came to rely upon Saddam to do his dirty work.[12]

At the time, Saddam likely had little appreciation for al-Bakr's effort to continue Arif's nationalization program and moved Iraq toward a highly centralized governing system, much akin to that of the Soviet Union. Of most importance, the Ba'athist regime succeeded in completely nationalizing Iraq's oil industry by the mid-1970s. Saddam certainly, however, appreciated al-Bakr's swift retribution against those who opposed the Ba'athist program. Frequent purges cleansed government and military ranks of dissenters while persuading fence sitters to get on the Ba'athist side of the fence. Al-Bakr shrewdly appointed Saddam vice president of the RCC, where Saddam played a key role in snuffing out opposition to the regime. Fiercely loyal to al-Bakr more through blood kinship than ideology, Saddam organized and ran al-Bakr's secret police and reorganized the Republican Guard into a Ba'athist militia that would ultimately grow over 50,000 men and later serve as Saddam's own security force.[13]

For the Iraqi military, all of the shortcomings that plagued its performance in the 1967 Six Day War again plagued its performance in the 1973 October or Yom Kippur War. Observers at the time rated the Iraqis a distant last among Arab forces in readiness, operational effectiveness, and discipline. Iraqi forces usually outnumbered that of the Israelis they faced, but even then field commanders failed to maneuver and concentrate their forces to strike heavy blows at the Israelis. Iraqi junior officers showed an appalling lack of initiative and subordinates froze when facing the enemy without a superior officer to tell them what to do. The successful integration of armor, artillery, and infantry eluded these mostly unimaginative Iraqi commanders. The Israelis later confessed, however, that though tactically ineffective the Iraqis remained tenacious fighters. The Israelis were impressed by the sacrifice Iraqi soldiers made in the face of defeat, a bitter compliment indeed.[14]

While the Middle Eastern crises of the 1970s swirled around him, Saddam worked to solidify his position as heir-apparent to al-Bakr. Saddam wielded immense power, which he brutally if not adroitly used to remove any threat to his position through exile, imprisonment, torture, and execution. Similar to the labeling of potential foes as communists in the United States during the McCarthy era, Saddam simply accused such individuals of being Israeli spies, whereupon kangaroo "revolutionary courts" would convict them and order imprisonment or, more likely, execution. Saddam quickly commanded loyalty throughout the army, several government ministries, and, of course, his own security forces. In 1973, for example, Saddam imprisoned Abd al-Khaliq al-Samarrai, a fellow Ba'ath Party member and challenger to replace al-Bakr, and then several years later had him executed. When the commander of Saddam's security forces, Nadhim Kazzar, grew too vocal in his criticism of the Tikriti cabal that controlled the Ba'ath Party and subsequently plotted to kill al-Bakr, Hussein took the opportunity not only to execute Kazzar but thirty-four other officers and officials as well. In essence, Saddam ruled a terror-based state that he had created, despite al-Bakr remaining in the presidency.[15]

Saddam made his move to take complete control of Iraq in July 1979. Announcing al-Bakr's resignation due to health problems, on July 17 Saddam had al-Bakr arrested then took over as president of Iraq. In the ensuing days and weeks, Hussein undertook a purge of the military and government that would have made Josef Stalin envious of its efficiency, thoroughness, and brutality. Saddam and the state of Iraq became one and the same.[16]

Saddam reorganized the Iraqi government to solidify his power. He consolidated ministries, appointed loyal followers and family members to key positions, and created a new National Assembly complete with the superficial trappings of representative democracy. Iraqi oil revenues, now reaching tens of billions of dollars per year, allowed Saddam to increase the size of the Iraqi armed forces and modernize its weapons systems. From France, Iraq bought Mirage F-1 fighters, Alouette attack helicopters, and surface-to-air missiles (SAMs). The Soviet Union eagerly sold to Iraq Scud missiles and various MiG jet aircraft as well as large numbers of tanks, enough to give Iraq one of the largest armored armies in the world. French and Soviet technicians taught the Iraqis to use and maintain their new equipment and weapons systems. Other countries, such as Germany and Yugoslavia, profited by selling a wide range of military vehicles and other equipment to Iraq. Most astonishing, however, is the fact that Iraq bought from the United States and European countries the key ingredients from which to build biological and chemical weapons. Iraq's arsenal included anthrax and other biological agents as well as Tabun and VX nerve gas. Obtaining nuclear capability ranked highest on Saddam's wish list. France helped Iraq build its first nuclear power plant at Osirak, which the Israelis promptly destroyed in an air assault in June 1981, fearing the plutonium could be used to make a nuclear weapon. By 1980, Saddam's Iraq had a frighteningly powerful military.[17]

In addition to building his military machine, Saddam built schools, hospitals, and other facilities and improved transportation networks. He also revealed his megalomania. Placing his image on just about everything imaginable in every city, town, and village across Iraq, the Iraqi dictator firmly embedded the "cult of Saddam." He compared himself to Hammurabi and other great historical figures from the region's past and portrayed himself as the new Nasser, who would unite all Arabs, destroy Israel, and make an Iraqi-led Middle East the cultural center of the world. The rise of the Islamic Republic of Iran, however, stood in the way of that dream.[18]

In 1975, Iraq and Iran signed the so-called Algiers Agreement to temper border tensions between the two countries, but Saddam's rise to power of and the overthrow of the American-supported Shah of Iran by Ayatollah Ruhollah Khomeini's Islamic Revolution, both in 1979, disrupted this fragile peace. Both leaders reached the daunting conclusion that there could not be two so ambitious and diametrically opposed hegemons in the Persian Gulf region. The subsequent 1980–88 war between these two nations would lead directly to Saddam's decision to invade Kuwait in August 1990.

Exiled from Iran to Najaf in Iraq in 1965, Khomeini, a Shia, espoused Islamic Revolution in Iran and once the Ba'athists took power also promoted the same for Iraq. An associate of like-minded Iraqi ayatollah Baqir al-Sadr, Khomeini plotted the overthrow of the Shah's secular regime to make Iran an Islamic republic. At the Shah's request and wanting to squelch any possibility of a Shia uprising in Iraq, Saddam exiled Khomeini to Paris in 1978, a move that ironically freed Khomeini to organize and gather support to overthrow the Shah.[19]

While Islamic nationalism played a predominate role in the Shah's downfall, Khomeini's anti-American rhetoric proved most effective in inciting young Iranians against the Shah. The United States had supported the Shah of Iran since 1953 and in the 1970s gave the Iranian leader carte blanche to purchase weapons and other military material from the United States. In this context the revolution occurred, beginning with student demonstrations in Tehran in 1978, the Shah's departure from the country in January 1979, then culminating with the establishment of the Islamic Republic of Iran in April 1979, under the tight political and religious control of Khomeini. In a rage of anti-Americanism, Iranian students stormed the American Embassy in Tehran on November 4, 1979, taking its occupants hostage and not releasing them until 444 days later. While Khomeini took no part in taking the embassy, he exploited the hostage situation to galvanize his own anti-American message, a tactic that brought disparate groups jockeying for political position in his new regime together in a newfound hatred of the "Great Satan"—the United States.[20]

Saddam found both concern and opportunity in the new Islamic Republic of Iran. Khomeini understandably focused much of his anti-Arab nationalism rhetoric on the Iraqi dictator, whose secular Iraq offended Khomeini's Shia nationalist philosophy. Having just come to power himself, Saddam spent a great deal of time attempting to convince Iraqis, Sunni and Shia alike, of his Islamic faith. Appearing during prayer at holy sites across Iraq, Saddam tried to counter Khomeini's accusation that the Iraqi leader was actually an infidel. Nevertheless, Khomeini's Islamic Revolution found traction in Iraq through Ayatollah al-Sadr and militant Shias, who attempted to assassinate Hussein's deputy prime minister, Tariq Aziz, in April 1980. Saddam ordered al-Sadr's execution and expelled thousands of Iranians from Iraq. This crackdown on militant Shias, especially those of the al Daawa sect, enraged Khomeini, who in turn loudly called for the overthrow of Saddam's Ba'athist regime while quietly supporting Iraqi Shia militant groups with money, weapons, and training in the hope of ultimately starting a civil war in Iraq.[21]

The Iran–Iraq War

Tension between the two countries mounted, as forces along the border between Iraq and Iran took potshots at one another in several minor clashes. The failed US attempt to rescue the hostages in the American Embassy in Tehran on April 24, 1980, perhaps encouraged Saddam to go to war against Iran. From Saddam's point of view, Iran, once the darling of the US under the corrupt Shah, now found itself economically and diplomatically isolated because of the excesses of the Islamic Revolution. Dependent upon the US for arms and equipment that built the military forces of the Shah, Iran now found itself without a supplier to maintain its tremendous arsenal of American military hardware. Already well supplied by the Soviet Union, Saddam could now also court American support if he chose to take action against Iran. He could position himself as both hero of the West and savior of Arab nationalism by leading the charge to overthrow Khomeini's extremist Islamic regime. Moreover, the opportunity to expand Iraqi territory and gain unrestricted access to the Persian Gulf, to increase its oil reserves, and to finally resolve the dispute with Iran over the Shatt al-Arab waterway, all at the expense of Iran, easily convinced Saddam that the potential strategic gain outweighed the possible costs of war with Iran.[22]

Saddam decided to strike. To prevent further Shia uprisings in Iraq, he concluded quite logically that he would have to destroy the source of those uprisings—Khomeini's regime in Iran. Still internationally isolated, Khomeini's fledgling government had yet to fully develop its wings. Saddam had to strike before the new Iran emerged from its nest to threaten the entire region. Saddam reckoned that a swift surprise attack could do to Iran what the Israelis had done to the Arabs in the Six Day War of 1967. The Islamic Revolution would be dead and Saddam would be the unparalleled leader of the Arab world, surpassing Nasser in importance, popularity, and even longevity, so Saddam dreamed. Success against Iran would place him in this vaunted position, from where he could then lead the Arab world in the final destruction of Israel. Iraq's history supported Saddam's strategy—political problems, foreign and domestic, found their solution in quick, decisive military action. This stratagem was most prevalent under the Ba'ath regimes. Already a master of violence in the domestic realm, Saddam easily transferred his penchant for violence to the international realm. He controlled officials in the government and officers in the military. He controlled all decision making. That Saddam decided to war against Iran should have surprised no one.[23]

In early September 1980, clashes between Iraqi and Iranian forces along the border northeast of Baghdad near Qasr Shirin, Khanqin, and Mandali prompted Saddam to invoke an obscure clause of the Algiers Accords to lay claim to the Iranian area near Zain al Qaws and Saif Saad, to the announcement of which Iran responded with artillery barrages across the border into Iraq. During the second week of September, Saddam took the disputed villages and border areas by force. On September 17, Saddam appeared before the Iraqi national assembly to declare that repeated Iranian violations of the Algiers agreement had convinced him to nullify it. He also declared Iraqi control of the Shatt al-Arab waterway bordering southern Iran and Iraq—the country that controlled the Shatt al-Arab controlled the flow of oil out of Basra. In response, on September 20 Iran mobilized its armed forces, including reserves. On September 23, Iraq invaded Iran in what it publically called a pre-emptive action, an action that Iranian-born international relations expert Shahram Chubin described as: "Motivated by fear, opportunism and overconfidence, a mixture of defensive and offensive calculations, Iraq's decision to resort to force was a compound of preventive war, ambition and punishment for a regional rival."[24] Thus began the Iran–Iraq War.[25]

The outbreak of hostilities brought predictable international condemnations and embargoes, though secretly Saudi Arabia and Kuwait, both fearful of revolutionary Iran, gave their blessing as well as money to Saddam's enterprise. The Soviet Union stopped all arms shipments to Iraq, whose military depended upon mostly Soviet equipment, in November 1980, but relented a year later with renewed shipments. The United States likewise refused to supply the predominantly American-built Iranian military, despite early overtures by the Iranians to free the hostages in exchange for much needed spare parts. Later in the war, however, the United States would come to the aid of Iraq. Like all warring nations, however, both belligerents found suppliers to keep their war machines moving.[26]

Both countries indeed had substantial war machines, built from ample oil revenues during the 1970s, when Iran boasted a larger and more modern military than neighboring Iraq. By the outbreak of war in 1980, however, the tale of the tape had changed. Purges of the military during the Islamic Revolution robbed the Iranian armed forces of much-needed technical expertise, particularly among pilots and mechanical specialists required for tanks and aircraft. At the beginning of the conflict, Iran had an air force of over 400 combat aircraft, including American-made F-14 Tomcats, but without American support much of this fleet of modern jets remained grounded. The Iranian army, with its 150,000 regulars and 400,000 reserves, faced similar problems, as the lack of spare parts and technicians to service such a large mechanized force made only half of its 1,700 tanks and 1,200 armored fighting vehicles serviceable. The Iranian navy fared much better despite similar maintenance issues, possessing a fleet of three destroyers, four frigates, and several so-called fast-action craft armed with SSMs. Where Iran had an edge over the Iraqi military in modern weapons in the 1970s, in the early stages of the Iran–Iraq War, Iranian supply problems allowed Iraq quickly to surpass Iran in superiority. Iraq's mostly serviceable air force had over 300 combat aircraft, including several dozen Soviet MiG-23 and French Mirage F-1 fighter jets. The Iraqi army of over half a million regulars and reserves also had over 2,500 serviceable Soviet-made tanks and a like number of armored fighting vehicles. The Iraqi navy, however, remained woefully behind that of Iran, with only one frigate and several fast-action craft. Iraq suffered as well in finding consistent combat leadership. Between purges and politicization of the military, Saddam could count only on an officer corps made up of political lackeys with next to no combat experience and a mass of levies with questionable combat effectiveness and dedication to the fight.[27]

In many ways, Saddam pursued a limited war against Iran. He hoped that Iraqi military action along the border with Iran would incite rebellion against Khomeini and his regime. The Iranians, however, refused to cooperate with Hussein's scheme. Casualties mounted and Iraq's oil revenues plummeted when Iran shut down Iraq's only oil port at Faw. In 1982, several of Saddam's closest advisors and supporters conspired in a failed attempt to get Iran to agree to a cease-fire. Saddam cleaned house in a purge reminiscent of Soviet leader Josef Stalin's purges in the 1930s. Wanting desperately to save face, Saddam vowed to continue the fight. He needed help, however, and considering future events that help came from an unexpected source—the United States.

To add to American concerns over heightened tensions in the Middle East, in 1979 the Soviet Union invaded Afghanistan, the infamous "graveyard of empires," to root out terrorist cells of Islamic extremists based in Afghanistan and operating in the southern areas of the Soviet Union, and to restore order following a coup that ousted the government of Muhammad Daoud Khan in 1978. The Soviet Union backed a new government under Nur Mohammad Taraki to replace the military junta that had overthrown Daoud, but with Taraki's murder in 1979 Afghanistan fell into chaos. The Soviets invaded, expecting the operation to be over in a matter of weeks. Faced with the prospect of an extremist regime in Iran destabilizing the entire Middle East and now Soviet military action in Afghanistan, President Jimmy Carter announced that the United States would act to deter any threat to the free flow of oil from the Middle East. The so-called Carter Doctrine intended to send a strong warning to the Soviet Union, but also to other countries tempted toward aggression in the region. "Let our position be absolutely clear," declared Carter, "An attempt by any outside force to gain control of the Persian Gulf region will be regarded as an assault on the vital interests of the United States of America, and such an assault will be repelled by any means necessary, including military force."[28]

The Carter Doctrine legitimized the decision to support Iraq against a country that had once been its ally in the Middle East and also gave Carter's successor, Ronald Reagan, support to increase the American military presence around the Persian Gulf—the United States beefed up basing in the Azores and Diego Garcia, and assisted the Saudis in the design and construction of King Khalid Military City in northeastern Saudi Arabia. King Khalid Military City in particular would play a pivotal role in the 1991 Gulf War. Built by the US Army Corps of Engineers from 1974 to its completion in 1986, King Khalid Military City was one of dozens of military building projects designed and built by the United States and funded by the Saudi government. Isolated amid a flat, stark desert landscape, King Khalid Military City had not only airfields, munitions depots, and communications centers, it also boasted several mosques, schools, a hospital, and swimming pools, along with housing and shopping facilities to satisfy the needs of over 65,000 people.[29]

In 1983, President Ronald Reagan sent Donald Rumsfeld, who had been former President Gerald Ford's White House Chief of Staff, as his special envoy to Iraq to open discussions on how the United States could best help Saddam in his war against Iran. Soon, the United States provided Iraq with satellite imagery and arms, as well as money to buy American grain to feed Saddam's army. Whether the United States sold Saddam chemical and biological warfare agents remains unclear. Perhaps most importantly, the United States policed the Persian Gulf, deploying the US Navy to protect Kuwaiti- and American-flagged oil tankers and stop illegal arms shipments from reaching Iran via the Gulf. In the process, the US Navy all but destroyed the Iranian navy, sinking fast-attack craft, destroying oil platforms used as bases by the Iranian navy, and shooting down several Iranian fighter jets and helicopters. From 1987 through 1988, the US Navy conducted such operations in the Persian Gulf, including Operations EARNEST WILL, NIMBLE ARCHER, and PRAYING MANTIS. The so-called Tanker War was not without its costs, however, as on May 17, 1987, the Iraqis mistakenly fired Exocet missiles at the Perry-class guided-missile frigate USS *Stark*, killing thirty-seven crewmembers. The US also caused a tragic accident when on July 3, 1988, the cruiser USS *Vincennes* mistook Iran Air Flight 655 for an Iranian F-14, shooting the airliner down and killing all 290 passengers and crew onboard. Overall, the Tanker War internationalized the conflict, as several nations contributed ships and other assets to perform escort duty in the Persian Gulf.[30]

Bolstered by American support and financial loans from Kuwait and Saudi Arabia, Saddam fought on, but the Iraqi dictator still had domestic issues with which to contend. The Kurds took advantage of the war to revolt in the north, gaining control of much of the countryside outside the northern cities of Iraq by 1987 in the process. In March 1988, Iran in desperation invaded the Kurdish region of Iraq in hope of fomenting a civil war. Saddam responded with a brutality not seen since World War II or perhaps in the killing fields of Cambodia. He had already used chemical weapons against Iranian soldiers on the field of battle, specifically in the 1987 Iranian assault on the southern Iraqi city of Basra. Now, Saddam used these same weapons against his own people. On March 16, 1988, Saddam's forces attacked the Kurdish town of Halabja with a variety of poison gasses, killing as many as 5,000 people and injuring thousands more.[31]

By 1988, both sides revealed signs of exhaustion, with Iran in perhaps worse shape than Iraq. With its economy in shambles, with the US Navy in control of the Persian Gulf, and with initiative on the battlefield in the hands of the Iraqis, Iran had little choice but to find a way out of the conflict. In 1987, the UN Security Council passed Resolution 598, which called for a cease-fire and status quo ante bellum. Although it took another year for the two sides finally to agree to the cease-fire, treaty talks nevertheless failed to produce an agreement acceptable to both parties, resulting in a purgatorial state of "no peace, no war."

Posturing on both sides made an accurate accounting of casualties impossible, as each side downplayed its own casualties while inflating that of the other. Conservative estimates, however, are harrowing enough. Among Iranians, 260,000 were killed, while Iraq lost 200,000. Each side had hundreds of thousands injured, and tens of thousands of civilians killed and wounded. Iran spent as much as $90 billion to fight the war. Iraq spent perhaps as much as $110 billion. Iraq's foreign exchange reserve held $35 billion in 1980; by war's end, Iraq had a foreign debt of over $80 billion, an amount in excess of two times Iraq's gross national product. In total, the war cost both the Iraqi and Iranian economies in excess of $1 trillion in lost revenue.

For such a costly war, neither side gained much of anything. No territory changed hands. Saddam remained in power in Iraq and the Islamic Revolution continued to rule Iran. Neither side accomplished what they had originally set out to accomplish back in 1980. Still, Saddam declared victory and Iraqis deluded themselves into believing they had achieved a victory of historic proportions. The Iranians turned inward and mythologized the conflict as one of heroic sacrifice while at the same time Iran became more anxious about its own security. Surrounded by states unfriendly to the Islamic Revolution, paranoid that the CIA was plotting to overthrow its government, and distressed at its loss of prestige in the Middle East, Iran, like Iraq, turned to weapons of mass destruction (WMD), particularly nuclear weapons, as the answer to a multitude of problems.[32]

Kuwait in particular drew Saddam's ire for declaring after the war that Iraq must repay what Saddam perceived as an investment—Iraq after all had prevented the Islamic Revolution from infecting Kuwait by warring with Iran. To Saddam, Kuwait had already earned a nice dividend and was now behaving most ungratefully in demanding repayment. While much of this may have been posturing on Saddam's part, the issue made for good coverage in Iraq's state-controlled press and thus gave Saddam a public reason to take action in 1990. In addition to foreign debt, Iraq needed $230 billion to repair its damaged infrastructure and rebuild its depleted armed forces. Annual oil revenues of $13 billion fell far short of the amount required simply to again get the Iraqi economy running. Saddam faced a daunting, if not impossible, post-war calamity, one of his own making.[33]

Faced with dire economic conditions and mounting opposition at home, like rulers of Iraq before him, Saddam gambled on risky action to preserve his hold on power. Threats appeared from several quarters, but the uprisings in Iraqi Kurdistan and murmurings of discontent within the colossal Iraqi military, Saddam's own army, presented immediate challenges to his rule. While he could and did keep the army occupied in dealing with the Kurds, Saddam dared not demobilize this expensive force in a dead economy that offered no jobs, an insight later lost upon American decision-makers in Iraq in 2003. Either way, Saddam needed money, at least for relief from huge debt payments to Saudi Arabia and Kuwait, and needed to give his military something to do.

Saddam found, so he thought, salvation in tiny but wealthy Kuwait. With Iran in similarly dire straits, he did not need to fear reigniting war with Khomeini. With a battle-hardened but still recovering army, Saddam felt assured of operational success in taking Kuwait. By controlling Kuwaiti oil reserves, production facilities, and port access, Saddam could quickly wipe clean Iraq's account books and rebuild Iraq's economy. In 1990, Kuwaiti leaders angered Saddam by their refusal to loan Iraq more money for reconstruction, by violating oil production quotas and pricing, and by, according to Saddam, tapping into Iraqi oil fields by slant drilling under the border between the two countries. With oil prices tumbling, Iraq could not convert its immense oil reserves into quick cash—Kuwait's refusal to reduce its production capacity to help drive up the price of a barrel of oil, in Saddam's view, testified further to Kuwait's ingratitude to Iraq for fighting Iran. Saddam's ace in the hole, however, remained Iraq's historic claim to Kuwait, which Iraq had consistently alleged and sometimes acted upon since the creation of Iraq and Kuwait following World War I. He could, and did, argue that Kuwait belonged to Iraq, a nationalist concept that resonated with Iraqis, many of whom detested the lavish lifestyle of wealthy Kuwaitis.

Saddam, however, not only thought of his own control of Iraq and of restoring the Iraqi economy, he had much grander objectives in mind than only invading and annexing Kuwait. In addition to expanding Iraqi territory and access to the Persian Gulf, the lack of which had long remained a strategic sore point for Iraq, a successful invasion of Kuwait would make Saddam the most powerful leader in the Middle East and therefore among the most powerful leaders in the world. He would control up to 30 percent of the world's oil reserves. He would be the new Nasser, indeed a modern Nebuchadnezzar. For Saddam, invading Kuwait satisfied both the practical needs of Iraq and his own grandiose megalomania. In reality, however, Saddam's decision would rank among the most poorly conceived strategic miscalculations in modern history.[34]

3

The Iraqi Invasion of Kuwait

Iraqi forces invaded Kuwait with brutal swiftness on August 2, 1990. Within days, the last pockets of Kuwaiti resistance collapsed, paving the way for an Iraqi looting spree the likes of which the world had not seen in decades. Saddam's great gamble appeared to work, for the moment. Hindsight, through which armchair generals and weekend diplomats view the past with great clarity, hints that the world community, especially the United States, should have recognized Saddam's true intent. Conditions at the time, however, offered no such clarity. Confusion, misperception, and very simply distraction muddied worldwide response to the events leading to the invasion. Once undertaken, the invasion startled the world community into quick condemnation and, indeed, action, as Saddam's plans after taking Kuwait appeared no less clear. With Saudi Arabia threatened, the United States led the world community to first protect the House of Saud, while working to get Saddam to leave Kuwait, by force if necessary.

Prelude to Invasion

Throughout the spring and summer of 1990, Saddam grew more belligerent in his public rhetoric, accusing Kuwait of stealing oil from the Rumaila oil fields through slant drilling underneath the Iraq border and of betraying nonexistent promises of debt forgiveness and further loans. Through OPEC and in the Arab Cooperation Council, and also through direct communiqué, Saddam turned up the diplomatic heat on Kuwait, as well as on Saudi Arabia and the UAE, to adhere to agreed-upon oil quotas and forgive Iraqi debt. Saddam demanded additional loans, even gifts, of tens of billions of dollars to help rebuild Iraq after a war Iraq had fought, in Saddam's view, so that other Arab nations need no longer fear the Islamic Revolution of Iran. Saddam desperately needed Saudi

Arabia, the UAE, and most of all Kuwait to ante up and pay for Iraq's sacrifice.

Kuwait and other Arab nations refused to budge. Saudi Arabia offered nothing and insisted Iraq repay its loans to the House of Saud. Kuwait rejected Iraq's repeated requests and subsequent demands to forgive Iraqi debt and decrease oil production to inflate the price per barrel of oil for Iraq's benefit. When Saddam told his fellow Arab leaders in May 1990 that their insistence on low oil prices could be equated with economic war against Iraq, they remained unmoved, dismissing the Iraqi leader's rants as mere grandstanding. Saddam even claimed that Kuwait's failure to maintain oil quotas weakened the economy of all Arab nations to the benefit of Israel. Only in June 1990 did Kuwait and the United Arab Emirates agree to decrease production to edge the price per barrel higher near Saddam's hoped for $25. Even then, an infuriated Saddam remained unsatisfied.[1]

In mid-July, Saddam ordered Iraqi forces to mass near the Kuwaiti border. By July 19, three Iraqi divisions, totaling over 35,000 troops, along with hundreds of tanks, had positioned themselves at various points only miles from Kuwait. By the end of July there would be over 100,000 Iraqi soldiers poised for invasion. On July 16, Iraqi Foreign Minister Tariq Aziz outlined Iraqi grievances against Kuwait in a terse memorandum addressed to members of the Arab League. Aziz listed the now familiar accusations, including the theft of Iraqi oil and Kuwaiti manipulation of oil markets. Aziz also included several demands, including a moratorium on Iraqi debts and the creation of an Arab-wide economic plan to repay Iraq for its sacrifices in the Iran–Iraq War. Border grievances also complicated matters, as both Saddam and Aziz accused Kuwait of violating Iraqi sovereignty by encroaching upon Iraqi territory. Saddam told his Ba'ath followers on July 17 that he would not compromise with Kuwait—either Kuwait would meet all Iraqi demands or face the consequences, including possible Iraqi military action.[2]

The Kuwaiti government had placed its insubstantial armed forces on alert when the Iraqi army first moved toward the border, but later issued a stand-down, choosing instead to interpret Saddam's moves as nothing more than bluster. The Kuwaiti cabinet met on July 20 and issued to the Arab League a strongly worded rebuttal of each of Iraq's accusations and stern rejection of all Iraqi demands. Believing it could negotiate a settlement, the possibility of actual Iraqi military action seemed to the Kuwaiti government distinctly remote. To alleviate the crisis, the Arab League sent Egyptian President Hosni Mubarak, who was also eager to play a Nasser-like role in the Middle East, to talk with both the Kuwaitis and Saddam. After meeting with Saddam, Mubarak reported with relief that Saddam had agreed to further negotiations with Kuwait, to begin on July 31 in Jeddah. Mubarak sensed no hint of Saddam's intent to use military force against Kuwait.[3]

The presence of Iraqi forces so near the Kuwaiti border and Saddam's increasingly provocative threats against Iraq's southern neighbor gave the United States pause to issue statements reiterating its dedication to stability in the Middle East and its hope that disputes among nations in the region could be resolved peacefully. Secretary of Defense Richard Cheney, a former Republican congressional representative from Wyoming and long-time Washington insider, told Washington reporters that the United States would defend American interests in the region and view any threats against American friends in the Middle East with grave concern. The State Department issued similar statements, but admitted to the media that the United States did not have a mutual defense pact with Kuwait and therefore had no legal obligation to come to the aid of the small Persian Gulf nation.[4]

On July 25 occurred one of the more controversial events during the run-up to the Iraqi invasion of Kuwait. The American ambassador to Iraq, April Glaspie, met with Iraqi Foreign Ministry officials in Baghdad to personally relay the State Department's concerns and remind the Iraqis that the United States would stand by its friends in the region. Within minutes of returning to the American Embassy, the Iraqi Foreign Ministry summoned Glaspie to return to meet personally with Saddam, a diplomatic courtesy Iraq had yet to extend her since her arrival in Iraq in 1989. Perhaps because the United States had appointed a woman as its ambassador in a Muslim country, Saddam embarked upon a barely coherent tirade directed at the United States via Glaspie. He demanded an explanation as to why the United States supported Kuwait and all but ignored what to him were Iraq's legitimate grievances and why it had dismissed his leadership in trying to resolve them.

Claiming the United States had now threatened war against Iraq through its joint exercises with forces of the UAE (in reality, only minor refueling exercises), Saddam threatened terrorist attacks against the United States. He went further, questioning American resolve since its debacle in Vietnam to fight for its interests—could Americans stomach losing "10,000 dead in one battle?" Saddam warned Glaspie that if the United States used "pressure" against Iraq, "we will deploy pressure and force." Glaspie assured Saddam of sincere US intentions, telling the Iraqi dictator that President George H. W. Bush "wanted better and deeper relations with Iraq." Glaspie praised Saddam's "extraordinary efforts" to rebuild Iraq after the disastrous war with Iran and appreciated the challenges he faced: "I know you need funds. We understand that and our opinion is that you should have the opportunity to rebuild your country." Concerning the border dispute between Iraq and Kuwait, Glaspie told Saddam: "We have no opinion on the Arab-Arab conflicts." Saddam excused himself to take a phone call from Mubarak, during which the Egyptian president confirmed the Jeddah talks. Visibly relieved, Saddam ceased his rant and spoke calmly of the upcoming talks with the Kuwaitis. Glaspie told Saddam she would fly to Washington on July 30 to confer with President Bush, a previously scheduled trip she had postponed because of "the difficulties" between Iraq and Kuwait. The Iraqi government later released a transcript of the meeting that Glaspie claimed the Iraqis had edited to make it appear that she had given Saddam the "green light" to invade Kuwait, causing her and the State Department much embarrassment.[5]

On the same day that Glaspie met with Saddam, a working group reporting to Under Secretary of Defense Paul Wolfowitz met to discuss the "heightened tensions in the Persian Gulf region," namely the possibility of an Iraqi attack against Kuwait. In its resulting position paper, the group warned of the situation's complexities: "The US must walk a tightrope in trying to provide support to Gulf friends without precipitating the Iraqi actions that the US is trying to prevent." Recognizing Iraq's "untenable economic position," the group took as a good sign Iraq's willingness to meet with Kuwaiti officials to resolve the crisis and believed Saddam appreciated American interests in the region and thus wanted to "avoid a confrontation" with the US. The US, however, had no means to stop Saddam from invading Kuwait, once he decided to do so. The group recommended providing the Kuwaitis as much intelligence as possible, but hoped the crisis could be resolved through American-backed "regional initiatives." If the situation warranted a US military response, the group insisted such action must "be clearly thought out with a stated purpose and definition of roles."[6]

As the talks in Jeddah approached while Saddam continued massing forces near the Kuwaiti border, many observers seemed convinced of a non-military resolution to the crisis. Opinion among Middle Eastern leaders held that Saddam intended only to intimidate the Kuwaitis into some sort of financial settlement to satisfy his desperate need for cash. In a meeting with Chairman of the Joint Chiefs of Staff General Colin Powell, Saudi Ambassador Prince Sultan bin Bandar confidently claimed that Saddam had no intention to invade Kuwait.

Powell would play a central role in the coming events and ironically play a similarly key role in the decision of Bush's son, George W. Bush, as president to invade Iraq twelve years later. Born in Harlem in 1937 to immigrant parents from Jamaica and commissioned in 1958 through the Reserve Officer Training Corps program at the City University of New York, Powell could not have been any more the opposite of the wealthy, privileged Bandar. Powell had made the Army his life, rising from his two tours of duty in Vietnam to become the youngest general appointed Chairman of the Joint Chiefs of Staff. Like many career Army officers, Powell's Vietnam experience transcended the evolution of the conflict over time. As a young captain, Powell served as an advisor with field units of the Army of the Republic of Vietnam during his first tour in 1962–63. After duty stateside, Powell returned to Vietnam in 1968 as a major in the Americal Division (23rd Infantry Division), serving as an operations officer. Units in the Americal had been responsible for the slaughter of Vietnamese civilians at My Lai on March 16, 1968— Powell had no direct link to the incident. After his final tour of duty in Vietnam as a lieutenant colonel, Powell won a slot in the prestigious White House Fellows program to begin his ongoing association with the White House that would ultimately see him appointed Secretary of State in 2001. It was his experience as a White House Fellow that convinced Powell to stay in the Army rather than retire after twenty years, as had been his original plan.

Powell's subsequent service under Defense Secretary Casper Weinberger and National Security Advisor Frank Carlucci prepared him well to serve as National Security Advisor to President Reagan during the last years of Reagan's second term and then as Chairman of the Joint Chiefs of Staff under President George H. W. Bush. Powell was in the vanguard of a new type of senior officer, one who could transcend and nimbly navigate the military and civilian political worlds, much like General Alexander Haig had done under Nixon. As an African-American from Harlem, his meteoric rise to the top military post in the Pentagon was doubly significant in the American social experience.[7]

Bandar, on the other hand, had family and wealth to thank for his position, but the Saudi prince also exercised a keen political sense that made him perfect to represent King Fahd in the United States. As a Saudi Air Force officer, Prince Bandar had served as the Saudi defense attaché in Washington before King Fahd appointed him ambassador in 1983. Well connected, outgoing, and for an Arab diplomatic representative unusually overtly pro-American, Bandar knew everyone in Washington important to Saudi Arabia, especially concerning security matters. Despite their divergent backgrounds, Powell and Bandar got on well, having developed a close personal relationship over their years in Washington as military men (Bandar flew F-5s and F-15s in the Saudi Air Force) and racquetball partners. Theirs was typical of long-established relationships that would prove pivotal in the coming months.[8]

Meanwhile, Egyptian President Mubarak encouraged President Bush to leave resolving the Iraq–Kuwait dispute to Arab leaders—an Arab solution for an Arab problem. Jordan's King Hussein claimed he had Saddam's personal assurance that the Iraqis did not intend to use military force against Kuwait. British sources offered similar assessments. Saddam, the world believed, had embarked on the long-held Arab tradition of saber-rattling intimidation to get his way.[9]

American intelligence services, however, slowly reached a different conclusion as the heretofore unknown invasion date approached. Initially, low communications traffic and slow movement of munitions and other supplies thought necessary for offensive action against Kuwait supported the intimidation theory. On July 16, analysts in the Defense Intelligence Agency (DIA) noticed the sudden appearance of a brigade of Iraqi T-72 tanks near the Kuwaiti border and trains loaded with military equipment to outfit a Republican Guard division headed south. On July 17, satellite images revealed the Republican Guard's Hammurabi Division, with its 10,000 troops and 300 tanks, near the border. In the following forty-eight hours, the Medina Division and the In God We Trust Division, both elite Republican Guard units, had arrived. Powell concurred with DIA assessments that because there had been no evidence of pre-combat rehearsals, as there had been on numerous occasions during the Iran–Iraq War, that Saddam's intent remained unclear. Powell nevertheless ordered General H. Norman Schwarzkopf, the commander of US Central Command (CENTCOM), to devise contingency plans both for a retaliatory response if Iraq undertook a strike against Kuwait and for militarily stopping an Iraqi strike.

By July 30, DIA concluded that Iraqi forces had now taken an effective offensive posture. At least eight Iraqi divisions had massed along the Kuwaiti border. Both the DIA and the CIA speculated that Saddam was about to unleash an invasion of Kuwait, but based upon the lack of any hard evidence to the contrary failed to convince Powell. On August 1, Iraqi tank units "uncoiled," communications traffic increased dramatically, and Iraqi fuel trucks moved in large numbers toward the border. CIA assessments confirmed the movements to reach the same conclusion—Saddam's game of bluff had ended. The United States could do little but stand by and watch if Saddam decided to actually pull the trigger. Powell, now convinced, worried that the Iraqi force far out-sized the number of troops and tanks it would take to overrun Kuwait. With no forces deployed forward, it would take weeks for the United States to build more than a minimal military presence in the region, especially against such a colossal Iraqi force, one that seemed far out of proportion to that required to invade and occupy tiny Kuwait. Still, the White House refused to accept the possibility that Saddam would actually commit such an aggressive act, one that seemed in the waning days of the Cold War to be very anachronistic.[10]

On July 31, delegations from Iraq and Kuwait met as planned in Jeddah. Iraq's lead representative, Izzat Ibrahim, promised that Iraq would substantially reduce its heavily armed presence along the border with Kuwait in exchange for restitution of $10 billion from Kuwait for oil depleted from the Rumaila oil fields. Speaking for Kuwait, Crown Prince Sa'd Abdallah al-Sabah countered that demand with an offer of $9 billion. For some reason, the Kuwaiti offer offended the Iraqis. Ibrahim and the Iraqi delegation walked out and returned to Bagdad, but not without first agreeing to continue talks with the Kuwaitis on August 4 in the Iraqi capital.

Also on July 31, in Washington, DC, John Kelly, the Assistant Secretary of State of Near Eastern and South Asian Affairs, testified before the House Foreign Relations Committee that the United States had no treaty obligations to defend Kuwait. That night, Jordan's King Hussein warned President Bush via phone of the potential for Iraqi military action but said that he still hoped for a peaceful resolution. The next day, Saudi King Fahd offered Bush a similar assessment of the situation. No one in the Middle East, it seemed, was convinced that Saddam would order his forces to invade Kuwait. Mubarak, King Fahd, King Hussein, and the Kuwaiti Emir all believed Saddam's bold moves were merely bluster, designed to give Iraq leverage at the negotiating table. Saddam, however, had already issued orders to launch the invasion of Kuwait.[11]

Iraq Invades

In the pre-dawn hours of August 2, 1990, Iraqi military forces crossed the border into Kuwait. Elite armored units of the Republican Guard, including the Hammurabi and Medina Divisions, reached Kuwait City within hours. Iraq Special Forces units attacked strategic targets in Kuwait City by helicopter and secured other important locations across Kuwait, including the disputed islands of Warba and Bubiyan in the Persian Gulf.

By August 3, Republican Guard units had occupied Kuwait's al-Burqan oil field and had reached the border with Saudi Arabia. The Emir and Kuwaiti Royal Family fled to Saudi Arabia, denying Saddam the coup of capturing them, if not executing them. The Emir's brother, Sheik Fahd, tragically died while defending the Kuwaiti Royal Palace against Iraqi invaders. While some Kuwaiti military units managed to resist for two to three days, the bulk of Kuwait's army of 16,000 and its small air force buckled in a matter of hours under the invading weight of at least 100,000 Iraqi troops and their 2,000 tanks. Surviving elements of the Kuwaiti military retreated into Saudi Arabia.[12]

Iraqi troops then pillaged and plundered their way through Kuwait City and other towns and villages, where they ransacked offices, hospitals, department stores, car dealerships, and countless other businesses and homes. Cars, furniture, clothing, appliances, money—anything they could take they did take. Iraqi soldiers set animals free from the Kuwait City Zoo, destroyed the Kuwait desalinization plant, and committed untold other acts of destruction, leaving a ruined city that would take the Kuwaiti government years to restore. Such heinous acts further confirmed Saddam's sadistic reputation and damaged all the more his standing in the Arab world.[13]

Troops rounded up Kuwaiti men, young and old, and even teenage boys, sending them across the border into Iraq for internment in squalid camps. Hundreds of thousands of Kuwaitis fled the country, with many reaching Egypt, Jordan (ironically driving across Iraq to get there), or Saudi Arabia, while Iraqi troops stopped an unlucky minority near border crossings, robbing them of all their possessions and in some cases shooting them. Of those who made it out, the lucky ones had either money or external help to reach a safe destination. Many of those less fortunate settled into crowded refugee camps. In Jordan alone, over 100,000 Kuwaitis sat out the war in camps. Many of Kuwait's nearly two million guest workers, mostly from Pakistan and India, found themselves abandoned, though their home governments managed to fly out several planeloads during and just after the invasion. During the few days following the invasion, allegations of horrific atrocities committed by Iraqi forces reached the outside world by telephone, fax, and word of mouth.[14]

The international community, led by the United States, quickly condemned the Iraqi attack. From Washington, initial statements from the White House condemned the invasion and called for Iraq to immediately withdraw from Kuwait with such conviction that they seemed to expect Saddam to pull out his forces the next day. Such expectations, though, underestimated the conviction of the Iraqi dictator. Interestingly, these statements put pressure on the UN Security Council and the Arab League to address the crisis, showing the Bush administration's willingness, publically at any rate, to work toward a solution through both international and regional organizations rather than through unilateral action. That same day, the UN Security Council passed Resolution 660 by a vote of 14 to 0 (with only Yemen abstaining), condemning the invasion and calling for Iraq's immediate and unconditional withdrawal from Kuwait, and also approved Resolution 661, which placed an embargo on Iraq to include oil and weapons. Nevertheless, according to the August 2 statement the United States was "reviewing all options in response to the Iraqi aggression."[15]

Early on August 2, President Bush addressed reporters in the Cabinet Room at the White House, where he first referred to the Iraqi invasion as "naked aggression," a phrase he would invoke repeatedly over the next several months. Bush informed the media that he had signed executive orders freezing both Iraqi and Kuwaiti assets in the United States to deny Saddam access to Iraqi funds and to prevent him from stealing Kuwaiti money held in the United States. Bush also announced that he was already working through the State Department to build a united international front to "act together to ensure that Iraqi forces depart Kuwait immediately." Later in the day on August 2, President Bush and British Prime Minister Margaret Thatcher appeared before reporters in Aspen, Colorado, where Thatcher strongly condemned Iraq and called for collective action through the United Nations if Iraq refused to leave Kuwait. "None of us can do it separately," the Iron Lady told reporters, "we need a collective and effective will of the nations belonging to the United Nations." When asked about possible military action, Bush cagily replied, "We're not ruling any options in, but we're not ruling any options out." Thatcher and Bush presented clear, united support for resolution of the crisis, peacefully or otherwise, through the UN. While Bush initially shied away from openly confirming his consideration of military options, by August 5 he subtly opened the door for such action when he rejected the legitimacy of any government Saddam had established in Kuwait. In response to a reporter questioning "how can you and other world leaders prevent the installation of what you term a puppet government" in Kuwait, Bush replied sharply, "Just wait. Watch and learn."[16]

Bush had the political experience to back up such bold pronouncements. Born to a political family (his father, Prescott Bush, had served in the United States Senate) in Massachusetts in 1924, Bush had attended Phillips Academy, and then entered the US Navy as a pilot in 1942. At the time, he was the youngest naval aviator at just under nineteen years of age. His wartime service in the Pacific theater had included over fifty combat missions flying the single-engine Grumman TBM Avenger torpedo bomber. On September 2, 1944, Japanese flak had hit his Avenger attack aircraft during a mission in the Bonin Islands. Despite flying a badly damaged plane and with one of his two crewmembers severely wounded, Bush had completed his mission. Unable to nurse his wounded plane back to the carrier *San Jacinto*, Bush and one his surviving crewmembers had bailed out. His crewmate had failed to survive the jump, but Bush had managed to cling to his tiny life raft for several hours until his rescue by an American submarine. Bush had been awarded the Distinguished Flying Cross and had also earned several Air Medals for over fifty combat missions he had flown in the Pacific.[17]

After the war, Bush had graduated from Yale, and then had gone to Texas to seek his fortune in the oil business, where by the mid-1950s he had indeed made that fortune. After an unsuccessful run for one of Texas's two senate seats in 1964, Bush had won the election in 1966 to the first of his two terms in the United States House of Representatives, beginning his long career in politics and distinguished record of public service. After losing a senate bid in 1970, Bush had served as the American Ambassador to the United Nations, and then as Chairman of the Republican National Committee. Then followed service as Chief of the U.S. Liaison Office in China, as Director of the CIA, and as the head of the Council on Foreign Relations before his election as vice president with President Ronald Reagan in 1980. Bush had won the presidency in his own right in 1988. As a president with a Distinguished Flying Cross, Bush certainly had clout with his military advisors and senior military leaders in the Pentagon. His continued interests in the oil business gave him exposure to Middle Eastern politics and culture and a keen appreciation for the volatility of both the Middle East and the oil market. While perhaps not the most accomplished public speaker, Bush had energy and gave his utmost personal attention to US national security policy. Few presidents can claim to have been better prepared for a crisis in the Middle East than Bush.[18]

Publically, Bush initially downplayed the possible Iraqi threat against Saudi Arabia and the potential for American military action in the Persian Gulf region. However, within his council of advisors, the so-called Gang of Eight, Bush fully recognized the seriousness of Saddam's action and its potential ripple effects across the region if not the world.[19] For Bush, all diplomatic, economic, and military options were on the table. The invasion had occurred at a time of stable if not good relations between the United States and the waning Soviet Union, and because industrialized nations around the world relied in varying degrees on Middle Eastern oil, countries such as China, Japan, India, and Brazil soon joined in the international chorus of condemnation. As Saddam could now control 20 percent of the world's oil reserves and would be able to control another 30 percent if he invaded Saudi Arabia, which Bush privately seemed convinced he would, the Iraqi dictator could wreak havoc on the global economy, and especially on that of the United States. The invasion had already caused deep dips in stock markets in Japan, Europe, and of course Wall Street. Oil prices rose, but stabilized at the end of August when OPEC increased production. After the invasion on August 2, Iraq moved heavy armored divisions near the Saudi Arabian border; that, combined with the excessively large force used to invade Kuwait, understandably led Bush, and the Saudis, to conclude that Saudi Arabia was next on Saddam's list of countries to intimidate if not to occupy. On August 8, Saddam announced annexation of Kuwait as the 19th Province of the Republic of Iraq.[20]

Defending Saudi Arabia

Saudi Arabia's King Fahd found himself in a difficult position. His small but well equipped army and air force could not hold out against an Iraqi onslaught. He desperately needed American help, realizing that only the United States had the military capacity and capability to defeat Saddam. Having earlier dismissed Saddam's threats to occupy Kuwait as mere bluster, Fahd now asked President Bush if he would send American ground forces to protect Saudi Arabia and if so, he wanted Bush's personal assurance that those forces would return to the United States when the threat had passed. Bush told the Saudi King that the United States would assist him in whatever way he requested and that he need not fear a permanent American military presence in the Saudi Kingdom. Accordingly, the Saudi Ambassador to the United States, Prince Bandar, met with Bush's National Security Advisor, Brent Scowcroft, and then received a full briefing from General Powell and Secretary of Defense Cheney on American contingency plans for sending a significant defensive force to Saudi Arabia. On August 6, Cheney, along with CENTCOM commander General Schwarzkopf, Deputy National Security Council Advisor Robert Gates, and Under Secretary of Defense Paul Wolfowitz, were in Riyadh to personally meet with King Fahd to obtain his blessing to dispatch as many as 200,000 American troops to Saudi Arabia.

Numerous factors influenced Fahd's unprecedented and risky decision to allow American forces into his country. Aside from the obvious Iraqi threat, which Schwarzkopf made painfully clear through satellite photographs showing Iraqi tanks near the Saudi border, Fahd, normally very pro-American, had to satisfy the concerns of those in his ruling circle who exhibited less than enthusiastic attitudes toward the United States. Many among the Saudi elite feared that such a large US force in their Islamic homeland would threaten religious and social traditions by personally exposing Saudis to American culture and western values. The thousands of women in the US military alone presented an enormous threat to the Saudi way of life. Others voiced not unwarranted concerns that an intended temporary US garrison might grow into a long-term, potentially destabilizing presence, while still others questioned the commitment of the United States to stay the course through difficult military crises.

Among those gravely concerned was the thirty-three-year-old son of a wealthy Saudi family named Osama bin Laden. Born in 1957, bin Laden had been a good student and by most accounts a normal Saudi boy until at age fourteen when he had some sort of socio-religious awakening. Bin Laden gravitated toward the teachings of Wahhabi theologians, who preached a return to the Golden Age of Islam, at a time when the faith had not been corrupted by Western influences—before the Crusades, before European imperialism, and before the creation of Israel. He matriculated in 1976 at Jeddah's King Abdul Aziz University, where his faith intensified and was augmented by the writings of the influential Egyptian leader of the Muslim Brotherhood, Sayyid Qutb. In 1979, bin Laden left Saudi Arabia to join the jihad against the Soviet invasion of Afghanistan. While bin Laden saw little combat, he became an effective organizer and fundraiser to engage and train Arab recruits to fight the Soviets. While his role in the Soviet–Afghan War is subject to intense debate, there is minimal dispute that he returned to Saudi Arabia in 1989 as an immensely popular folk hero. Bin Laden was appalled at the lavishness of the Saudi royal house, but put these concerns aside when he learned that American—that is, Christian—troops numbering in the tens of thousands would soon be stationed in his Islamic homeland. Bin Laden loudly protested the presence of US troops in Saudi Arabia, causing King Fahd no end of embarrassment in front of his American allies and potential saviors if Saddam decided to attack. Fahd gladly had bin Laden banished from his kingdom. From that point, bin Laden channeled his enormous energies into ridding the Islamic world of the influence of the decadent West, resulting in al Qaeda's attack on the United States on September 11, 2001.[21]

While not as fanatical toward the West as bin Laden, for many Arabs across the Middle East the thought of US and European troops in the region brought back memories of imperialism. American and Western support of Israel, too, complicated matters among Arabs who feared foreign troops could be used to that end rather than against Saddam. The quick American withdrawal from Beirut in 1983 and tensions between the United States and Iran remained fresh memories for many Saudis as well as for others in the Middle East. Realizing the immediate danger that his kingdom faced, Fahd put aside his usual political tactic of building consensus among the royal family on major decisions to instead make the choice alone. Bush's strong statement to reporters on the White House's south lawn on August 5 should have reassured Fahd: "This will not stand. This will not stand, this aggression against Kuwait."[22]

Fahd quickly gave his approval, but conditioned his go-ahead on US commitment to tough it out through to the end of the crisis, to leave Saudi Arabia once the threat had passed, and to respect Islamic traditions (to the point that American troops had to hide crucifixes underneath clothing and restrict Bibles to US bases—Jewish troops ultimately had to be flown out of the country to a US naval vessel on station in the Persian Gulf to attend services).[23]

On August 8, President Bush delivered a nationally televised address announcing his decision to send forces to help defend Saudi Arabia. While not mentioning Adolf Hitler directly, Bush made the analogy linking unchallenged Nazi expansion in the 1930s to Saddam as "an aggressive neighbor threatening his neighbors" after promising not to invade Kuwait—like those promises of Adolf Hitler over fifty years before, Saddam's "promises mean nothing." Bush then laid the groundwork for what would become one of the most widespread, diverse, and effective coalitions of nations during the twentieth century, declaring that "this is not an American problem or a European problem or a Middle East problem: It is the world's problem."[24] By revealing intent to defend if attacked, Bush had now opened the door to the possibility of war. In Powell's view as Chairman of the Joint Chiefs of Staff, early in the crisis Bush had clearly come to accept use of force as the only means to get Saddam out of Kuwait. The "tail-end option," Powell later wrote, "suddenly became the front-end option."[25]

As part of its Cold War contingency planning, the US military already had the beginnings of an operational plan for defending Saudi Arabian oil fields from external attack, in this case from the Soviet Union. Now, with Iraq as the chief threat to Saudi Arabia, General Schwarzkopf and his planners at CENTCOM pulled Operational Plan (OP PLAN)

1002-90 from the shelf to tailor it to the current situation. Earlier in 1990, CENTCOM had exercised a variant of OP PLAN 1002-90 under the operational name INTERNAL LOOK 90 to test the plan's joint command functions, and General Schwarzkopf had mentioned the plan's existence in a crisis briefing the day before Iraqi forces invaded Kuwait. The plan, however, had remained incomplete as a usable unified campaign plan, lacking component force lists and the necessary final approval of the Joint Chiefs of Staff. Regardless, the plan assumed a thirty-day advance notice just to get the requisite forces (including squadrons of F-15s, the Ready Brigade of the 82nd Airborne Division, and a Marine Expeditionary Brigade, among other assets) prepared to deploy. Saudi Arabia might not have that sort of time.[26]

The Iraqi invasion naturally sped up the evolution of OP PLAN 1002-90, and throughout the coming months CENTCOM constantly updated and altered the plan, especially when the mission shifted from defending Saudi Arabia to ejecting Iraqi forces from Kuwait with military force. Meeting the Iraqi military machine toe-to-toe required a months-long buildup of US forces in the region. With no sizable forward deployed forces, the United States would have to move everything—troops, vehicles, tanks, artillery, aircraft, fuel, and munitions—to Saudi Arabia. Carrier fleets had to be positioned in the Persian Gulf. Permission from various nations had to be gained for use of airspace as well as for basing aircraft combat missions. All of this would take time; indeed it would take months to get US forces in position to defend Saudi Arabia, then later undertake offensive operations if directed to do so.[27]

The United States, nevertheless, exercised its rapid-deployment muscle. By August 8, two F-15 fighter squadrons and the Ready Brigade of the 82nd Airborne Division were deployed to Saudi Arabia. More units from the XVIII Airborne Corps at Fort Bragg, North Carolina, arrived daily. B-52 bombers, the mainstay of Strategic Air Command (SAC), were deployed to the upgraded American base on the island of Diego Garcia in the Indian Ocean. Two carrier battle groups, the *Dwight Eisenhower* and *Independence*, made their way to the Persian Gulf. Thus began DESERT SHIELD, ultimately the largest concentrated movement of American military forces since World War II. During its first month, however, DESERT SHIELD still moved at a trickle compared to the influx of forces that would pour into Saudi Arabia in the coming months. At the moment, the relative handful of American forces deployed to Saudi Arabia found themselves at Saddam's mercy, should he choose to move against Saudi Arabia.[28]

The US Military in 1990

For the United States, DESERT SHIELD came at a pivotal moment in the recovery of the US military from its calamitous experience in the Vietnam War that had ended in January 1973. Wracked by drug and racial problems, severe discipline issues, and a poor public perception because of Vietnam and the draft, the US Army in particular had found itself at a low ebb in the early 1970s. The bold move to an all-volunteer force (AVF), however, put the US military back on course to rebuilding its force structure, restoring its public image, and returning to its focus on fighting the Soviet Union. Doubts nonetheless remained as to whether the AVF could fight a "big war."[29]

The US military had restored its public image in part through aggressive advertising and recruiting campaigns, both of which were necessary to reach recruiting goals under the new AVF, which some criticized as nothing more than a glorified federal jobs program. In 1980, the Army had rolled out its very successful "Be All You Can Be" recruiting campaign that lasted through 2001. The Marine Corps, also deeply affected by Vietnam, had promoted the uniqueness of being a Marine through "We're Looking for a Few Good Men," while the Air Force offered such slogans as "Look Up; Be Looked Up To!" and "Aim High!" The Navy had told young Americans, "It's Not Just a Job, It's an Adventure!" The Department of Defense had hit television with such ads as "Army! Navy! Air Force! Marines! It's a Great Place to Start!" In addition to implied service to country, the armed forces had pitched the long-term benefits of military service, especially job skills and money for college tuition. One recruiting commercial had proudly proclaimed: "We don't need experience, we give it!" So successful were these campaigns that all of the services, including Reserve and National Guard components, had met recruiting goals by the early 1980s. Some wondered, however, if these "soldiers" who had enlisted to get job training or money for college could actually "pull the trigger" when called upon to do so.[30]

The US military also had to refocus, restructure, and reequip to fight a large conventional, industrialized enemy after fighting a hybrid conventional–counterinsurgency war in Vietnam for so many years. While the Air Force had tried to refocus on its strategic strike capability through SAC, the Army had gained the upper hand as the principal American force to stop a Soviet invasion of Western Europe with the introduction of AirLand Battle doctrine. Initiated in the mid-1970s in response to the modernization of the Soviet military and the lethality of modern weapons used in the 1973 Arab-Israeli War, the AirLand Battle doctrine had provided the American military with basic guidelines to fight and quickly win a conventional war against a similarly equipped and manned Soviet Union. The primary concepts of AirLand Battle had matured over the course of a decade, appearing in successive updates of Army Field Manual 100-5. AirLand Battle had integrated air and land assets to counter a Soviet invasion of Western Europe by holding the front line with heavy armored units while using air, artillery, and other assets to strike deep behind enemy lines to disrupt reinforcement and logistics, all with the assumption that American and Allied forces would be outmanned. Such doctrine had encouraged commanders to utilize maneuver on the battlefield and maintain and capitalize on initiative to act independently of enemy action. Because of its nature, AirLand Battle gave primacy to land warfare, using air power in an integrated role and providing the military guidance on force structure and future procurement.[31]

This emphasis on AirLand Battle also fit perfectly with the Army's rediscovery of Clausewitz. In 1976, Princeton University Press had published Michael Howard and Peter Paret's landmark translation of Clausewitz's *Vom Krieg—On War*—with the expressed intent to make the Prussian's classic treatise, first published in German in the 1830s, accessible to professional military officers. Colin Powell in particular had found the new edition of *On War* appealing. Having just graduated from the Army War College at Carlisle Barracks, Pennsylvania, Powell had found in the Prussian's study on war answers to what had happened to his Army and his country during the Vietnam War. Linking military action and policy was the key, as one had to be clear in how to fight the war at hand so that the appropriate military action would achieve the desired political objective. If the political objective was unclear, then clarity would elude military leaders while they devised their strategic and even tactical approach to the war. The Army's interpretation of Clausewitz's integrated (and controversial) trinity—military, government, people—convinced many officers that the lack of integration of these three pillars was the Achilles' heel for the American war in Vietnam.[32]

What married Clausewitz and AirLand Battle was the concept of operational war. Speed, depth, and decisiveness, delivered by a technologically superior and expertly trained military force, would achieve the political objective. There is much debate on what Clausewitz actually meant by "operational" and the Prussian himself was inconsistent in his references to the operational aspect of war. While he did write that in war the defensive is preferable to the offensive, operationally Clausewitz seemed to prefer a "unitary conception of war" that many Western theorists throughout the twentieth century interpreted as meaning the use of all available resources in a decisive manner to annihilate the enemy. The Germans had attempted this in World War I. The Allies had actually achieved this in World War II. The United States had turned its back on Clausewitz and failed to do this in Korea, and had ignored this in Vietnam.[33]

This post-Vietnam period represented the coming together of another Clausewitz-like trinity of martial philosophies that historian Brian McAllister Linn calls that of the Guardians, the Heroes, and the Managers. The American approach to war that developed after Vietnam, indeed in response to Vietnam, resulted from the fluid tension of this triad of values. The Guardians, in Linn's framework, consider war an engineering problem in which the answer is derived from "immutable scientific principles." For the Guardians, a formula that equates military capabilities with the accepted national security policy, then contrasts the same to that of potential competitors, determines success. Victory in war, then, can be predicted if not predetermined. Heroes, predictably, rely upon traditional battlefield values—such as courage, honor, and tactical skill—as the determining factors for victory in battle and in war. Only when "other factors" subvert the legitimacy and worth of these values does defeat enter the equation. For the Heroes, the failure of Vietnam lay in the "betrayal" of these martial values by the Johnson and Nixon administrations and American society (two legs of the Clausewitzian trinity failed at the expense of the third). Managers, as they are called by Linn, reduce war to an organizational problem—"the rational coordination of resources, both human and materiel." Using Linn's framework, then, Powell could be viewed as a Guardian, Schwarzkopf as a Hero, and the bureaucrats of the American defense establishment, the heirs of Secretary of Defense Robert S. McNamara's approach to defense policy, as the Managers. The three philosophies of the Guardians, the Heroes, and the Managers worked with, pushed against, and even subverted each other as the post-Vietnam military tried to right itself and rethink its approach to war against a peer enemy. Each assumed that enemy to be the Soviet Union. The first real test of this trinity, however, came in the Gulf War against Iraq.[34]

Now past Vietnam and refocused on the Soviet military colossus in Europe, the US military, particularly its army, had to revisit its organization, procurement, and doctrine to defend Western Europe from possible Soviet attack. In assaulting these challenges, Clausewitz provided at least some inspiration for the Guardians, Heroes, and Managers jostling to provide answers. The result included the AVF, AirLand Battle, and a new reliance on cutting-edge technology.

The post-Vietnam American military establishment certainly needed reorganization. Since the expansion of the American defense establishment in 1947, decades-old inter-service rivalry over mission, command and control, budgets, and procurement had stifled creativity, encouraged waste and redundancy, and intensified service parochialism to the point that some speculated that the American military might be incapable of preparing for a large conventional war, much less capable of fighting one. The aborted Operation EAGLE CLAW rescue of American hostages in Iran in 1980, the 1983 terrorist bombing of the Marine barracks in Lebanon, and the 1983 American invasion of Grenada (Operation URGENT FURY) highlighted these inefficiencies. The establishment of the Rapid Deployment Force (RDF) by President Carter had been a step in the right direction to quickly project US military power to crisis points around the world, but the creation of the RDF and all of its service components, however, hit numerous roadblocks because of service parochialism, competition over limited funding, and other issues.

The 1986 Department of Defense Reorganization Act, commonly known as the Goldwater–Nichols Act after its sponsors Senator Barry Goldwater of Arizona and Representative William Nichols of Alabama (both of whom were combat veterans of World War II), attempted to address these shortcomings in the most sweeping reorganization of the Pentagon since the 1947 National Security Act. Goldwater–Nichols transformed the Chairman of the Joint Chiefs of Staff from a sort of general manager to the principal military advisor to the president. The act gave the service chiefs control over training and procurement within their respective service at the expense of operational control, which now flowed from the president to the Secretary of Defense, bypassing the Joint Chiefs, down to the regional commanders-in-chief (CINCs). Goldwater–Nichols gave regional CINCs operational command over all assets in their theaters regardless of service, establishing for the first time truly integrated joint commands. To facilitate this "jointness," the act allowed each regional CINC to have a staff made up of personnel from each service. The Chairman of the Joint Chiefs of Staff, too, now had a similar joint staff. "Jointness" was the common theme of Goldwater–Nichols. Select officers of each service would now attend professional military education (PME) schools of other services, such as the Army Command and General Staff College at Fort Leavenworth, Kansas, or the Air War College at Maxwell Air Force Base in Alabama. Joint billets would now count more toward promotion, particularly for flag rank.

"Jointness" even reached into the realm of procurement, mandating that the services share technology and cooperate in developing new weapons systems to both avoid redundancy and improve overall effectiveness, something the services had been loath to do during the Cold War expansion of the military establishment. After Goldwater–Nichols, as a play on combining the traditional distinctive uniform colors of each service, the tongue-in-cheek question among officers became "Are you purple?" when asking if one had completed newly required joint assignments.[35]

Goldwater–Nichols, however, did not resolve all of these problems overnight. The intense debates surrounding the act ironically intensified service loyalty. Overcoming service parochialism would take years, if not decades, if it could be overcome at all. Indeed, such deeply entrenched service rivalries made establishing some sort of joint culture nearly impossible. The Army, Navy, Air Force, and Marines did recognize, however, that they had better try to get along and work together, lest civilian bureaucrats or political appointees make important military procurement, strategic, and organizational decisions for them. In 1990, Goldwater–Nichols had only been in effect for a few years—thus, while unified commands existed according to the law, changing service culture remained beyond its reach at the time of the Persian Gulf crisis.[36]

Reorganization resulted in five regional commands around the world, and by 1990 a special operations command and a space command.[37] CENTCOM evolved from the old RDF to include the Persian Gulf region. Any US military operation in Saudi Arabia, Kuwait, or Iraq would fall under CENTCOM and its burly commander Army General H. Norman Schwarzkopf. Schwarzkopf's father, Herbert Norman Schwarzkopf, Sr., had been a veteran of World War I and had served for several years as the superintendent of the New Jersey state police, where among other things he had played a leading role in investigating the Lindbergh baby kidnapping. During World War II, the elder Schwarzkopf had been posted to Iran, where he had helped organize the Iranian gendarmerie. As a major general, Schwarzkopf, Sr., had returned to Iran as part of the CIA's Operation AJAX to train paramilitary forces in support of the CIA's bid to return the Shah of Iran, Muhammad Reza, to power. As a boy, the younger Schwarzkopf had lived in Iran, attending school in Tehran as well as in Geneva.

A graduate of the United States Military Academy at West Point (Class of 1956), Schwarzkopf had served on two tours in Vietnam that bookended the American experience in that ultimately fruitless conflict. Like Powell, Schwarzkopf had spent his first tour as an adviser with the South Vietnamese army in 1965–66. He had returned to Vietnam in 1970 as lieutenant colonel, and was awarded the Silver Star for bravery in rescuing several wounded men from a minefield. The bear-like officer had stayed in the Army after Vietnam, helping it recover and transition to the AVF. In 1983, he had served as the Army commander for Operation URGENT FURY in Grenada, and then in the Army's Operations and Plans division in the Pentagon before taking command of CENTCOM in 1988. Schwarzkopf knew the Middle East perhaps better than any senior American military officer; that, combined with his Vietnam experience, gave him ample cause to approach any US use of force in the Persian Gulf with confidence and caution.[38]

As the CENTCOM CINC, Schwarzkopf had access to whatever resources from each service he required to carry out military operations in accordance with American interests and objectives. Through Goldwater–Nichols, the services literally trained, equipped, and organized to provide Schwarzkopf with the tools of war necessary to carry out DESERT SHIELD, then later DESERT STORM. While the Goldwater–Nichols reforms continued to evolve through their various stages of implementation, the crisis in the Persian Gulf nonetheless forced the first full test of the new "joint" American military establishment.[39]

While the AVF and reorganization helped the American military put behind the ghosts of Vietnam, the military also needed to replace and update its arsenal to meet the Soviet threat through the new AirLand Battle doctrine. The Department of Defense reviewed just about everything from transportation to the most sophisticated weapons systems. The new systems that would see action in the Persian Gulf included the M1A1 Abrams tank, the M2 and M3 Bradley infantry fighting vehicles, the AH-64A Apache attack helicopter, and the UH-60A Black Hawk utility helicopter. The M1A1 Abrams tank had been in the US Army's arsenal since 1980 and had been designed to fight Soviet armor in Western Europe—it would face off against Soviet-made tanks in the Iraqi desert. The Bradley Fighting Vehicle had joined the Army's arsenal in 1981 and was designed to carry a squad of infantry into close combat. The Bradley also had a TOW (tube-launched, optically tracked, wire command data link, guided missile) missile system capable of destroying tanks and other armored vehicles. The Apache attack helicopter had come on line in 1986 to eventually replace the Vietnam-era Cobra attack helicopter. It had been used in Panama in 1989 but would see its first widespread combat test in the Persian Gulf and had day-and-night flight capability. With its radar and other electronics, the Apache could fly also in adverse weather conditions. Its weapons package, including Hellfire missiles and a 30 mm chain gun, made it especially lethal. The Black

Hawk, introduced in 1979 to replace the Vietnam-era UH-1H Iroquois (or Huey) utility helicopter, provided a multipurpose function, including air assault, medical evacuation, and other capabilities. The Patriot air defense missile system had also come on line just in time for service in the Persian Gulf, as had the HMMWV (high mobility multipurpose wheeled vehicle or Humvee, also called a Hummer) that like its predecessor the Jeep would later be made available for public purchase by its maker General Motors as the Hummer.

The Air Force introduced so-called "stealth" technology to the world during the crisis. Though the F-117 Nighthawk had been used in Operation JUST CAUSE in Panama in 1989, the radar-avoiding flying-wing aircraft were generally unknown to the general public—that would change in the coming months. Radar and communications platforms, such as the Air Force's Airborne Warning and Control System (AWACS), new satellite mapping through the Global Positioning System (GPS), and the latest generation of everything from precision-guided munitions (PGMs) to night-vision goggles gave the American military an unprecedented though largely untried technological advantage. Despite these advancements in technology and weapons development, few of these systems and tools operated flawlessly and their use in the coming months would reveal a range of shortcomings. While the American military's equipment and personnel made it the most advanced and lethal armed force in the world, neither had been tested in battle on a large scale.[40]

Along with the long shadow of the Vietnam syndrome, the serious problems revealed by the aborted hostage rescue in Iran, the Grenada invasion, and the Beirut peacekeeping operation, had also led President Reagan's Secretary of Defense, Casper Weinberger, to offer conditions for US use of force. In a speech to the National Press Club in November 1984, Weinberger had outlined these in what had become known as the Weinberger Doctrine. To avoid future Vietnam-like debacles, Weinberger had favored using appropriate force to achieve limited political objectives, but only if the use of force met six tests. First, the United States should "not commit forces to combat overseas unless" the situation "is deemed vital to our national interest." Second, the United States should commit military forces "wholeheartedly, and with the clear intention of winning." Third, American military forces should only be committed under "clearly defined political and military objectives." Fourth, once committed, forces should be "reassessed and adjusted" as objectives and conditions change. Fifth, the United States should commit forces only with public and congressional support. Only "candid"

explanation of the purported threat and "continuing and close consultation," according to Weinberger, could assure and sustain such support.
Finally, Weinberger had maintained that the United States should commit
military forces only "as a last resort," after exhausting all other available means to achieve the political objective at hand. While warning that
his conditions should not be interpreted as an "abdication of America's
responsibilities" or that the United States "is unwilling" to send its military into harm's way, Weinberger had offered the conditions as a "note of
caution" that had to be considered before committing American forces to
combat: "When we ask our military forces to risk their very lives in such
situations, a note of caution is not only prudent, it is morally required."[41]

Each of Weinberger's six conditions had clearly addressed long-
simmering issues, many of which stemmed from the so-called Vietnam
Syndrome. As national security advisor to President Reagan and then
as Chairman of the Joint Chiefs of Staff for President Bush during the
Persian Gulf crisis, Colin Powell held principles on the use of military force similar to that of Weinberger. Powell, a combat veteran of
the Vietnam War, espoused these beliefs more clearly after the Persian
Gulf crisis, but certainly adhered to them before and during 1990–91.
Powell's variation on the Weinberger doctrine offered similar principles
stated in a slightly different way. In addition to having a vital interest
at stake, a clear and attainable political objective, and public and congressional commitment, Powell wanted thorough cost–benefit analysis
and an examination of possible unintended consequences. Among his
conditions, Powell also included substantial international support and a
clear exit strategy. Additionally, he warned against half-measures and
gradualism—the United States should use only "overwhelming" military force, unlike its gradual escalation during the Vietnam War. Such
principles reflected Powell's interpretation of Clausewitz, especially the
admittedly often misunderstood but nonetheless prevalent trilogy of military, government, and people, and their synergy leading to decisive
victory in pursuit of clear political objectives.[42]

By the time of the Persian Gulf crisis in 1990, the Vietnam Syndrome
had become fully engrained in any consideration of US use of force. Use
of force now had to be low casualty for the US military and the American
public while being technologically lethal on the enemy, reliant upon an
AVF extremely small in comparison to a largely noninvolved American
public, and supported by the American people while having a clear exit
strategy. The so-called Weinberger–Powell Doctrine, the Goldwater–
Nichols Act, the AVF, and other structural, doctrinal, and procurement
changes had given the US military a more lethal conventional capability,

but with an extreme cautiousness, even a reluctance, to use it. In essence, the US military had reconfigured itself into a technologically lethal force that when used for appropriate military objectives in pursuit of legitimate political ends could do so with less cost to American blood. Such a force would, so hoped Weinberger, Powell, and others, allow the US military to finally overcome its Vietnam demons and again be an effective tool in defending American national security.[43]

4

Building DESERT SHIELD

From the first day of the crisis in August 1990 through the end of the conflict in March 1991, the United States worked to build and then maintain a broad coalition of diverse nations to initially condemn the Iraqi invasion, and after that to coerce Iraq into withdrawing from Kuwait through sanctions, and later to both participate in and contribute troops, material, and money to DESERT SHIELD and DESERT STORM. In the early days of the crisis, President Bush determined to use international pressure, especially through the UN Security Council rather than unilateral American action, to restore Kuwait. For Bush, the world emerging from the Cold War, one that appeared to leave the United States as the lone superpower, presented a historic opportunity for the United States to lead the international community. While a superpower could exercise power unilaterally, Bush understood the importance of international consensus and of pursuing American aims through multilateralism, in this case through the UN. Moreover, Bush appreciated the need to enhance the legitimacy of the UN in the world community. Successfully forcing Saddam to abandon Kuwait either peacefully or by use of force through American leadership in the UN, Bush hoped, would achieve both purposes.[1]

The Coalition

In addition to Saudi Arabia, the Coalition had some obvious partners. Under Thatcher's and her successor John Major's leadership, Great Britain stood up to play a traditional role in the Middle East. Having previously helped Kuwait defend itself against aggressive Iraqi posturing in 1961 and having exercised over a century's worth of influence in the region, Great Britain unhesitatingly deployed naval assets and several Tornado fighter–bomber squadrons in tandem with initial US deployments in August 1990. While Thatcher had to do a delicate political dance to convince members of Parliament that Great Britain should play a leading role in resolving the crisis by peace or by force, by October 1990 Great Britain had forces in the region second only in number to that of the United States. These included the 7th Armoured Brigade (the famous Desert Rats), a mechanized infantry battalion, and air and missile defense assets.

Not wanting to appear too closely allied to American leadership in the crisis, France not surprisingly attempted to exercise an independent approach to enhance its standing in the region now that the Cold War appeared ended. France had been perhaps the closest Western ally of Saddam's Iraq; now, France faced the embarrassment of the Iraqi invasion of Kuwait. France first dispatched several envoys to various countries in the region to seek a resolution of the crisis and to assure French allies in the Middle East of the defensive nature of the French reaction. Among French President Francois Mitterrand's cabinet, several ministers worried that a large deployment of Coalition forces, even for the defense of Saudi Arabia, would in turn certainly guarantee war with Iraq. For its part, the United States paid little notice to French unilateralism, which largely appeared inept to American observers. After following its own path for over two months, by the end of October France slowly gravitated toward the American-led Coalition. Iraqi treatment of French diplomats and other citizens both in Iraq and Kuwait forced the issue, leaving France with little choice but to grudgingly join the Coalition.[2]

China also presented the United States with some challenges in building support against Iraq. With the Tiananmen Square incident still fresh in public memory, China wisely decided to take a backseat in the crisis. While wanting to be seen as the staunch supporter of lesser developed countries, especially in Africa, and to avoid too close an affiliation with the American-led Coalition, China nonetheless had to closely watch the crisis as it developed in the late summer and fall of 1990. With heavy investment across the Middle East and deep trade interests in Europe and the United States, China had much to risk as it cautiously considered its approach to the crisis. Bush's long relationship with China (he had been head of the US Liaison Office in China in 1974–75) and his controversial *laissez-faire* approach to the Tiananmen Square crisis in 1989, helped him to garner Chinese support in the UN Security

Council throughout the crisis. The Bush administration had to be aware of possible public backlash in its dealings with China during the crisis, while China, too, had to be cognizant of repairing its own international image.[3]

Constitutional issues restricted both West Germany and Japan's ability to participate in the Coalition. Neither could contribute actual troops, which in the case of Germany may have been for the best since the presence of German forces so near Israel would have posed obvious symbolic problems. Moreover, for Germany the crisis erupted amid forthcoming elections and burdensome financial commitments to unify East and West Germany. Ultimately, Germany found ways to support the Coalition. In addition to contributing over DM3 billion, Germany allowed the United States to move troops and equipment from US bases in Germany on public roads and railways and also contributed various military vehicles for Coalition use in Saudi Arabia. Dependent in part on Iraqi oil, the Japanese government condemned the Iraqi invasion but had difficulty finding consensus on how to participate, if at all, in the Coalition. After failed attempts to amend its constitution to allow the deployment of military forces outside Japan, the Japanese government did manage to put together a significant financial aid package worth several billion dollars, some of which went to Turkey and Egypt, while the bulk supported the cost of transporting and maintaining Coalition military forces in the Persian Gulf.[4]

Several other countries also had to overcome obstacles to do more than simply condemn the Iraqi invasion. The Soviet Union, for example, faced its own internal issues and also had to consider the safety of several thousand of its citizens working in Iraq, a problem faced by other countries as well, including Turkey, India, and Egypt. All told, almost two million foreign nationals worked in Iraq and just fewer than one million did so in Kuwait, mostly as day laborers. Several countries had significant trade agreements with Iraq, and more still relied to varying degrees on Iraqi oil. Turkey in particular relied heavily on oil from Iraq and depended upon a lucrative revenue stream from a major oil pipeline from Iraq that passed through Turkey. Moreover, Turkey, a member of the NATO since 1952, feared Saddam might indeed attack it in addition to Saudi Arabia. In order to secure support for the embargo and basing rights in Turkey, the United States and the Emir of Kuwait gave Turkey billions of dollars in direct aid and other inducements. Militarily, Turkey's involvement in the Coalition forced Saddam to maintain a large troop and equipment presence along its northern border at the expense of much needed forces positioned in Kuwait and near the Iraqi border with Saudi Arabia.[5]

Getting Arab nations to join the Coalition proved equally challenging. For many in the Middle East, the very idea of joining the United States, the principal ally of Israel, in a coalition against a fellow Arab country presented enormous political and economic difficulties. Balancing long- and short-term national interests with delicate political and domestic support at home also involved significant risks. The United States, often under the guidance and skill of Secretary of State James Baker, utilized old-fashioned "checkbook" diplomacy to align as many Arab states as possible against Iraq.

For Baker to be secretary of state during the crisis was most fortuitous. A native of Texas and a former Marine Corps officer, Baker had become a bedrock player among Washington insiders. A lawyer by profession and classicist by education, Baker understood economic and diplomatic relations between nations and, like his long-time friend President Bush, did not underestimate the power of oil. Baker had served as presidential campaign manager for Gerald Ford, Ronald Reagan, and Bush, serving also as secretary of commerce, secretary of the treasury, and White House chief of staff along the way. His experience, calm demeanor, and political acumen served well during the crisis, though Baker's strong sense of initiative sometimes caught his boss by surprise despite his good intentions.[6]

To secure Egyptian support, President Bush forgave Egypt's $6 billion debt to the United States. In exchange, Egyptian President Hosni Mubarak allowed US warplanes to cross Egyptian airspace and Coalition warships priority to traverse the Suez Canal en route to the Persian Gulf. More importantly, Mubarak committed over 5,000 troops to the Coalition. Although Mubarak wanted to exhibit and enhance his own Arab leadership and also had little regard for Saddam, his agreement to join the Coalition against the Iraqi dictator had broad impact across the Arab world. For Bush, Mubarak proved critical in recruiting and holding together Arab participation in the Coalition.

Syria, too, presented a challenge to the Coalition. Long the sworn enemy of Israel, Syrians also had little affection for Saddam and Iraq, and had supported Iran in the Iran–Iraq War. Like Turkey, Syria shared a lengthy border with Iraq, making it strategically important to the enforcement of the embargo and possible military action against Iraq. With American encouragement, the UAE, Saudi Arabia, and Bahrain arranged a financial aid package worth some $3 billion for Syria. In exchange, Syria enforced the UN embargo against

Iraq and provided troops for both DESERT SHIELD and DESERT STORM.

Along with Saudi Arabia, several other Persian Gulf states had good reason to feel threatened by Saddam's aggression. Accordingly, leaders in the UAE, Bahrain, Qatar, and Oman quickly overcame their initial hesitation to eagerly support the American-led Coalition with money and military forces. Of all the Middle Eastern countries, however, Israel presented the greatest challenge. Despite Israeli offers to militarily and financially participate in the Coalition, the United States worked feverishly to both tactfully decline Israel's offer to help and to convince Arab countries that they need not worry about having to fight Iraq while serving alongside Israeli troops. Most importantly, the United States had to prevent Israel from intervening unilaterally if attacked by Iraq, the result of which would, analysts assumed, assuredly destroy Arab participation in the Coalition.[7]

The United States also needed more immediate help to pay for military operations to enforce the UN embargo, police the Persian Gulf, and to help pay, if necessary, for what Bush and his advisors hoped would be a short war to oust Iraqi forces from Kuwait. In addition to securing military and political support through the various aid packages mentioned above, Baker also had great success in getting money on his "Tin Cup Trip" during September 1990. Most significantly, Baker secured $15 billion from both King Fahd of Saudi Arabia and the Kuwaiti Emir to support DESERT SHIELD and later DESERT STORM. As Baker later put it: "The President was prepared to bear the brunt of the burden, in that if force were required to eject Iraq from Kuwait, Americans would die in the Gulf. The very least we could expect in return was that the countries we were helping, and all our other allies with stakes in the crisis, should join not only in supplying forces to the extent they could, but also in financing the costs."[8]

In all, thirty-four nations contributed military forces and/or equipment of varying size and type, while several others made financial contributions to support aid packages to affected countries in the Middle East as well as to help pay for military operations to enforce the embargo and then ultimately for the war itself. US envoys, namely Secretary of State Baker and Secretary of Defense Cheney, flew tens of thousands of miles from August 1990 through January 1991 to meet with Middle Eastern and other leaders. President Bush, too, made long trips. He personally visited King Fahd in Saudi Arabia, for example, while also making numerous phone calls to dozens of world leaders to create and sustain the Coalition.[9]

Figure 1   *President H. W. Bush and Saudi King Fahd discuss the situation in Iraq during Bush's visit to Saudi Arabia, November 21, 1990.* *Source*: George Bush Presidential Library and Museum.

Linkage, Sanctions, and Strategic Miscalculation

Saddam worked diligently to undermine the Coalition, yet his incompetent efforts had the opposite effect. From the outset, Saddam's actions strengthened international opposition to his invasion and annexation of Kuwait, even among Arab nations, with whom Saddam blundered opportunities to reach a peaceful settlement, perhaps even to his advantage. The formal annexation of Kuwait drew immediate international reaction, including an overwhelming UN condemnation of his illegal act.[10] The Arab League, with the exception of Libya and the Palestinian Liberation Organization (PLO), refused to recognize what Saddam considered a *fait accompli*. Saddam's attempts to link a settlement over Kuwait with Israeli concessions to the PLO also had no chance of success. Saddam had long attempted to portray himself as a Nasser-like proponent of Arab nationalism and hoped to gain support among Middle Eastern countries by linking Kuwait and Israel in a settlement. Israel provided the obvious fissure point, which Saddam would again try to exploit during DESERT STORM by launching SCUD missiles at Israeli cities in an attempt to draw Israel into the war and thereby undercut Arab participation in the Coalition against him.

Saddam's most egregious miscalculation in this regard came in attempts to manipulate the presence of thousands of foreign nationals, or "guests" as he often referred to them, in both Iraq and Kuwait. Hussein detained thousands of citizens from Western countries, including the United States, while allowing those from lesser developed nations to leave piecemeal in a vain attempt to appeal to other "victims" of Western imperialism. As many nations had thousands of nationals working in Iraq, sending home money that in turn supported local economies, and as neighboring countries, such as Syria and Jordan, had to deal with the sudden influx of foreign nationals exiting Iraq, Saddam's strategy did not go as planned, for images of desperate refugees heavily influenced public opinion in the developing world against him. Few countries took the bait to support the Iraqi dictator.

Saddam also used several Western nationals as human shields, placing American, British, and other European citizens near probable Coalition military targets in and around Baghdad. The UN Security Council condemned the practice in Resolution 664 on August 18, 1990, but Saddam continued to use Westerners as a bargaining chip to convince Coalition forces to abandon their positions in Saudi Arabia and the Persian Gulf. President Bush deplored Saddam's treatment of detained foreign nationals and their use as human shields, strongly condemning Saddam's use of "hostages" in a speech on August 20, 1990: "They know, as we do, that leaders who use citizens as pawns deserve and will receive the scorn and condemnation of the entire world."[11]

As the crisis wore on into the fall of 1990, diplomatic efforts to find a peaceful resolution coexisted with diplomatic efforts to build consensus on the potential use of military force to restore Kuwait. Time worked both for and against a peaceful resolution. While many nations supported giving economic sanctions more time to deeply affect Saddam's Iraq and giving negotiations more time to seek an unconditional Iraqi withdrawal from Kuwait, more time would also allow Saddam's forces to fortify along the Saudi border and entrench in Kuwait, making the use of military force all the more costly and uncertain. President Bush appreciated the increasingly tricky dilemma. If he acted with force too quickly, he would be criticized for not giving sanctions and talks a real chance; if he waited too long to use force, he risked a bloodbath against one of the largest, best-equipped, and most experienced military forces in the world and repercussions from a casualty-averse American public.

Several efforts were made to convince Saddam to withdraw peacefully from Kuwait and stand down his forces along the Saudi border. UN Secretary General Javier Pérez de Cuéllar of Peru met with Iraqi representatives in Amman, Jordan, where he offered UN peacekeeping forces to maintain order during and after the Iraqi withdrawal from Kuwait and to mediate negotiations to settle outstanding issues between the two countries. The Iraqis, however, remained obstinate and seemed to be using de Cuéllar's goodwill to buy time to strengthen their position in Kuwait. De Cuéllar also took a hands-off approach to Security Council action, letting the United States lead the way in passing multiple resolutions calling for Iraq to withdraw from Kuwait, in placing and enforcing sanctions and embargoes on Iraq, and in finally setting an ultimate deadline for withdrawal. These actions empowered the American-led Coalition to act for the UN, which under de Cuéllar seemed glad to hand over actual diplomatic initiatives to the United States and other countries willing to try to resolve the crisis. Rather than taking the lead, the UN instead provided the legitimacy through which the Coalition could act.[12]

For the United States, using the UN was not without risks. China and the Soviet Union supported establishing the embargo against Iraq with few quibbles. Support for actual enforcement, however, proved more difficult to obtain. Secretary of State Baker and the American Ambassador to the UN, Thomas Pickering, worked hard to reach common ground with China and the Soviet Union to approve Security Council resolutions to allow Coalition forces to use force to stop and search vessels of all types that might be carrying contraband to or from Iraq. Like the United States, both countries had veto power as permanent members of the Security Council. Both countries also worried that giving the "cowboy" United States too much leeway to enforce the embargo would result in an incident that might send the crisis spiraling out of control.

Ultimately, both China and the Soviet Union agreed to specific language in UN Security Council Resolution 665 that allowed enforcing states to "use such measures commensurate to the specific circumstances as may be necessary under the authority of the Security Council" to enforce the embargo. While the United States could have acted unilaterally under existing Security Council resolutions, Bush recognized the value of UN legitimacy in keeping together the Coalition through international consensus. Chinese support was critical to gaining the approval of so-called nonaligned countries on the Security Council. Saddam, too, recognized the importance of 665 and tried to convince Iraq's traditional ally, the Soviet Union, to vote against and cause a significant crack in the fragile Coalition. The Soviets instead tried to give Saddam a way out of the crisis by offering to host a Middle East peace conference to consider all territorial disputes in the region, including those between Israel and the PLO. For his part, President Bush reluctantly acquiesced to the Soviet effort, so long as Iraq agreed to withdraw from Kuwait before such talks could begin. Saddam, of course, rejected any notion of withdrawal as a precondition to talks, killing the Soviet initiative, which was probably the result Bush had bargained for in the first place.

Soviet Foreign Minister Eduard Shevardnadze, however, coolly played Saddam's gambit, buying Saddam a few days' time before a final vote, while knowing full well that the Iraqi dictator would not compromise. Saddam rejected flatly Soviet President Mikhail Gorbachev's joint demand with French President Mitterrand that Saddam withdraw Iraqi forces from Kuwait and release all foreign nationals held by Iraq as hostages. Saddam's refusal paved the way for Soviet support for Resolution 665, which was passed on August 25. To reinforce Soviet solidarity with the UN-backed Coalition, Gorbachev warned Saddam not to "base his calculations around the idea of dividing us, of creating a split among [us] . . . . If he thinks like this, he is very wrong." The Soviet Union, like France, had the clout of permanent membership in the UN Security Council, which, along with its resistance to its own decline as a superpower, made Soviet attempts to resolve the crisis understandable.[13]

Saddam also tried to create fissures in the Coalition by exploiting French unilateralism. France fell somewhat in the same category as the Soviet Union—a declining power with a permanent seat in the Security Council, desperate to show the United States that it still mattered in world affairs. Saddam understood France's situation and motivation, but nonetheless failed in his attempts to exploit France to his advantage. France attempted to act apart from the American-led international reaction to the crisis, but Saddam's treatment of French nationals in Kuwait and Iraq undermined French commitment to reach a settlement, representing yet another opportunity squandered by Saddam. The leader of the PLO, Yasser Arafat, also tried to exploit French eagerness to mediate the crisis by acting as a go-between for the Iraqis while attempting to link a settlement over Kuwait to other Middle Eastern issues, namely the existence of Israel and an independent Palestinian state. Arafat tried to tie in concessions to Israeli-occupied territories along the West Bank and in Gaza, but these efforts came to naught. If the Gorbachev–Mitterrand statement demanding withdrawal from Kuwait and release of all hostages did not signal to Saddam that his attempts at "linkage" had failed, US Vice President Dan Quayle's response to a CNN interviewer that "Palestine is not an issue on the table" should have put to rest any hope Saddam, and Arafat, may have had for a broad Middle Eastern settlement favorable to Iraqi and PLO interests.[14]

Interestingly, while countries such as France acted unilaterally to free their citizens held in Iraq and Kuwait, individuals also made trips to Baghdad to plead for the release of hostages. With hundreds of American, French, British, Japanese, Austrian, German, and other citizens held against their will, many as human shields at strategically important sites in Iraq, Saddam hoped to use them to manipulate their home governments and public opinion. He shamelessly exploited hostages in front of eager television cameras, in one case appearing with a seven-year-old British boy who looked sincerely frightened as an awkward Saddam attempted to appear fatherly by patting him "clumsily" on the head.[15] These reckless tactics backfired. Facing strong international criticism for holding hostages, Saddam lost face with his traditional allies, especially the Soviet Union and even Libya, and among his fellow Arabs. Still, the steady stream of former world leaders, celebrities, and other supposedly important people making the trek to Iraq to beg for the release of hostages fed Saddam's perception of his own self-importance. By releasing a few hostages here and there, Saddam hoped to appear magnanimous in the face of the growing number of countries aligning against him in the Coalition. The Austrian president and former UN secretary-general Kurt Waldheim, the American Reverend Jesse Jackson, former German prime minister Willy Brandt, former British prime minister Edward Heath, former world heavyweight boxing champion Muhammad Ali, and even recording artist Cat Stevens (using his Muslim name Yusuf Islam) appeared before Saddam, who reveled in the celebrity of his visitors while releasing a number of hostages to each, apparently according to each petitioner's potential positive impact for Iraqi propaganda.[16]

King Hussein of Jordan also tried to work a deal with Saddam. A one-time friend of the United States and Great Britain, King Hussein had gravitated closer to Iraq in the years leading to Iraq's invasion of Kuwait, in part because of his close relationship with the PLO and in part because of Saddam's popularity in Jordan because of the Iran–Iraq War. King Hussein made several high-profile trips to Iraq, Algeria, Libya, Washington, DC, and London, in a haphazard attempt to broker a deal based on Arafat's PLO plan that would withdraw Iraqi forces from Kuwait and Coalition forces from Saudi Arabia, allow the insertion of UN peacekeepers, and then initiate negotiations between Iraq and

Kuwait that would be sponsored by the Arab League. King Hussein also proposed the reestablishment of Kuwait as a constitutional monarchy, with Kuwait having a relationship with Iraq similar to that of Monaco and France. King Hussein, however, found no traction for his proposals, especially with other Arab leaders, who considered him a sell-out for his overt support of Saddam.[17]

Oil and Food

UN restrictions on Iraqi trade worked alongside diplomatic initiatives to resolve the crisis. The dilemma of sanctions and embargoes presented itself in the form of oil and food. In addition to uncertainties in the oil market caused by the crisis itself, preventing Saddam from exporting oil, thereby cutting off over 90 percent of Iraq's oil-related income, risked another worldwide oil crisis similar to the two price shocks of the 1970s caused by the Arab–Israeli War and the revolution in Iran. A war to oust Saddam's forces from Kuwait would, potentially, exacerbate that situation even more. Similarly, cutting off food exports to Iraq risked similar consequences. While meant to cause the Iraqi people some pain in the hope that they would pressure Saddam to change his tactics, starving the Iraqi people into submission ran counter to accepted norms of warfare. The oil embargo and sanctions prohibiting the export of food and medicine to Iraq also had other, unintended consequences, hurting trade balances for several nations while sending much needed revenue streams spiraling downward for several others.

As it had done more effectively in the 1970s, OPEC again tried to place quotas on crude oil output to control the price per barrel of oil during the crisis. While tensions between Iraq and Kuwait worsened, the price per barrel increased from $18 in July 1990 to $21 when Iraq invaded Kuwait, then to $27 in mid-August amid fears that Saddam would take Saudi oil fields near the Iraqi and Kuwaiti borders. The International Energy Agency estimated that the world's industrialized nations had petroleum reserves to last over ninety days, with some having enough for five months, and major oil companies held the legal minimum reserve of sixty-five days. Nevertheless, the embargo of Iraqi oil, which now included Kuwaiti oil, took as much as 7 percent of the world's daily oil demand offline. Even if other oil-exporting countries increased production to make up the difference, this would be a major cause for concern not only among Western nations dependent upon Middle Eastern oil but also for many developing countries in Asia, Latin America, and Africa that depended upon oil imports to an even larger degree. While it might have appeared advantageous to OPEC countries and oil companies to let the price per barrel increase, such was not wholly the case. Short-term profits from higher oil prices would suffer in the longer term, as rapidly increasing oil prices would cause an economic recession wherein consumers would cut back on petroleum consumption and seek cheaper energy alternatives, hurting OPEC even more.

OPEC had to control the price per barrel with deft consideration for the world market, global consumption demands, and the political consequences of supporting the Coalition. Not all oil-exporters supported the Coalition, however, as Iran and Libya, for example, enjoyed the increase in revenue at the expense of the West and Iraq. In addition to these two emergent antagonists of the West, countries like Nigeria and Indonesia, too, had little sympathy for Western economic issues while enjoying increased profits. OPEC did increase its production quotas to meet the embargo shortfall, but prices nevertheless steadily climbed, hitting $35 per barrel in late September 1990. Some feared that if war broke out between Iraq and the Coalition, the price per barrel could exceed $100, bringing untold calamity upon the global economy.

The so-called Third Oil Shock caused by the Persian Gulf crisis indeed had serious economic consequences for the global economy. While the strategic reserves of the United States, Germany, and other Western countries remained largely untapped (the United States, for example, did release five million barrels of its reserve of over 600 million barrels), increases in the price per gallon of gasoline and heating oil during the winter of 1990–91 put the pinch on consumer spending, feeding fears of an economic recession taking hold by 1991–92. Other nations, however, suffered more deeply, as the embargo on importing Iraqi and Kuwaiti oil and exporting other goods to Iraq cost nations ranging from India to Sudan to Poland to Sri Lanka billions of dollars. Jordan, for example, lost nearly 30 percent of its national income due to the embargo and other sanctions placed on Iraq. For the developing world, $40 barrels of oil would cost a collective $120 billion over the course of a year, a deficit from which these economies would take years to recover. Eastern European states, just coming out from under the thumb of the Soviet Union with astronomic reconstruction costs and now paying the market price for oil from the Soviet Union rather than the old subsidized price, already had mountainous economic troubles—the crisis in the Persian Gulf exacerbated these problems, so much so that the World Bank estimated Eastern European countries were losing close to 5 percent of their Gross Domestic Product (GDP).

Various aid packages offered by the United States, the European Economic Community, and Saudi Arabia help relieve some of this intense financial pressure. Early in the crisis, President Bush, an oil man at heart, established the Gulf Crisis Financial Coordination Group (GCFCG) to monitor the impact of the fluctuating oil market and recommend fixes in the form of loans, aid packages, and other means. Twenty-four nations participated in the group, including several members of the Coalition. Much of the aid went to Egypt, Turkey, and Jordan, but several other states benefitted from the recommendations of the GCFCG.

Saddam's use of the oil card proved to be yet another example of the Iraqi dictator's strategic incompetence. While hoping to erode public will in Coalition countries to support removing Iraqi forces from Kuwait, Saddam's oil play instead deeply affected the Third World, the very developing countries that he could have courted for international support. Conversely, the Coalition likewise caused these same nations to suffer while attempting to coerce Saddam into abandoning Kuwait, revealing a shortcoming in Coalition strategic thinking. Oil in the Persian Gulf crisis proved to be the poster-child for the unintended consequences of strategic policy.[18]

While the oil embargo meant to coerce Iraq had global economic and political implications, UN sanctions banning the export of any goods, notably food, to Iraq added a moral element to using embargoes and sanctions as a coercive measure. Even though Iraq had hundreds of millions of barrels of oil worth tens of billions of dollars, it could not sell a single drop. With no money from oil revenue or anything else under the sanctions, Saddam could buy not a single morsel of food, of which Iraq normally imported over 75 percent, to feed the Iraqi people. Sanctions often achieve little in the short-term and even their long-term success can be questioned if one looks at South Africa and Cuba as examples. The sanctions against Iraq, however, brought both an immediate severity and intense armed enforcement to the table. Sanctions actually affected Iraq mainly because Iraq had only oil as a tradable commodity. Unable to trade oil and having invaded Kuwait in an attempt to economically recover from the costly war with Iran, Iraq had no revenue with which to continue public works projects, subsidize gasoline, and keep millions of people in wage-earning jobs, resulting in a population with little money to buy increasingly scarce food at inflated prices.

Iraq had previously been through similar trying times, though not without some sort of external support, as it now was. Saddam outlawed hoarding and black-marketeering of food and other necessities, making such acts punishable by death. Ration cards allowed Iraqis to purchase preset allotments of basic food items, but over the course of the crisis items once plentiful in August 1990 became scarce by January 1991. Flour, sugar, powdered milk, cooking oil, and other basics slowly evaporated from public availability. Iraqis, however, put their war-time experience to work, growing their own vegetable gardens, planting crops in once fallow farmland, and even fishing to keep food on their tables.

At first, US and UN estimates of Iraqi food stocks gave Saddam only months before serious shortages would force him to comply with UN Security Council resolutions. Reassessments, however, gave Iraq more time, perhaps as much as a year, before it would reach such a crisis point. Even though Iraqis stood in long queues to buy bread, for example, the CIA forecasted another bountiful harvest for Iraq in the spring of 1991 that would keep Iraq fed another year. Getting to Saddam through the stomachs of his people, in the CIA's estimate, would not work.

Another wildcard giving Iraq more "food time" involved the hundreds of thousands of foreign nationals still in Iraq. With no ration cards, many of these foreign workers had to fend for themselves, which left more food for Iraqi citizens. Various countries did try to get food shipments to their own citizens in Iraq, a development that gave Saddam some hope that the Coalition's resolve would crack. India, Bulgaria, Yugoslavia, and the Philippines, among other nations, desperately wanted to get food to their nationals trapped in Iraq, but doing so would violate UN-established sanctions. China, Cuba, and Colombia, and others supported some sort of humanitarian relief for foreign nationals and Iraqi children. For Saddam, a propaganda bonanza awaited if UN sanctions resulted in starving children.

The main problem for the UN and the Coalition concerning food lay in logistics. Who would distribute this food? If left to Iraqi authorities, the food would assuredly go to the Iraqi military, as Saddam had ordered, or to Iraqis, but assuredly not to foreign nationals. The UN Security Council's Sanctions Committee explored various options for getting humanitarian relief into Iraq, but all proposed solutions required some sort of UN oversight that Saddam would surely reject. Even President Bush and Soviet President Gorbachev conceded that food relief needed to reach Iraq, but, as they announced at their summit in Helsinki in September 1990, only through an international agency such as the Red Cross could they be assured that relief would reach those intended. Saddam, not surprisingly, rejected any external oversight of Iraqi internal affairs, especially humanitarian aid.

This predicament brought to the fore the very notion of food as a weapon. The Geneva Convention of 1949 forbade using starvation as a weapon in warfare. To reject Iraq's "naked aggression" and then to resort to the generally accepted immorality of using food as a weapon undermined the moral high ground upon which the American-led Coalition and the UN assumed they so firmly stood. The food problem presented a true strategic dilemma that remained unresolved.[19]

By November, President Bush and his advisors realized that Saddam did not intend to withdraw Iraqi forces from Kuwait as part of any unconditional or even conditional agreement. Saddam gambled on time—the longer he held out, the more likely the American-led Coalition would collapse. Saddam, like President Bush, also appreciated the difficulty in keeping the Coalition together in the face of possible offensive military action to force Saddam from Kuwait. Bush and Secretary of State Baker had overcome several challenges to line up an impressive international front to dissuade Saddam from further aggression and to put the coercive screws on the Iraqi dictator through sanctions but had nonetheless failed to convince Saddam to abandon his coveted 19th Province. For Bush, convincing the Coalition to militarily remove Iraqi forces from Kuwait presented an altogether different and more difficult set of challenges.

5

Moving to the Offensive

Bush and his military advisors realized that the longer Saddam held out, the more time Iraqi forces had to reinforce themselves along the Iraqi and Kuwaiti borders with Saudi Arabia and to build defenses along obvious amphibious assault areas along the Kuwaiti coast. Indeed, while the United States and other Coalition partners had over 220,000 troops in the region by the end of October 1990, Saddam had increased the size of Iraqi forces to nearly 400,000 in southern Iraq and Kuwait.[1]

An Offensive Option

Other factors weighed on Bush in his decision to pursue the offensive option against Saddam. Militarily, he realized a viable offensive option required a much larger force of perhaps as many as half a million troops and commensurate equipment to war against what appeared on paper to be a seasoned, well equipped and trained, and expansive Iraqi military machine. Moreover, Bush knew Saddam had used chemical weapons before and had little doubt that he would not hesitate to use biological and chemical weapons against Coalition forces, a possibility that would give any leader pause before ordering troops into harm's way. Time was also factored into the military equation. In addition to Iraqi reinforcement in Kuwait and southern Iraq, commencing offensive operations too late in the spring of 1991 would deplete personnel and machines with equal ferocity due to the oppressive summer heat in the desert and the violent sandstorms.

Domestically, Bush had to convince a wary public and Congress that going to war against Iraq was worth American lives. He had laid the groundwork for this potential scenario from the beginning of the crisis, telling the American public, and indeed the international community, at every opportunity that such aggression in the new world order could not "stand" unopposed. As the leader of the free world, the United States had a vital national interest in exercising leadership among the international community against "naked aggression." As an oil-consuming nation, the United States had a vital national interest in not letting a single dictator control so much of the world's oil reserves. As the world's leading military power, only the United States had military forces capable of making good a threat to use force to remove Saddam from Kuwait. While Iraq had not attacked the United States directly, Saddam's assault on Kuwait nonetheless threatened American national security. Had it, however, been threatened enough to warrant war? Bush had to make the case for a war of choice, if Saddam did not first back down.

From the beginning, Bush reluctantly sought congressional cooperation and support for his handling of the crisis. For his part, Bush unenthusiastically followed the spirit of the 1973 War Powers Resolution, which legally obligated the president as commander-in-chief to notify Congress within sixty days of putting American military forces in harm's way. Passed by a Vietnam-weary Congress, the War Powers Act was clearly a reaction to the blank-check approach Congress had given President Lyndon Johnson through its 1964 Tonkin Gulf Resolution early in the Vietnam War. Intended to ensure joint consultation between Congress and the president before committing the United States to military action, the War Powers Resolution had not enjoyed much popularity among presidents. From Nixon to Bush, all had mostly flaunted and sometimes outright ignored the War Powers Resolution, considering it an affront to the Constitutional responsibilities of the president as commander-in-chief. Technically, failure to follow the War Powers Resolution could result in Congress withdrawing funding for the action in question or, at the extreme, the impeachment of the president.

As for actual congressional authorization to use force, Bush initially sought from Congress a Tonkin Gulf-like resolution that would leave him legislatively unrestricted. Bush's approach revealed a lack of historical understanding among his advisors of the congressional backlash against presidential authority because of the Tonkin Gulf Resolution. For Congress, the Tonkin Gulf Resolution was the ultimate example of what not to give a president—congressionally authorized unrestricted war powers. While Congress through various resolutions had applauded President Bush's handling of the Gulf crisis throughout the fall of 1990, for Bush to consider obtaining a Tonkin Gulf-like blank check from Congress was at best misguided and at worst foolhardy.

Bush nevertheless moved forward to find common ground with Congress as he transitioned from a defensive to a more offensive posture in the Persian Gulf. As with the UN, Bush had to time his dealings with Congress perfectly. Mid-term congressional elections took place on November 8, 1990. Bush delayed publically announcing more deployments until the next day so as not to hurt Republican candidates. Nevertheless, when the new 102nd Congress convened in January, Bush faced a somewhat hostile Democrat-controlled Congress and had little help from his own party leaders in the House of Representatives and the Senate in brokering a way forward to resolve the crisis so that it would be satisfactory to both parties. Bush met with congressional leaders regularly to inform them of his actions in the crisis, but this generosity failed to alleviate their fears that Bush was taking the United States headlong into a war without proper congressional authorization and support. While the War Powers Resolution only required the president to inform Congress of the initiation of force rather than to obtain actual congressional authorization for military action, many believed that Bush had to adhere to Constitutional requirements and ask for a declaration of war.

Dozens of House Democrats actually petitioned for a federal court injunction to block Bush from ordering military action unless first authorized by Congress. Led by Representative Ron Dellums of California's 8th District, the group complained that for Bush to act without a congressional declaration of war would violate the enumerated powers given to Congress in Article 1, Section 8, of the United States Constitution. In December 1990, a federal court rejected the petition for an injunction on the grounds that because Congress had passed no resolution either to authorize or prohibit the use of military force, no federal court could consider such a petition. Moreover, the court affirmed that there was no provision in the Constitution for federal courts to have any say as to whether the United States could declare war in any given instance.[2]

Members of Congress were near universal in their calls to give sanctions more time to force Saddam's hand. Republican leaders tried to find common ground with their Democrat colleagues by offering to debate the issue on the floors of both houses of Congress. Bush at first resisted, fearing such an open debate might reveal lack of American resolve, which would potentially benefit Saddam and weaken the Coalition. As a compromise, Bush and congressional leaders agreed to delay debating the issue until the new Congress convened in January 1991, though Bush held little hope of getting congressional authorization and, like presidents before him, seemed determined to unilaterally exercise his authority as commander-in-chief, as loosely interpreted in the

Constitution. That debate would be one of the most anticipated and closely watched in Congress in decades.[3]

UN Security Council Resolution 678

To convince the international community via the UN that force was warranted, Bush also had to time his diplomatic strategy perfectly. As a former American ambassador to the UN, Bush understood the workings and eccentricities of the Security Council. His own ambassador to the UN, Thomas Pickering, also knew his way around the Security Council. Pickering would lead the Security Council in November as the United States took its turn in the rotating chair of the UN's principal policymaking body. Bush wanted a UN Security Council resolution that would both set a deadline for Iraq to withdraw from Kuwait and authorize the Coalition to use force if Saddam ignored the deadline. Such a resolution would not only give the American-led Coalition international legitimacy but would also make Bush's job of convincing Congress to authorize force a bit easier, so he reasoned. Bush also realized that in setting a deadline for Saddam to leave Kuwait, he had committed the United States and the Coalition to military action if Saddam again thumbed his nose at the UN Security Council, as the Iraqi dictator had earlier done with impunity at each of the UN resolutions addressing the crisis.

In early November, the Bush team drafted a resolution for the UN Security Council to authorize enforcement of previous Security Council resolutions through "all necessary means." The draft explicitly included "use of force" and a deadline for Iraqi withdrawal from Kuwait set in mid-January. Secretary of State Baker set out on another world tour with the draft in hand, meeting with several heads of state, including Soviet President Gorbachev, and foreign ministers to gain support for the resolution. Time was of the essence, as Yemen would take over as chair of the Security Council in December, all but assuring a US-sponsored resolution regarding Iraq would not get on the agenda that month. As permanent members of the Security Council, Great Britain and France supported the resolution while China and the Soviet Union agreed not to oppose the resolution (a veto from any permanent member would kill the resolution). As rotating members currently serving on the Security Council, Malaysia, Zaire, Ivory Coast, Ethiopia, Colombia, and Romania agreed to support the resolution after intensive talks with Baker. Because the United States had no formal diplomatic relations with Cuba, Baker did not visit Fidel Castro nor confer with the Cuban foreign ministry at this time (though he did meet with the Cuban foreign minister in New York later in November, the first high-level meeting between US and Cuban representatives since before the Cuban Missile Crisis of 1962). He wasted no time with Yemen, which had supported Iraq with unabashed bravado throughout the crisis.

In Paris on November 18–19 at the meeting of the European Council on Security and Cooperation, Bush met with Gorbachev to iron out objectionable language in the draft, namely "use of force." Through Baker and Soviet Foreign Minister Shevardnadze, the two reached a compromise on language that satisfied the Soviets while maintaining the intent of the American-sponsored resolution. The two agreed that using instead "all possible means" implied the use of force without explicitly saying so. In addition to agreeing to a deadline, Bush bent to Gorbachev's desire for a specific period of negotiations before undertaking military action.

On November 29, 1990, the UN Security Council met to consider Security Council Resolution 678. Foreign ministers, including Baker acting as chair in place of Ambassador Pickering, represented most member states. Secretary of State Baker opened the session by quoting former Ethiopian leader Haile Selassie's plea to the then League of Nations to respond to Italy's invasion and occupation of his country in 1936:

> There is ... no precedent for a people being the victim of such injustice and of being at present threatened by abandonment to an aggressor. Also there has never before been an example of any government proceeding with the systematic extermination of a nation by barbarous means in violation of the most solemn promises, made to all the nations of the earth, that there should be no resort to a war of conquest and that there should not be used against innocent human beings terrible poison and harmful gases.[4]

Baker set a stern tone through his use of the famous Selassie speech connecting Italy's brutal assault on Ethiopia to Saddam's invasion of Kuwait and his use of chemical weapons in war and on his own people, strongly implying as well that the Emir of Kuwait could have just as easily stated Selassie's words. Baker reminded his colleagues that in 1936 Selassie's plea "fell on deaf ears" and that the League of Nations failed to stand up to aggression, clearly alluding to the League's inaction in the face of Adolf Hitler and Nazi Germany in the 1930s. Noting that "History has now given us another chance ... to make this Security Council and this United Nations true instruments for peace and justice across the globe," Baker reminded the Security Council both of its obligations and of the historical moment: "With the Cold War now behind us, we now have the chance to build the world envisioned by the founders of the United Nations." To do so, Baker said, "We must meet the threat to international peace created by Saddam Hussein's aggression."[5]

Now that Baker had laid down a gauntlet challenging the Security Council to fulfill its purpose and back up its resolutions with force, the US Secretary of State opened the floor for discussion on Resolution 678. Yemen's representative tried to link the Kuwait crisis to Palestinian demands that Israel withdraw from the occupied territories, while Cuba also supported Iraq by not surprisingly deriding UN-mandated sanctions and embargoes. China, too, objected to the potential use of force authorized in the resolution, a position that struck Baker as odd considering China's brutal crackdown against protesters in Tiananmen Square less than eighteen months before, in 1989.

The Kuwaitis, of course, pleaded for their liberation, fully supporting the resolution. The Iraqis, as expected, railed against it, declaring that an authorization of the use of force played to "America's imperialistic ambitions" and delivering a rambling soliloquy complaining of the injustice of the UN Security Council resolutions and the harm caused by UN-mandated sanctions and embargoes. The Iraqis to no one's surprise offered no concessions.

After honoring all requests for time to speak, Baker called for the vote. In what may have been the most important meeting of the Security Council since the inception of the UN following World War II, Resolution 678 was passed, with the expected no vote of Cuba and Yemen, which for Yemen meant losing over $70 million in US aid—Baker later called it "the most expensive no vote they ever cast." Resisting the urge to use its veto power, China instead abstained. Key to the resolution's successful passage was the clause calling for "one final opportunity, a pause of goodwill" for Iraq to comply with all relevant Security Council resolutions. Using "all available means" rather than explicitly stating "use of force" also smoothed some ruffled feathers, namely those of the Soviets. As of November 29, 1990, Iraq had until January 15, 1991, to comply. If not, Resolution 678 authorized the Coalition to "use all necessary means to uphold and implement resolution 660."[6]

The Extra Mile

On November 30, President Bush applauded the UN Security Council's "historic" passage of Resolution 678 and reaffirmed his commitment to seeking a resolution to the Persian Gulf crisis, peacefully or otherwise.

In remarks before answering questions from reporters, Bush continued to prepare Congress, the American public, and the international community for the possibility of war. "No nation," declared Bush, "should be able to wipe a Member State of the United Nations and the Arab League off the face of the earth." For Bush, the "immoral" invasion of Kuwait, the misuse and mistreatment of hostages, the threat against American personnel in the US Embassy in Kuwait City, the brutalization of Kuwaiti citizens and other foreign nationals, and Saddam's growing obsession with obtaining a nuclear weapon and unflinching use of chemical and biological weapons justified a settlement of the crisis through implementation of UN Security Council resolutions. Bush downplayed any comparisons between Vietnam and possible military action in the Persian Gulf, and made it clear that he wanted "peace, not war." Bush remained steadfast in his conviction "to see Saddam's aggression reversed," telling the Iraqi dictator, "Time is running out." Then Bush offered a surprise olive branch to the Iraqis, to "go the extra mile for peace," by inviting Iraqi Foreign Minister Aziz to Washington for talks as well as offering to send Secretary of State Baker to Baghdad to meet with Saddam. Bush now put the ball in Saddam's court, showing that he was willing to "exhaust all means for achieving a political and diplomatic solution" that removed Iraqi forces from Kuwait, restored the government of Kuwait, and freed all hostages held by Iraq.[7]

Baker later recalled that the "extra mile" initiative "confused and confounded our friends, delighted our critics, and fuelled whispers about a weakening of America's resolve." On the one hand, the initiative was Bush at his best—a seasoned, smart politician who seized the political initiative in a coercive effort to achieve his political objectives. On the other hand, Bush's sometimes-elusive oratory failed to explain his real intent. Frustrated allies worried that he had undermined the Coalition and had handed Saddam invaluable fodder for Iraqi propaganda. Bush, however, held a different view. He could tell Congress he was doing all he could while maintaining a credible and now UN-authorized threat of military force. He could also now show the international community— in particular the countries of the Middle East— that he had given Saddam every opportunity, and then some, to withdraw from Kuwait. Although the tactic gave him a dual path to resolving the crisis, the January 15 deadline remained the line in the sand.[8]

Saddam's reaction to this "extra mile" initiative disappointed those clinging to some hope of a peaceful resolution. Whereas Bush intended his remarks as a firm statement of his unwavering resolve while offering Saddam a way out, Saddam played it as just the opposite. In an old-fashioned game of political one-upmanship, Saddam twisted the president's words to make Bush appear weak and uncertain, as some of Bush's advisors had earlier feared. Saddam touted public opinion polls in the United States that indicated that a majority opposed going to war over Kuwait, claiming Bush's offer to talk testified to lack of American resolve and that a subsequent invitation from the European Community for talks on the crisis indicated Bush no longer led the fragile coalition. Iraqi media portrayed a weak President Bush submitting to the ever-strong Saddam Hussein, now also ever generous, as Saddam promised to release all remaining foreign hostages, including Americans held in Iraq and Kuwait. Now that the deadline had been set, Saddam realized hostages no longer had value as a deterrent or as a distraction. Saddam told Iraqi state television on December 2 that he believed a one in two chance of resolving the crisis existed so long as Bush wanted to have a "real dialogue." If Bush wanted to stage talks simply for the sake of showing the world, and Congress, that he had exhausted all options and the Iraqis refused to budge, "then in that case we are closer to war."[9]

For Arab members of the Coalition, Bush's "extra mile" could not have sent a more conflicted message to Saddam. To Arab leaders, Bush had inadvertently given Saddam a way to "save face" while signaling possible weakness in the Coalition. Prince Bandar, the Saudi ambassador to the United States, told Bush's National Security Advisor Brent Scowcroft that sending Baker to Baghdad would only tell Saddam "you're chicken." Because Bush had not consulted Coalition members, especially the Arab states, about his peace initiative, a meeting with Saddam would prove pointless—Saddam only had to announce that he would not abide by any agreement reached without consultation with his Arab brothers.

Moreover, Bush's rogue diplomacy opened the door for other countries to communicate with Iraq in an attempt to settle the crisis. The European Community had already invited Aziz to discuss a settlement. Saudi King Fahd urged Saddam to accept Bush's peaceful way out, as did a joint communiqué from the foreign ministers of Saudi Arabia, Egypt, and Syria. Bush's advisors worried that the "extra mile" would cost the United States the initiative as the leader of the world community in dealing with the crisis. For Saddam to work a deal with another country, perhaps with conditions, would be disastrous for US interests and prestige in the Middle East if not the world. While these communiqués intended to reinforce to Saddam the strength of the Coalition but also to avoid war, he instead portrayed these extra-American contacts as indicators of the Coalition's weakness.[10]

Saddam now played into Bush's hands. Instead of quickly arranging Aziz's visit to Washington and agreeing to meet with Baker in Baghdad, Saddam squandered an opportunity to upstage Bush and the United States in the eyes of fellow Arabs across the Middle East. Whereas Saddam could have negotiated a withdrawal from Kuwait with some minor concessions that would have made the United States look ridiculous for considering going to war, he instead haggled over meeting dates and the substance of proposed talks. Ultimately, Bush and Saddam settled on a January 9, 1991, meeting between Baker and Aziz in Geneva, Switzerland. At that late date, just six days before the deadline established in Security Council Resolution 678, there would be no negotiating. Either Iraq withdrew from Kuwait, or the Coalition would initiate a war to force an Iraqi withdrawal.[11]

Secretary of State Baker and Iraqi Foreign Minister Tariq Aziz did indeed meet on January 9 at the Hotel Inter-Continental in Geneva. Baker hoped to impress upon Aziz the wrath of destruction his country faced if Iraq did not withdraw from Kuwait by January 15. Within Bush's close circle of advisors, there existed an underlying concern that Saddam's sycophants had intentionally hidden the true seriousness of the situation out of fear. To Bush, moreover, Saddam had placed far too much faith in the Vietnam syndrome, convincing himself that Bush and the American people had no stomach for war. This cavalier attitude, combined with his brutal rule and quick punishment of any dissenters around him, convinced Bush that Saddam was not getting the full story. In his meeting with Aziz in Geneva, Baker hoped to rectify that. "Aziz may wear suits tailored in Paris and speak English more typical of Oxford," Baker offered, "but underneath this veneer, he is as tough as they come and a Ba'ath Party loyalist through and through."[12]

As the meeting opened, Baker and Aziz gave photographers the standard handshake-across-the-table pose, though Baker refused to look Aziz in the eye and kept a stern, serious expression that contrasted starkly with Aziz's nervous smile. Then Baker and Aziz, along with their interpreters and a few staff, sat down to begin the diplomatic dance, much like countless other diplomats had done over the course of centuries. The tension revealed itself quickly, as Baker struggled to maintain his usual calm, courteous demeanor and Aziz visibly sweated, his hands shaking nervously. Baker told Aziz that he had no intention of negotiating; his mission was to "communicate." He then handed Aziz an envelope containing a letter from Bush addressed to Saddam as well as a copy for Aziz to review. Baker had anticipated that Aziz had been told not to accept any letter from Bush, so Baker cunningly had the copy on hand to give to Aziz, assuring that at the very least Aziz would see the letter if he refused to accept the sealed original. The gambit worked. Aziz refused the envelope after taking time to read the copy, telling Baker that the "threats" included in the letter were "alien to the manner of communications between heads of state." In the letter, however, Bush had made clear his intent to "inform" Saddam of the gravity of his situation rather than to "threaten" the Iraqi dictator.[13] Baker replied to his Iraqi counterpart that the letter was entirely appropriate and expressed clearly Bush's intentions if the January 15 deadline passed unheeded.

Baker left the sealed envelope and copy of the president's letter in the middle of the table, directly between himself and Aziz. He then gravely warned Aziz that should war come, "it will be massive.... This will not be another Vietnam.... God forbid, it will be fought to a swift, decisive conclusion." He warned Aziz of the terrible retribution the Coalition would inflict should Saddam use chemical or biological weapons against Coalition forces, consequences that would include the elimination of the Ba'ath regime. Baker nevertheless concluded his opening remarks with a hopeful gesture: "This is the last, best chance for peace."

Aziz responded with a lengthy, defensive diatribe, attacking American imperialist ambitions in the Middle East and reminding Baker of Iraq's war capacity and, as if Baker needed a lesson in classical history, that Iraq, despite its comparatively young Ba'ath government, had existed for over six thousand years: "We have outlasted coalitions like yours in the past.... We are not afraid." To Baker, Aziz "spoke of war with a fatalism of someone for whom peace no longer held any real meaning." After a break, Aziz continued, defending Iraq's invasion of Kuwait with wild unsubstantiated allegations of American and Israeli designs to control the entire Middle East while trying once again to link the crisis to the Palestinian issue.

After over six tense hours, the meeting ended. Just before it ended, Aziz offered to arrange a meeting between Baker and Saddam, which due to the preparations that were necessary could not take place before January 15. Baker, however, blocked Aziz's effort to push back the deadline, countering that President Bush had offered the same meeting weeks before and that the Iraqis had done nothing but stall in making a decision. Baker pointedly told Aziz, "It's too late for that, ... This meeting is your chance. If you aren't prepared to act now, forget it. Time runs out in six days." Afterwards, Baker returned to his room to phone Bush, informing the president that the talks had failed. To his credit, Aziz probably had no leeway to negotiate anyway and had impressed Baker with his diligence under such circumstances. Outside the hotel, Baker told the press,

"Regrettably, ladies and gentlemen, in over six hours I heard nothing that suggested to me any Iraqi flexibility whatsoever on complying with the United Nations Security Council resolutions." The price per barrel of oil rose from $23.35 to $31, and the Dow Jones Industrial Average lost its forty-point gain from earlier in the day.[14]

In his diary, Bush called January 9 "one of the toughest days of my presidency," as he waited to hear from Baker in Geneva.[15] Upon receiving the disappointing but not unexpected news that Aziz offered only intransigence, Bush addressed reporters, telling them the Iraqi response at Geneva "was a total stiff-arm . . . a total rebuff." Bush insisted that "the choice of peace or war is really Saddam's to make," as it had been since Iraq invaded Kuwait. Still, not wanting to "misrepresent" the gravity of the situation, Bush made it clear that while he would do all he could to work toward a peaceful resolution, with only six days until January 15, he fully intended to implement Security Council Resolutions 660 and 678 if the deadline passed without Iraqi compliance.[16]

The Great Debate

As the drama played out with the passage of Resolution 678 in the UN Security Council and in Baker's meeting with Aziz in Geneva, Bush also had to build domestic consensus for his "line in the sand" in the Persian Gulf. Bush, along with Baker, Cheney, and especially Powell, understood that threatening to use force without domestic support undermined American credibility.[17] On January 8, Bush asked Congress to consider a resolution supporting the American use of "all necessary means" pursuant to UN Security Council Resolution 678. In a letter to congressional leaders of both parties, Bush tactfully took Congress to the woodshed for not passing a supporting resolution earlier in the crisis. "It would have been most constructive," Bush wrote to congressional leaders, if in Geneva the next day Baker had a congressional resolution in hand to show unity with the Coalition and "send the clearest possible message" to Saddam. "As you know," he shot at Congress, "I have frequently stated my desire for such a Resolution." Concluding with a more conciliatory tone, Bush urged Congress to "act to strengthen the prospects for peace and safeguard this country's vital interests." "I can think of no better way for Congress to express its support for the President at this critical time," Bush wrote, "This truly is the last best chance for peace."[18]

At his January 9 press briefing, Bush again downplayed the necessity of a congressional resolution while at the same time welcoming and even urging congressional support. As commander-in-chief, Bush believed he already had authority as the leader of a UN member state to act accordingly to implement UN Security Resolution 678. Still, as he related to reporters, "I don't think it's too late to send a consolidated signal to Saddam Hussein," and with his approval ratings up to over 60 percent in early January from a low of 54 percent in November 1990, Bush believed he had the momentum of public support on his side.[19]

Many congressional representatives and senators of both parties believed the president must either ask for a declaration of war or at the very least request a resolution authorizing use of force. For the president to follow merely the spirit of the War Powers Resolution was not enough. Moreover, many Democrats wanted to give sanctions more time, perhaps as much as a year, to compel Iraqi compliance. Some doubted that going to war over Kuwait was worth American lives, much less a threat to American national security. While many Republicans supported the president and backed an authorizing resolution, some in the president's party also wanted to give sanctions and the possibility of negotiations more time. Asking for a resolution authorizing use of force placed Bush in a tenuous position; if approved, Bush could truly present a united domestic and international front against Saddam, but if Congress rejected such a resolution, a humiliated Bush would have to decide whether to go it alone.

Public opinion favored congressional authorization, a fact that certainly drew the attention of both Congress and President Bush. In early January, 57 percent of Americans agreed the time had come to use force rather than give sanctions another chance. The United States, 60 percent believed, had done all it could to resolve the crisis through other means. Sixty percent nevertheless believed Bush must obtain congressional authorization to use force before taking military action against Iraq. Americans had no doubt that Coalition forces would prevail, and 70 percent believed victory very likely. With troops deployed, Americans reluctantly concluded that the time had come to use them. As with Bush, for the American people Saddam's time had run out.[20]

Throughout the fall and into December and January, congressional hearings gave members of Congress the opportunity to air their views on the crisis while considering the viewpoints of past and present government officials. Testimony centered upon the merits and choice of American response to the crisis, as few members of Congress disagreed that Iraq should ultimately withdraw from Kuwait. If anyone had doubts as to the brutality of the Iraqi occupation, witnesses who had fled Kuwait testified to looting, rape, and murder committed by Iraqi forces. Despite the fact that some witnesses (including a woman who alleged that Iraqi troops tossed newborn babies from incubators in Kuwaiti hospitals) had been coached by a public relations firm hired by the Kuwaiti government, the gruesome testimony of alleged Iraqi atrocities made it all the easier for political leaders and pundits alike to say that the Hitler analogy was prescient and to reject any sort of appeasement of Saddam's aggression.[21]

Congressional committees called a distinguished list of very important people to testify, many expressing serious concerns about the viability of war in the Persian Gulf against such a formidable foe as Iraq. Former Chairman of the Joint Chiefs of Staff Admiral William Crowe, for example, recommended giving sanctions more time to avoid what he anticipated would be a bloody and costly war. Former Secretary of Defense James Schlesinger warned that an American war in the Middle East would at best be unpredictable and the subsequent costs in occupation and reconstruction risked the financial ruin of the United States. Others, such as former Secretary of the Navy James Webb, argued that if there was to be war, then Congress should declare it in accordance with the Constitution. Fear of "another Vietnam" haunted the committee rooms. Only former Secretary of State Henry Kissinger, a classic realist in the realm of state-to-state relations, supported the Bush administration's approach to the crisis while arguing that the United States and the world community must firmly face aggression, such as that committed by Saddam, in the interest of balance of power and the international order.[22]

Both houses of the 102nd Congress began debating on January 10. These debates, the most historic and momentous in years, riveted television audiences in the United States and around the world for three days, culminating in dramatic roll-call votes in the House of Representatives and Senate on January 12. Ultimately, the Democrat-controlled Congress (62 percent of the House and 58 percent of the Senate) delivered to President Bush what he wanted but what he nonetheless maintained technically he did not need.

Two different resolutions reached the floor of both houses: one put forth by Democrats and the other by Republicans. The resolution put forward by the Democrat majority leadership called for President Bush to give sanctions more time and to continue seeking a peaceful resolution to the crisis, then return for authorization to use force once all peaceful efforts had been exhausted. The Republican resolution gave clear authorization for the president to use force in accordance with UN Security Council Resolution 678 once Bush had delivered to Congress written notice that all peaceful measures had failed. Both resolutions required the president to include Congress in a decision to go to war in accordance with Constitutional prerogatives.[23]

Bush expected the House to pass an authorizing resolution by a comfortable margin, as enough hawkish Democrats would join Republicans in supporting the president. Still, most House Democrats and some Republicans needed to be convinced that war remained the only option to force Iraq to withdraw from Kuwait. Many believed Bush had rushed to war by including an arbitrary deadline of January 15 in UN Security Council Resolution 678. President Bush, they argued, should give sanctions more time while keeping the military option on the table.[24]

Jim McDermott, a Democrat from the state of Washington, questioned if the Bush administration had really gone the "extra mile," while calling for the president to "slow the headlong rush to battle, give the sanctions time to work, pursue all diplomatic efforts, and talk this thing through fully and rationally" before taking the United States to war. McDermott concluded his remarks with an emotional appeal to resolve the crisis peacefully: "Let it be said that America brought to this crisis not simply the will to do battle, but the way to achieve peace."[25] Representative Robert Wise, Jr., a Democrat from West Virginia, asked, "Did anyone think seriously in September and October, when sanctions were imposed . . . that this was a process that would be over by December?" "Just as you cannot conceive of a five-day war in serious terms," Wise cautioned, "You cannot have two months of sanctions and expect them to work."[26] Gerry Sikorsky, a Democrat representing Minnesota's 6th Congressional District, declared, "Perhaps the time will come when war is absolutely and clearly and unarguably necessary. That is not yet the case." Said Sikorsky : "I cannot support a decision to throw our children's bodies at each other because we are out of patience."[27] Democratic Representative Edward Markey of Massachusetts also urged patience while cautioning against a Tonkin Gulf-like resolution that would remove Congress from the discussion: "We can either give the administration the blank check for war it wants or the reality check for peace that it needs. Let's vote for a policy of patience and prudence."[28]

Bush supporters tried to counter these pleas for patience with arguments for urgency. Time only gave Saddam the opportunity to strengthen his position, making it even more difficult to force him out of Kuwait, they argued. Representative Tom Coleman, a Republican from Missouri, put the case for supporting the president in stark historical terms: "More than half a century ago there were those who thought peace could be purchased by appeasement and turned a deaf ear to the cries of those who had fallen victim to tyranny. They sacrificed weak and peaceful nations to ruthless dictators while murmuring 'peace in our time.' But they did not buy peace: They bought time for the dictators to grow stronger and bolder. And they earned for themselves the condemnation of history."[29] Failing to support the president only played into Saddam's hands, declared Republican Jack Fields of Texas: "This body should be talking in a unitary voice so that we do not send a conflicting signal."[30]

Bush had less confidence in gaining the support of the Senate. Traditionally and constitutionally more involved in foreign affairs than the House of Representatives, the Senate prided itself as an equal colleague to the president in the conduct of American foreign relations. Precisely because of this, many in the Senate from both sides of the aisle chided Bush for abusing his power by not including Congress at important decision points since the crisis had begun in August 1990, namely in the decision to deploy more American troops in November 1990. A US president, according to many senators, had to do more than simply inform; the president had to consult. For his part, Bush maintained he had done his diligence and had consulted Congress throughout the crisis. As in the House, few senators doubted that Iraq must leave Kuwait; the question lay in peaceful versus military means, and what congressional authority, if any, the president must obtain before undertaking military operations to force Iraq from Kuwait.[31]

With fewer members than the House, the Senate debates attracted more attention as members of the upper house of Congress enjoyed more public notoriety if not perceived expertise in military matters and foreign affairs. Democrats led the charge against conceding to Bush the war-making authority that the Constitution reserved for Congress. George Mitchell of Maine, the majority leader for the Democratic Party in the Senate, began the historic Senate debate by reminding his colleagues that the United States Constitution "is not and cannot be subordinated to a UN resolution." Mitchell laid out the central issue before the Senate: "the question is whether Congress will give the president an unlimited blank check to initiate war against Iraq, at some unspecified time in the future, under circumstances which are not now known and cannot be foreseen, or whether, while not ruling out the use of force if all other means fail, we will now urge continuation of the policy of concerted international economic and diplomatic pressure."[32] Patrick Leahy of Vermont warned that a vote authorizing President Bush to use military force would "set a precedent which says that in the most powerful Nation known in history, one person, whoever is president, has the sole power to unleash that enormous power in a war that can engulf any part of the world."[33]

Senator John Kerry of Massachusetts, a combat veteran of Vietnam and young leader in the veterans' anti-war movement during the latter years of the Vietnam War, urged President Bush to give sanctions time to take effect while downplaying the direct threat Saddam posed to American national security. Kerry argued that the United States should only go to war "when the Nation as a whole has decided that there is a real threat and that the Nation as a whole has decided that we all must go." "I do not believe this test has been met," Kerry urged, "There is no consensus in America for war and, therefore, the Congress should not vote to authorize war."[34]

Like their fellow members in the House, Senate Republicans countered that Congress must act to support the president, as delay only benefitted Saddam. Pennsylvania's Republican Senator, Arlen Spector, declared that he would have preferred a deadline much later than January 15. "However," Spector said, "I believe as a matter of US policy that we are well beyond that alternative." Spector reluctantly agreed with President Bush that the time had come for action: "If we do not follow through at this stage, if Iraq does not withdraw voluntarily from Kuwait, and if the UN resolution does not proceed, we will be building a more powerful Iraq, and we will be fighting this war at another day and in a more destructive way with greater loss of life, American lives."[35] Republican Senator Orin Hatch of Utah told his fellow senators that "it is time for Congress to help rather than hinder the President." For Hatch, an overwhelming vote would "maximize the pressure on Iraq," while a close vote would convince Saddam that "he can divide our country if [he] will only hold out." Hatch believed a clear authorization to use force would pave the way for a peaceful resolution: "The only way to avoid war, in my opinion, in this particular situation, is to be prepared to go to war and to show our resolve is for real."[36] Richard Lugar, the Republican Senator from Indiana, argued that as the "only remaining" and "reluctant superpower," American "credibility" was at stake: "The moment for accountability has come."[37]

The debates in both houses of Congress expressed concern over whether war was warranted and if so what the desired end state would be. Members compared Saddam to Hitler and made analogies with Vietnam, generally agreed Iraq must leave Kuwait, and universally supported the troops. On January 12, in front of packed galleries and a live television audience, the House and Senate voted. Two hundred and fifty members of the House (including eighty-six Democrats) said "yea" to House Joint Resolution 77, while 183 (including three Republicans) answered "nay," with two not voting.[38] Senate Joint Resolution 2 was passed in a close vote, fifty-two (including ten Democrats) in favor to forty-seven (including two Republicans) against, with California Democrat Alan Cranston abstaining.[39] In identical phrasing, the joint resolutions "authorized the use of United States Armed Forces pursuant to United Nations Security Council Resolution 678" once the president "has used all appropriate diplomatic and other peaceful means" to free Kuwait from Iraqi occupation. In keeping with the War Powers Resolution of 1973 and to ensure presidential consultation with Congress, the resolution required President Bush to report to Congress every sixty days "on the status of efforts to obtain compliance by Iraq with the resolutions adopted by the United Nations Security Council in response to Iraq's aggression." Bush signed the resolution as Public Law 102-1.[40]

Congress had spoken and despite significant opposition to the use of force, members of both houses made it a point to present a unified front to support the president once the resolutions passed. Later in the day on January 12, President Bush met with reporters at the White House, telling them he was "gratified" to have congressional support for UN Resolution 678. Clearly relieved, Bush declared, "This action by the Congress unmistakably demonstrates the United States commitment to the international demand for a complete and unconditional withdrawal of Iraq from Kuwait." Praising this latest "last, best chance for peace," Bush told the world, "we've now closed ranks behind a clear signal of our determination and our resolve to implement the United Nations resolutions. Those who may have mistaken our democratic process as a sign of weakness now see the strength of democracy. And this sends the clearest message to Iraq that it cannot scorn the January 15th deadline."[41]

Bush had managed perhaps the most impressive diplomatic, political, and military alignment in the twentieth century—UN Resolution 678, congressional authorization to use force, and a military coalition quickly approaching offensive capacity. Bush later wrote that he would have "acted and ordered our troops into combat" without congressional authorization. Having avoided making such a decision without the support of Congress and possibly the American people, Bush felt the "heavy weight" of possible impeachment for acting in defiance of Congress lift from his shoulders.[42]

Meanwhile, UN Secretary-General Perez de Cuéllar's last-minute visit to Baghdad on January 11 failed to budge the intransigent Iraqis, who insulted the secretary-general by making him wait until January 13 to personally meet with Saddam and in the interim suffer lengthy diatribes from Aziz and PLO leader Yasser Arafat. Saddam offered his usual platter of anti-American rhetoric and Arab solutions to the crisis. Perez de Cuéllar could find no sign that Saddam had the slightest intention of withdrawing from Kuwait. The secretary-general left Iraq on January 14, disappointed despite having little hope of success before making the trip: "You need two to tango. I wanted to dance but I did not find any nice lady for dancing with."[43] On January 15, Perez de Cuéllar made a final vain attempt to bring Saddam to his senses. In a public statement, the secretary-general appealed to Saddam "to turn the course of events away from catastrophe and towards a new era of justice and harmony based on the principles of the Charter of the United Nations." If Saddam began the total withdrawal of his forces "immediately," Perez de Cuéllar assured him that UN-backed forces would not attack. In his last year as secretary-general, Perez de Cuéllar lamented that "no disappointment would be greater and more tragic than to find the nations of the world engaging in a conflict that none of their peoples want." Saddam made no reply.[44]

The French, too, made a last-second effort to avoid war. At the behest of Arafat, the French government attempted to submit a new resolution to the Security Council that called for Iraq to announce its intention of withdrawing from Kuwait and also linked settlement of the Iraq–Kuwait dispute to other regional issues, including the Israeli-Palestinian problem. French Foreign Minister Roland Dumas met with the Iraqi ambassador to France to plead with Saddam to offer at least a signal that he was willing to make a last-second deal, but Dumas received only disappointment for his effort. Regardless, President Bush rejected the French draft resolution, as did the Security Council in a meeting behind closed doors on January 14. Time, it now seemed, had run out for Saddam.[45]

For Bush, obtaining both UN and congressional authorization to use "all available means" to force Saddam from Kuwait was critical to maintaining the solidarity of the Coalition, gaining domestic support in the United States, and leaving Saddam with little doubt as to American resolve to expend its own blood to restore Kuwait. To coordinate these political objectives with General Schwarzkopf's timetable for offensive capability to time perfectly with the January 15 deadline was a masterful exercise in politics, diplomacy, and organization. Now, all that remained was the deadline itself, which if ignored by the Iraqis would set into action Schwarzkopf's plan to oust Iraqi forces from Kuwait.

The Plan

Schwarzkopf and his staff at CENTCOM had begun planning for just such a war days after Saddam's forces invaded Kuwait in August 1990.

The plan-on-the-shelf, OP PLAN 90-1002 provided for deploying 100,000 troops to the Persian Gulf region over the course of twelve to sixteen weeks, preceded by an additional four weeks of preparation before shipping out to the Persian Gulf. This plan had been the foundation for the initial deployments of DESERT SHIELD, the defensive deployment operation to protect Saudi Arabia from an Iraqi invasion. At a crisis meeting at Camp David on August 4, Schwarzkopf had briefed the president on alterations to OP PLAN 90-1002 that could get a deterrent force of over 200,000 to Saudi Arabia in about four months. Shifting to an offensive capability would require a completely different force, a much larger one than the deterrent and one that would require calling up the Reserves and National Guard units to field a force of over 500,000 troops, which along with requisite equipment, aircraft, fuel, and the like would take several months to deploy to Iraq.[46]

Relying solely on airpower provided another tempting option, as Iraq offered a target-rich environment, and had never faced an onslaught of such modern aircraft and precision-guided weaponry, even during the Iran–Iraq War. Moreover, an air campaign could have chaotic effect on Iraq's highly centralized command-and-control structure and perhaps break the will of the Iraqi people to continue supporting Saddam. Air Force Colonel John A. Warden designed the initial concept of the air campaign, using his ideas of concentric rings and centers of gravity as the foundation for a three-phased plan. Warden's rings represented an enemy's "system," overlapping outward in descending order of strategic importance and effect. Leadership and central command occupied the center ring of highest importance, followed by key production commodities, such as electricity and fuel, and then by infrastructure (bridges, roads, rail networks). Population also occupied a strategic ring, as one might expect for an air campaign. Breaking the will of the population had been a hallmark of airpower theorists dating back to the advent of military use of air in World War I. Hitting targets to affect the population, in Iraq's case the middle class, the Ba'ath party apparatus, and military elites, would theoretically cause the population to lose faith in Saddam's cause. The last outward ring contained fielded forces. Thus, in Warden's construct, attacking as many targets in each ring as possible while hitting the center ring especially hard would collapse the entire enemy "system." Like airpower theorists before him, Warden envisioned such an air campaign to achieve the political objective without having to use ground forces, thus avoiding mass casualties.[47]

Schwarzkopf, Powell, and Secretary of Defense Cheney, however, doubted airpower alone could fulfill its much-ballyhooed capability and force Saddam out of Kuwait through a strategic bombing campaign. Warden disagreed, but was not present to defend his ideas. The Air Force Chief of Staff, General Michael J. Dugan, later publically espoused an air-only campaign to oust Saddam's forces from Kuwait, a gaff that gave Secretary of Defense Cheney cause to fire Dugan. Airing such views, apparently, had no place in the post-Goldwater–Nichols joint environment, at least not in Bush's inner circle of advisors. Kicking Saddam out of Kuwait by force, Powell, Cheney, and others concluded, required a joint approach involving both air and ground forces. Warden's air campaign plan, nevertheless, became the genesis for INSTANT THUNDER, the air component of Operation DESERT STORM.[48]

While CENTCOM's primary focus early in the crisis remained the DESERT SHEILD deployment, Schwarzkopf nevertheless established a planning cell to devise a military campaign to liberate Kuwait. By mid-September, Schwarzkopf's vision of DESERT STORM began taking shape, consisting of a major ground thrust from Saudi Arabia north across Kuwait to the Rawdatayn oil fields to shut the door on Iraqi forces retreating from Kuwait City and heavily fortified areas along the Kuwaiti coast. Even at this early stage, the Iraqis expected an amphibious assault as a principal part of any Coalition offensive against them in Kuwait. Schwarzkopf understood this as well. This initial iteration of the offensive plan involved a single corps sweeping across the Kuwaiti frontier to strike Iraqi Republican Guard units while bypassing strongly defended areas to lessen the cost in casualties as much as possible. In deciding to hit Saddam's Republican Guard, Schwarzkopf determined that Saddam's elite troops represented a key center of gravity, a core component of an enemy's force, economy, or political structure that if destroyed would cause the enemy's fighting ability to collapse. Schwarzkopf had also realized, as had Saddam, that the Coalition's center of gravity was indeed the Coalition itself.[49]

Planners had much to contend with as they considered the many factors that could influence not only how the campaign might unfold but if it would even be successful. Schwarzkopf's planning cell evaluated mission, enemy, terrain, troops, and time available (METT-T) constantly throughout the planning stage and well into the war itself. Summer, for example, made offensive operations prohibitive. The heat, often above 120 degrees Fahrenheit, would debilitate troops and equipment alike. January through March would be the ideal months as far as temperature was concerned, but even then sudden deluges of rain would flood the wadies that often ran along a northeast to southwest axis near the Saudi-Iraqi border. Wind and sandstorms also presented problems regardless of the time of year; the superfine desert sands of the region had already wreaked havoc on equipment deployed as part of DESERT SHEILD. Logistics, too, plagued planners, as hundreds of miles separated primary bases, such as King Khalid Military City, from necessary logistical points near the border. Few highways connected these desolate areas. While the rocky plain along the Saudi-Iraqi border could support the heavy mechanized style of warfare that the American military had equipped and trained for during the Cold War, the exact geologic conditions of the Iraqi interior remained largely unknown.[50]

Then there was the enemy itself. On paper, Iraq appeared well equipped and experienced. The Iraqi army outsized the German forces that had defended against the Allied landings in Normandy in 1944. At the base, the Iraqi army relied upon conscript-driven infantry divisions equipped with often dilapidated equipment and led by second-rate officers. These infantry divisions had declined in quality beyond the questionable level that they had practiced during the Iran–Iraq War, so much so that American analysts speculated that even a static defense might be beyond their capability. Saddam made sure his regular heavy divisions were better maintained with better equipment, better troops, and career officers of better quality than that of the basic infantry divisions. The core of Saddam's military machine was of course the Republican Guard, which in 1990 consisted of twenty-eight combat divisions, including armor, infantry, mechanized infantry, and special forces, in eight named divisions. These were the battle-hardened, ideologically committed troops fanatically loyal not to Iraq but to Saddam. Many senior officers hailed from Saddam's native Tikrit and most of the troops were, like Saddam, Sunni Muslims. While regular army units suffered logistical wants, the Republican Guard lived a comparative life of military luxury. The Republican Guard most concerned Powell, Schwarzkopf, and American analysts.

Highly mechanized, the Iraqi army boasted several armored divisions with an armada of mostly Soviet-made tanks. Regular army armored divisions included 250 T-54, T-55, and T-62 tanks, while Republican Guard armored divisions had over 300 modern T-72s, with a select few armored brigades in the Republican Guard boasting the top-of-the-line Soviet T-72M1. From its war with Iran, Iraq had the latest French, Austrian, and South African-made artillery. Modern defenses ringed Baghdad and other strategic centers and protected field forces in the desert. The Iraqi air force—while its over 750 aircraft made it appear sizable on paper—maintained an uneven assortment of aircraft, including large numbers of Soviet-built MiG-29s, with aircrews of equally uneven quality. The very best pilots flew the best fighters in the Iraqi air force—the French-made Mirage F1. Iraq also maintained a large and diverse arsenal of SSMs and SAMs, including dozens of fixed-site and mobile-launched Scud missiles, some of which had a range of over 600 kilometers. Saddam's arsenal of chemical and biological weapons presented the gravest threat to Coalition forces, which took every precaution to defend against potential chemical and biological attacks.

Iraq's military juggernaut was not without its weaknesses. Such a large force depended upon conscription of many reluctant levies. While CENTCOM planners expected Republican Guard units to fight to the death, the will of the vast majority of conscriptees remained open to question. Reaching a high rank required an officer to be a sycophant to Saddam, a practice that brought the military capability of Iraq's senior military leadership into question, as the wrath of Saddam made taking the initiative not worth the risk. Thus, Iraq's officer corps had questionable strategic and tactical abilities beyond mass-fire operations, such as those that characterized the Iran–Iraq War of the 1980s. The most telling weakness in the Iraqi military, though, was Saddam himself. A megalomaniac due in part to the very nature of his existence as a dictator, Saddam commanded his forces with both strategic and tactical ineptness and exercised uncompromising centralized command-and-control, so much so that commanders in the field could rarely act on their own accord—one did so at one's peril.

Thus sat Saddam's military, a diametric force that simultaneously exhibited characteristics as a juggernaut and as a paper tiger. His army dug in behind impressive defenses along the Saudi border. Although also dug in behind formidable defenses, Iraqi forces in Kuwait were nevertheless isolated at the extreme end of an extremely long logistical tail. Moreover, the Iraqi air force could not provide those forces with air support once the fighting started. The Republican Guard would not come to their rescue. Instead, these soldiers from the lower rungs of Iraqi society would be sacrificed once the shooting started. Schwarzkopf reckoned the Republican Guard would let Coalition forces advance, then counterattack, much as they had during the Iran–Iraq War against Iranian forces.[51]

Getting US and Coalition troops and equipment ready, deployed, and then positioned probably caused Schwarzkopf's planners their more intense headaches. With American forces scattered literally around the globe, getting both specific units and large divisions to Saudi Arabia required the most delicate and creative logistical planning. With limited transport for personnel and equipment, planners had to prioritize what they wanted, where they wanted it, and when they wanted it. This included coordinating the arrival and deployment of Coalition partner forces and equipment, both of which rarely honored CENTCOM's logistical time-tables. Time, indeed, provided the greatest challenge. Synchronizing the arrival, positioning, and use of troops and equipment, including food and fuel, required adroit skill and patience. As Army General Robert Scales later wrote, "Schwarzkopf's task would be to orchestrate the movements and actions of many disparate parts to bring them harmoniously to exactly the right place in time to achieve a single aim." Such issues made both Powell and Schwarzkopf apprehensive about engaging in such a war; both knew from history and their own experience the Clausewitzian dictum that "friction" could derail the best-planned campaign. "Countless minor incidents—the kind you can never really foresee—combine to lower the general level of performance," the Prussian officer wrote in the nineteenth century, "so that one always falls far short of the intended goal." How well Powell and Schwarzkopf and their subordinates dealt with the unforeseen once the campaign began would, as had been the case in wars before and since, determine the outcome.[52]

Much to the frustration of Schwarzkopf, Bush requested a briefing on an offensive plan in early October. At this stage, a real plan did not exist, thus Schwarzkopf could offer only ideas and talking points. Nevertheless, Schwarzkopf sent his chief of staff, Marine Major General Robert B. Johnston, to Washington on October 10. In the Pentagon's secure "Tank," Johnston outlined what CENTCOM had to date to Powell and Secretary of Defense Cheney. With only one corps deployed in the Kuwait Theater of Operations (KTO) and limited air assets in the region, Johnston explained, the plan involved a three-phased air campaign resembling Warden's INSTANT THUNDER scheme from early August, followed by a fourth ground-centered phase.

Dissatisfied with Warden's air-only plan, Air Force Lieutenant General Chuck Horner, CENTCOM's Joint Force Air Component Commander (JFACC) had tasked Brigadier General Buster C. Glosson, director of campaign planning for CENTCOM's air forces, to derive a combined air plan that would both attack strategic targets and support the ground phase of the liberation of Kuwait. Glosson's planning team called their workspace the Black Hole, meeting in a secure bunker within the CENTCOM command complex in Riyadh, Saudi Arabia. Within the Black Hole group, USAF officers along with representatives from the other services developed a more comprehensive air campaign plan for Washington's consideration. Their plan transitioned from the initial phases to establish control of the air by destroying Iraqi air defenses, decapitating the Iraqi leadership and command and control, and degrading Iraqi NBC capability, and then to battlefield preparation and support for the ground campaign by targeting logistics and transportation and Iraqi fielded forces, especially the Republican Guard.[53]

While the air plan would continue to evolve in scope and scale, the basic concept of the plan that General Johnston included in his brief to Powell and Cheney would remain the same. The Black Hole group had given Schwarzkopf an air plan easily integrated into an overall campaign that assumed ground action. Johnston gave Powell and Cheney CENTCOM's four-phased plan. Phase 1 targeted Saddam's command and control network to isolate both the top Iraqi political and military leadership and Iraqi forces in Kuwait. Also in Phase 1, Coalition air forces would destroy the Iraqi Air Force as well as Iraq's air defense system, and target Iraq's known weapons of mass destruction (WMD) assets. Phase 2 involved intensive bombing of the Iraqi logistical network, hitting bases and transportation nodes, as well as rail stock and trucks, to shut down Iraq's supply to its fielded forces in Kuwait and southern Iraq. Iraq's fielded forces would suffer massive bombardment in Phase 3. Then, the Coalition ground assault would begin, involving either an Army strike head-on against Iraqi defenses along the Kuwaiti border or an amphibious landing by Marines on the Kuwaiti coast, or both. During the briefing, the idea of using the Marines as a feint to pin down Iraqi forces on the Kuwaiti coast surfaced, but neither the amphibious landing nor the "go-up-the-middle" approach gained much support, as both implied heavy casualties. Powell and Cheney criticized the ground plan for lacking mobility and creativity, but seemed pleased with the air component. Johnston briefed President Bush on October 11, telling the commander-in-chief that Schwarzkopf needed two corps rather than one to create a better offensive option. An additional corps would give Schwarzkopf more flexibility and power, and would allow him to use more space for movement in the desert in southern Iraq as an alternative to a straight-up-the-middle assault into Kuwait.[54]

Bush approved the deployment of a second corps in early November as part of his announced troop increase, signaling the transition to an offensive capability. Schwarzkopf wanted the VII Corps, based at the time in Germany. Considered the best equipped and trained because of its position as the first line of defense against a possible Soviet invasion of West Germany, the VII Corps included heavy mechanized and armored divisions that Schwarzkopf required to battle Iraqi armor. In addition to the XVIII Airborne Corps already deployed to Saudi Arabia, the First

Infantry Division, I Marine Expeditionary Force, numerous Marine and Air Force wings, and a range of National Guard and Reserve units joined VII Corps in Saudi Arabia. CENTCOM estimated the buildup to an American force of over 400,000 would be complete on January 15, with other deployments continuing afterward.

To incorporate Coalition military partners into the campaign, Schwarzkopf established Joint Forces Command (JFC) North and South. In addition to his CENTCOM joint command staff, Schwarzkopf established a Coalition command to include Lieutenant General Prince Khalid bin Sultan al-Saud of Saudi Arabia, French General Michel Roquejeoffre, and Lieutenant General Peter de la Billiere of Great Britain. Prince Khalid proved masterful as the Saudi government's primary contact with Coalition forces and acted as co-commander of Coalition forces, while General de la Billiere brought long experience in the Middle East and his expertise in special operations to the command table.

Coalition members contributed a wide array of troops, equipment, and capabilities to Schwarzkopf. One destroyer and two frigates from the Australian Navy patrolled the Persian Gulf, along with ships from Argentina, Belgium, Denmark, Canada, Germany, France, Great Britain, Greece, Italy, The Netherlands, Norway, Poland, and Spain, and augmented the large US Navy presence in the Persian Gulf, the Red Sea, and the Mediterranean. Afghanistan, Bangladesh, Czechoslovakia, Egypt, France, Great Britain, Kuwait, Oman, Bahrain, Qatar, Saudi Arabia, Honduras, Italy, Morocco, Niger, Pakistan, Romania, Sierra Leone, Senegal, Singapore, Syria, and Turkey contributed combat troops, medical teams, support troops, and other units in support of both DESERT SHIELD and DESERT STORM, totaling over 300,000 personnel. Several of these countries and others also contributed aircraft, mostly transports and tankers but some fighters and bombers, to the fight. Turkey and Saudi Arabia, among others, proved critical militarily by providing basing and flyover rights to Coalition forces. Many gave money, totaling tens of billions of dollars, to help pay for the deployment of Coalition forces to the Gulf and, ultimately, the war. Saudi Arabia, Kuwait, and other Arab states alone paid for close to two-thirds of the cost of the war, while Japan and Germany contributed $10 billion and $6 billion, respectively.[55]

The developing two-corps plan shied away from the all-out straight-up-the-middle assault, favoring instead a classic end-run maneuver similar to that used during the American Civil War by Union General Ulysses S. Grant at Vicksburg in 1863 or during World War II by Wehrmacht General Erwin Rommel at the Battle of Gazala in 1942. Grant had swung his force south of Vicksburg, for a time breaking its logistical line, to approach the Gibraltar of the Confederacy from the east and to ultimately lay siege to the city and capture it on July 4, 1863. More directly akin to the developing Coalition plan, Rommel, the "Desert Fox," had used his armor to flank the British Gazala line in his campaign to take the Libyan port of Tobruk. Rommel's use of maneuver in the desert had been daring, stretching his logistical line, especially fuel, to swing his tank divisions toward the southern flank of the British line after a deception demonstration to convince the British that he intended to assault the northern British line closer to Tobruk head-on. In less than four weeks, Rommel had taken Tobruk. Rommel had utilized maneuver, speed, and deception—the hallmarks of AirLand Battle doctrine.[56]

Both American corps would make a Rommel-like swing west, and far west, into the desert and enter Iraq through the back door while the two JFCs and IMEF kicked in the front door along the Kuwaiti border with Saudi Arabia. VII Corps would swing around as a hammer hitting the anvil of IMEF and the JFCs to destroy Iraqi fielded forces. XVIII Corps would make a wider swing to envelope Kuwait, catching any Iraqi forces, especially Republican Guard units, that may have escaped the hammer and anvil. Later called the "Great Wheel" and the "Hail Mary," the westward swing would allow American forces to go around the major Iraqi defense networks of anti-tank ditches and berms, extensive minefields, and flammable oil pits. Deception was the key to the plan. The Iraqis had to be convinced either of an amphibious assault or of a frontal attack. In the interest of Coalition solidarity, planners placed select British and French forces in both American corps and ensured that Saudi-commanded Arab troops would be the first to enter Kuwait City.

With Iraqi forces in static positions and unaware of the massive two-corps force moving west, Schwarzkopf anticipated that it would be too late for the Republican Guard and Iraqi forces to react when they realized what had happened. Deception would play a pivotal role in the coming weeks as Schwarzkopf kept Marine amphibious assault units aboard ships in the Persian Gulf and teased reporters into expecting a classic Inchon-like amphibious landing near Kuwait City. Keeping the Great Wheel part of the plan secret, however, became a key matter of concern for Schwarzkopf, as moving two corps of over 200,000 troops to new jump-off locations hundreds of miles west of their current positions without tipping off the media or Saddam presented an immense security challenge that Coalition forces ultimately largely met.[57]

With the plan and requisite forces in place, then, January 15 came and went, with no Iraqi move to leave Kuwait, nor any word from Saddam.

6

INSTANT THUNDER

On January 17, 1991, at approximately 0300 hours local time, American and Coalition air forces attacked Iraqi forces in Kuwait and southern Iraq as well as strategic targets in the heart of Baghdad. CNN, the world's first twenty-four-hour news channel, had its top anchor Bernard Shaw and veteran correspondent Peter Arnett in Baghdad reporting live as the city's air raid sirens blared in the night to be followed by heavy explosions and the distinct ack-ack bursts of Iraqi anti-aircraft fire or AAA. Shaw and Arnett stayed on the air for almost sixteen hours either on the phone or through their fuzzy satellite connection, bringing television audiences around the world the dramatic sights and sounds of the opening salvos of DESERT STORM. In Washington, DC, at just after 1900 hours local time on January 16, White House Press Secretary Marlin Fitzwater appeared before White House press corps to announce, "The liberation of Kuwait has begun."[1]

Airpower Unleashed

Just before the first bombs fell, President Bush met with the Kuwaiti ambassador to inform him that the war to free his country was about to begin, then made phone calls to several world leaders to let them know war was imminent. Secretary of Defense Cheney telephoned his counterpart in Israel, Moshe Arens, to alert him that the offensive was underway and to expect Iraqi retaliation. Much depended upon Israel's restraint, as many expected Saddam to fire missiles at Israel in an attempt to goad Israel into attacking Iraq, thereby breaking up Arab participation in the Coalition. The White House delivered letters to House and Senate leaders formally notifying Congress that President Bush had given the green light to Schwarzkopf to begin military operations on the Coalition commander's order. In the White House that evening, Bush, his wife Barbara, and the Reverend Billy Graham sat in front of a television tuned to CNN.[2]

President Bush delivered a live televised speech from the Oval Office at 2100 hours local time, telling them "the battle has been joined" to force an "intransigent" Saddam to abandon his occupation of Iraq's "small helpless neighbor." Bush reiterated to the American people and to the world that Saddam had brushed aside "with open contempt" every opportunity for a peaceful resolution to the crisis, that sanctions had failed to compel Iraqi compliance, and that timing dictated immediate military action lest Saddam's forces entrench too deeply in Kuwait. Said Bush, "The United States, together with the United Nations, exhausted every means at our disposal to bring this crisis to a peaceful end. However, Saddam clearly reckoned that by stalling and threatening, indeed defying, the United Nations, he could weaken the forces arrayed against him." Exhaustive diplomacy, numerous UN Security Council resolutions, the diverse but admittedly fragile Coalition, congressional support, and the impressive military force now deployed in Saudi Arabia and the Persian Gulf, among other signs, left little doubt that Kuwait would soon be free of its Iraqi occupiers. Bush repeated that the war in the Persian Gulf would "not be another Vietnam . . . . We will not fail."[3]

With a further nod to the Vietnam syndrome and in keeping with the Weinberger/Powell Doctrine, Bush also laid before the American public the objectives of military action in the Persian Gulf. Iraqi forces would leave Kuwait and the Kuwaiti government would be restored. Iraq would comply with all relevant UN Security Council resolutions, and then, Bush hoped, Iraq could "live as a peaceful and cooperative member of the family of nations, thus enhancing the security and stability of the Gulf."[4] The previous day, Bush had approved National Security Directive (NSD) 54, explaining his use of military force to implement UN Security Council Resolution 678 and clearly stating the political objectives military action would achieve. Specifically, the objectives included the following:

a) To effect the immediate, complete, and unconditional withdrawal of Iraqi forces from Kuwait;
b) To restore Kuwait's legitimate government;
c) To protect the lives of American citizens abroad; and,
d) To promote the security and stability of the Persian Gulf.

In support of these objectives, NSD 54 outlined the following objectives for Coalition forces:

a) Defend Saudi Arabia and other GCC states against attack.
b) Preclude the Iraqi launch of ballistic missiles against neighboring states and friendly forces.
c) Destroy Iraq's chemical, biological, and nuclear capabilities.
d) Destroy Iraq's command, control, and communications capabilities.
e) Eliminate the Republican Guards as an effective fighting force.
f) Conduct operations designed to drive Iraq's forces from Kuwait; break the will of Iraqi forces; discourage Iraqi use of chemical, biological, and nuclear weapons; encourage defection of Iraqi forces; and weaken Iraqi popular support for the current government.[5]

If Saddam used chemical, biological, or nuclear weapons, initiated terrorist attacks "anywhere in the world," or attempted to destroy Kuwaiti oil fields, NSD 54 stated starkly and unmistakably that President Bush would then "replace the current leadership of Iraq" and possibly authorize "additional punitive actions." Aside from the vague assertion of weakening "popular support" for Saddam mentioned in objective "f" above, this was the only reference to overthrowing the Iraqi dictator. Otherwise, Bush did not include getting rid of Saddam as an overt political or military objective, nor did Bush wish to change Iraq's borders or maintain a long-term American military presence in the Persian Gulf after the conflict. While Bush's address to the nation on January 16 may not have been his best oratorical effort, the speech and NSD 54 specifically outlined not only the political objectives Bush sought to achieve, but also gave clear guidance to military leaders pursuant to those political objectives.[6]

On January 20, Saddam addressed the Iraqi people, telling his "O glorious Iraqis" that the planes of the "infidel tyrant" Bush "are falling out of the skies." According to Saddam, Iraq had not yet begun to fight, but would soon "use all the means and potential that God has given us" to bring "great victory in the mother of all battles." With victory, declared Saddam, "the skies in the Arab homeland will appear in a new color and a sun of new hope will shine" to overcome "the darkness in the hearts of the infidels, the Zionists, and the treacherous, shameful rulers, such as the traitor [King] Fahd." Saddam again attempted to tie the conflict to the "liberation of beloved Palestine" and the "release from bondage" of Jerusalem. Saddam called Iraqis and all Arabs to "holy war" against the United States and the Coalition.[7]

Just before 0300 hours in Iraq, Task Force Normandy, consisting of several Army AH-64 Apache and Air Force MH-53 Pave Low helicopters, attacked two Iraqi early warning radar sites in Iraq's western desert to give Coalition aircraft already en route on bombing missions clear passage. Although Task Force Normandy destroyed the radars, news of the attack quickly reached Baghdad, thus limiting the element of immediate surprise. In Baghdad and other locations, anti-aircraft crews manned their guns and armed missiles as air-raid sirens blared across the country. Across the world, people watched CNN's live coverage of the first strikes against Baghdad, as F-117A stealth fighters dropped 2,000-pound laser-guided bombs on targets in the Iraqi capital. Simultaneously, B-52 bombers that had left their home at Lackland Air Force Base in Louisiana some fifteen hours earlier dropped their bomb loads on designated targets in Iraq, then returned home for an ultimately thirty-five hour round trip of over 14,000 miles. The opening salvo also hoped to get the Iraqis to turn on their radar tracking systems and SAM sites, which they did, allowing Coalition aircraft to pinpoint and destroy much of the Iraqi air defense network during the initial phase of the air campaign. From that point, the Iraqis rarely turned on radars for fear of almost instant attack. In all, over 700 aircraft, including American F-4 Wild Weasels, F-111 Aardvarks, F-15 Strike Eagles, and F-16 Falcons, along with British Tornados and Saudi F-16s, flew combat sorties that first night from bases in Saudi Arabia, Turkey, Qatar, Bahrain, and UAE as well as from aircraft carriers in the Persian Gulf. For the first time in combat, US Navy ships in the Persian Gulf fired over 100 Tomahawk land-attack missiles (TLAMs), hitting targets considered too well guarded by anti-air defenses, including Saddam's presidential palace.[8]

Far from dire predictions of significant losses of aircraft and crews, of the over 1,300 sorties dropping over 18 kilotons worth of bombs (the atomic bomb used against Hiroshima, Japan, on August 6, 1945, was about 20 kilotons by comparison) flown during the first twenty-four hours of the air campaign, only three Coalition aircraft were lost. This trend continued throughout the three-phased air campaign and the ground war, as Coalition air forces lost only forty-six aircraft (including twenty-seven American aircraft), of which twenty-three were shot down by Iraqi SAMs, nine lost to Iraqi AAA fire, and only one shot down by Iraqi ground fire. Coalition air forces shot down thirty-four Iraqi aircraft, while destroying over one hundred Iraqi planes on the ground. Dozens of Iraqi planes fled to neighboring Iran where Iranian authorities impounded them. Not a single Coalition aircraft was lost in air-to-air combat with Iraqi MiG or Mirage fighters. By the end of Operation

Figure 2   *A Tomahawk land-attack missile (TLAM) is fired from the battleship* USS Missouri *at the start of DESERT STORM. Photograph by PH3 Dillon.*
Source: United States Department of Defense, DefenseImagery.mil.

DESERT STORM, over 90,000 tons of bombs had been used. To put this in perspective, consider that two smart bombs dropped by a single USAF bomber had the same effectiveness as 108 World War II B-17s, with over 1,000 aircrew members, loaded with almost 650 bombs. Coalition bombs shut down Iraq's oil refining capacity, for example, with roughly half the tonnage of bombs that Allied air forces used to destroy a single oil refinery in Germany during World War II.[9]

Coalition air forces struck Iraqi command and control centers, disrupted communication between Baghdad and Iraqi fielded forces in Kuwait and in southern Iraq, and destroyed key bridges across the Tigris and Euphrates Rivers. Electrical grids, water systems, gas stations, and pipelines crumpled under the onslaught of Coalition bombs and missiles. Iraqi government buildings and Saddam's many palaces were hit, as was the Ba'ath Party headquarters in Baghdad as well as targets in Saddam's hometown of Tikrit. To keep Iraq's military power in check for the long term, far beyond the current conflict to force Saddam from Kuwait, Schwarzkopf's air campaign planners targeted Iraqi defense industries, known chemical and biological weapons sites, any sites affiliated with Saddam's nascent nuclear weapons program, defense depots, and other military targets across Iraq, in addition to the more pressing targets in southern Iraq and Kuwait. Initial estimates projected it would take Iraq's chemical weapons program at minimum three years to restart and Iraq's biological capability one year to recover after these attacks. Saddam's nuclear program, which had been advanced before the war, had been set back years by Coalition attacks, though after the conflict defecting Iraqi nuclear scientists claimed Saddam's nuclear program remained largely intact despite the bombing. Indeed, by January of 1992, Iraq claimed to have a uranium enrichment program in place with the goal of producing a nuclear weapon.[10]

The impact on Iraq was immediate and real. Iraqi authorities quickly rationed gasoline, limiting each vehicle to less than ten gallons of fuel for every two weeks. Within three days, INSTANT THUNDER had cut Iraqi oil production by 50 percent; within ten days, it had been shut down completely. Coalition bombs knocked out Basra's water supply system, shutting it down for the duration of the conflict. Hundreds of thousands of people fled Baghdad, leaving its streets and shops comparatively deserted. Baghdad lost electricity the first night of the war and did not regain even intermittent electrical service until several months after the war. Later, critics of the air campaign pointed to the disconnect between bombing Iraq's electrical grid and the subsequent impact on the outcome of the war. While destroying electrical grids can be advantageous in a long-term war of attrition, they charged, doing so in support of a short-term war of limited objectives had little effect, resulting in excessive damage for little gain while inflicting undue hardship on the civilian population. In all, the air campaign destroyed one-quarter of Iraq's electricity generating capacity while significantly damaging an additional 50 percent of the country's electrical grid. Such destruction had ripple effects, such as the shutting down of sewer treatment plants and water systems, that caused more extensive and expensive damage.[11]

Collateral Damage

The air campaign was not without its pitfalls and mistakes. While everyone from planners to pilots made every effort to avoid collateral damage and limit civilian casualties, errant bombs and other accidents contributed to both. Part of the issue lay in unreasonable expectations for the accuracy of precision-guided munitions (PGMs). These laser and radar-guided weapons wowed the media and public, who watched captivating video footage shown at press briefings depicting bombs striking bridges, buildings, tanks, aircraft, and other targets "square in the crosshairs." Television viewers watched in awe as bombs and missiles entered through windows and doorways, even down ventilator shafts. At one briefing, Schwarzkopf revealed the "luckiest" person in Iraq, as a laser-guided bomb destroyed a bridge just after a speeding pick-up truck crossed it. Such footage gave an impression of the infallibility of modern weaponry. The "surgical strikes" delivered by such weapons were, in fact, the exception rather than the rule in 1991. In reality, only 10 percent of munitions used in the air campaign were PGMs; 90 percent were so-called "dumb bombs," delivered in much the same manner as their predecessors fifty years earlier in World War II.

The impact of collateral damage became the centerpiece of determining fact from fiction, as portrayed by pronouncements from both the Iraqi information office and American press briefings in Saudi Arabia and Washington. Much of this involved actual as well as falsified damage to neighborhoods and other non-military areas and civilian casualties therein. Yet, while Saddam's information ministry played up claims of Coalition bombs hitting civilian targets, it also downplayed the true extent of damage and casualties so as not to alarm the Iraqi people or, more accurately perhaps, not to give them cause to rebel against Saddam. Of course, Coalition forces went to great lengths to avoid civilian casualties, trying not to alienate the Iraqi people and world opinion. Even with PGMs, air campaign planners severely restricted targeting to avoid collateral damage near hospitals, schools, residential areas, and public spaces.

Saddam quickly took advantage of Coalition sensitivity to collateral damage. Iraqi forces moved communication centers and SAM sites so that they were near and even on top of schools. Military units moved into neighborhoods and small villages. Tanks and other vehicles sat protected in front of mosques, schools, museums, and other historic sites, even hospitals. Coalition air commanders had little choice but to attack many of these targets in the interest of protecting Coalition forces. Sadly, Iraqi authorities undertook little effort to evacuate people from these areas. Moreover, few air-raid shelters existed and other than air-raid sirens last updated early in the Iran–Iraq War, the Iraqi government had few civil defense measures in place to protect its citizens. Estimates vary as to civilian casualties, ranging from hundreds to as many as 15,000 killed and thousands more wounded. An exact number will never be known, but a moderate estimate is that approximately 3,000 Iraqi civilians died and 6,000 were wounded during the war.[12]

By far the most tragic incident involving civilian casualties occurred when on February 13 two American F-117A fighter-bombers released their bomb load on what intelligence had indicated was an Iraqi bunker complex in Amiriyah, just north of Baghdad. The clear presence of military vehicles and personnel around the reinforced concrete structure suggested the Iraqis were using the building as some sort of military facility. Inside, however, several hundred civilians from the area were taking shelter from the bombing raids, as they had since the beginning of the air campaign. The blasts killed over 400 civilians, including women and children. The Iraqis claimed the building was a designated air-raid shelter, while Coalition spokespeople countered that the Iraqis had intentionally allowed civilians to seek shelter inside a military facility that was a legitimate military target. The Iraqis quickly brought news media to the site to record and report the carnage, the footage of which shocked people around the world and briefly intensified the small but vocal anti-war protests in the United States, Europe, and several Arab countries. The fragile Coalition shuddered in the face of the tragedy, as several nations, including Spain, France, the Soviet Union, and Jordan, publically expressed concern over targeting that appeared obsessed with decapitating the Iraqi leadership rather than attacking fielded forces in southern Iraq and Kuwait. Some even called for a complete ban on bombing Baghdad.

These incidents, combined with Iraqi propaganda that claimed the Coalition had intentionally attacked several Muslim holy sites in Iraq, caused mass demonstrations in several Arab countries. There appeared to be excessive destruction of Baghdad with little regard to the safety of civilians or the protection of culturally sensitive sites. While the USAF indeed focused much of its bombing effort on the political leadership and command and control targets in and around Baghdad, US military and political leaders from Schwarzkopf to President Bush were keenly aware of and concerned about civilian casualties. Under pressure to keep the Coalition together and calm demonstrating peoples in Arab countries and elsewhere, Secretary of Defense Cheney ordered a review of the target list, resulting in the removal of several targets similar to the bunker complex in Amiriyah.[13]

Iraqi authorities often blocked media attempts to verify collateral damage and were not beyond inventing incidents for propaganda purposes. Iraqi officials reported, for example, that a Coalition air attack had killed over 135 civilians in Nasiriyah, a claim that could not be independently verified. When reporters were shown purported civilian casualties in a hospital, the occupants of ward beds turned out to be Iraqi soldiers posing as civilian wounded. Iraqi authorities tried to claim that damage actually caused during the Iran–Iraq War was caused by the Coalition. The more controversial incidents included the destruction by an American Tomahawk missile of what Iraq claimed had been a baby milk factory but that CENTCOM maintained had been a key Iraqi biological weapons facility. Iraq authorities paraded journalists through the rubble, pointing out destroyed containers of baby formula. In the White House, Bush worried about the impact of Iraqi attempts to manipulate the members of the media, especially CNN's Peter Arnett, who reported his belief that the factory had indeed produced nothing but baby formula. Five years later, the UN Special Commission (UNSCOM) in Iraq confirmed that the facility had been a biological munitions factory hidden by the façade of a baby milk plant. The incident remains controversial.[14]

Saddam and Prisoners of War

Saddam also took advantage of the Coalition air campaign to exploit captured pilots and aircrews for propaganda purposes, much like the North Vietnamese had done to American prisoners of war (POWs) during the Vietnam War. The Iraqis paraded American and Coalition POWs in front of television cameras, forcing some under clear duress to repeat denunciations of American and UN policies. Such was the case for Navy Lieutenant Rob Wetzel and his bombardier Lieutenant Jeffrey Zaun, who lost their Grumman A-6 Intruder to a SAM missile the first night of the war. Although Wetzel had been severely injured when ejecting from the A-6, the grainy television images clearly indicated both aviators had been physically beaten. Italian air force officers Major Gianmarco Bellini and Captain Marizio Cocciolone, captured after Iraqis shot down their Tornado fighter-bomber, were also forced before Iraqi television cameras as part of Saddam's ill-guided propaganda effort.[15]

For the Americans, rescuing downed pilots was a priority. The pain of POWs in Vietnam and later the hostages in Iran remained fresh in the minds of many Americans. Images of captured American POWs in Iraqi hands would, Bush and his advisors feared, crush American support for the war. Pre-war estimates had predicted fifty to one hundred Coalition aircraft could be lost in the air campaign. Precautions, such as mandating minimum bombing altitudes and of course destroying as much of Iraq's air defense system as possible early in the campaign, had been taken to minimize the risk. Special operations units were placed along the Saudi border as well as in Turkey to rescue downed crews. Some rescue missions were successful. Others, such as that to find downed Navy pilot Lieutenant Commander Michael Scott Speicher, who lost his F/A-18 aircraft to Iraqi fire on the opening day of the air campaign, failed. Speicher remained listed as missing in action (MIA) after the war, and some speculated he had been captured and was still held in an Iraqi prison. Efforts to determine Speicher's ultimate fate were renewed following the 2003 invasion of Iraq. Ultimately, in 2009, Bedouins in the Iraqi desert led investigators to where they had buried Speicher near where his plane crashed in 1991. Speicher had apparently died during the crash.[16]

The difficulties inherent in rescue operations in such an expansive environment as Iraq were highlighted in the failed effort to save "Corvette Three," the codename for Air Force Colonel David W. Eberly and his crewman Major Thomas E. Griffith, who had been shot down in their F-15 on January 19. Faulty radio equipment, the inability to pinpoint their exact location, and lack of cooperation from Syria in granting timely permission for an American air rescue team to traverse Syrian airspace contributed to Corvette Three's ultimate capture by Iraqi forces near the Syrian border. Others were also captured with no chance of eluding the Iraqis. Those crews flying missions over concentrations of Iraqi troops, especially in southern Iraq, were often captured moments after crashing or parachuting to the ground. Others, however, had the best of luck. Flight Lieutenant Rupert Clark of the British Royal Air Force (RAF), for example, was rescued within thirty minutes of his incident. Despite the efforts of combat search and rescue teams, most downed aircrews who survived were captured by the Iraqis. The Air Force Special Operations Forces Combat Search and Rescue (CSAR) teams, for example, could rescue only about 10 percent of crewmembers who were shot down or crashed in Iraq. Thirty-four percent of these crewmembers became POWs. The remainder, unfortunately, lost their lives. Post-war studies found that of those crew captured by the Iraqis, only a small percentage were actually "rescuable." These figures should not belie, however, the enormous effort and risk CSAR teams and other units exercised in attempting to rescue their comrades in arms.[17]

Eberly and Griffith were imprisoned in isolation, starved, and physically abused during their captivity, much the same as all American and Coalition prisoners of war captured by the Iraqis. Iraqi interrogators blindfolded Eberly and then demanded information on the Coalition attack. Eberly, of course, refused to respond. His captors beat him, clubbing him in the head several times as well as whipping his legs. They tried to break his will with outlandish stories—thousands of American soldiers had died; both Bush and Mubarak had been killed; American soldiers had surrendered in droves. Several times, the Iraqis put a pistol to his head. Eberly could hear the distinct clicks of the hammer as his torturer cocked the pistol. Then, he could hear the hammer fall as the muzzle pressed hard against his head. Time and time again the pistol was not loaded. That the pistol was never fired, however, did not lessen for Eberly the brief but dramatic swing of unspeakable fear to relief at still being alive. From his cell he could hear the screams of other POWs as the Iraqis delivered similar treatment. Because of his isolation, he had little idea of who or how many other prisoners shared his cell block, which he dubbed the Biltmore after the gaudy, ostentatious Vanderbilt mansion in Asheville, North Carolina.[18]

Other POWs experienced similar treatment. Iraqi captors sent multiple jolts of intense electricity through Air Force Major Jeffrey Tice in attempts to get him to reveal information about American forces, but Tice, who had a tooth "explode" out of his mouth during one of the shocks, remained defiant. Captured members of Bravo Two Zero, a British Special Air Service (SAS) team operating in Iraq as part of an intelligence-gathering operation, suffered severe physical and mental torture. That two American women survived their ordeal is testament to their strength and courage, and will. Major Rhonda Cornum, an Army flight surgeon, was captured on February 27 when the UH-60 Black Hawk she was aboard was shot down while searching for a downed F-16. As a flight surgeon, Cornum was there as part of the rescue mission to give medical aid to the F-16 pilot. The Black Hawk crash broke both of her arms and severely injured her knee. She had also been hit in the shoulder by one of the bullets passing through the helicopter. Though she was held captive for only one week before the war ended, Cornum suffered sexual assault and physical beatings. Specialist Melissa Rathbun-Nealy was also assaulted and beaten by her Iraqi captors. The

POW experience of both women, along with the role women played in the conflict, brought much needed attention to the issue of women in combat. Twenty-one Americans were held as POWs by the Iraqis during the war. Several Coalition personnel were also captured. Torture and abuse link their experiences. All were repatriated at the end of the war. Another twenty-five Americans were listed as "MIA presumed KIA" but their remains except for that of two pilots were ultimately recovered.[19]

The air campaign continued through its three phases with great effect at minimal cost to Coalition lives and aircraft. Considering that the air campaign ultimately included over 110,000 sorties (75,000 of which were flown by American air components, with approximately 50,000 flown by the USAF and the remainder by the Navy and Marine Corps) over the course of the thirty-eight-day air campaign and 100-hour ground war, and had significantly degraded Iraqi capabilities in accordance with Warden's five rings, the efficacy of airpower in DESERT STORM was nothing short of remarkable. Ironically, bad weather hindered the air campaign more than Iraqi air defenses, but this did not prevent air forces from destroying 1,300 of Iraq's 4,200 tanks, 1,100 of its 3,100 artillery pieces, and 850 of its 2,800 armored personnel carriers. Complete air superiority had been achieved. Airpower, nevertheless, could not do it alone, as Warden and others had hoped. Schwarzkopf's ground campaign would deliver the final blow against Saddam's invasion and occupation of Kuwait. And it would have to happen soon, as the Coalition was held together by a thread and world opinion bristled at the intensity of the war to this point.[20]

The Iraqis had hoped to weather the air phase with minimal damage, but were surprised by the scale, intensity, and length of INSTANT THUNDER. American F-4 Wild Weasels using high-speed anti-radiation missiles (HARMs) that locked onto Iraqi radar signals had all but destroyed Iraq's French-built Kari air defense system during the first few days of the campaign, making it impossible for Iraqi SAM, AAA, and radar installations to receive any advanced warning of incoming attacks and negating any centralized coordinated response. Iraqi SAM crews, for example, stopped turning on their radar sets early in the campaign because of the effectiveness of HARMs. Iraq's air force, proved ineffective, leading Saddam to first ground the air force in its protective bunkers, then after American bunker-busting bombs began taking effect he ordered planes that could to flee to Iran. Saddam's decisions to launch Scud missiles and to attack Ras al Khafji were calculated to goad Schwarzkopf into starting the ground war early.[21]

The Great Scud Hunt

The air campaign was very nearly derailed just as it got underway when on January 18 Iraq fired seven Scud missiles into Israel. In the late 1950s, NATO had listed these Soviet-made missile systems as the SS-1 (surface-to-surface), SS-1b, and so forth, as the missile evolved through the 1970s. Given the codename "Scud" by NATO, the missile could be fired either from static sites or massive mobile launching tractor-trailer rigs. The Scud had a wildly inaccurate range of anywhere from 150 to 350 miles depending upon modifications. The Iraqi variant, branded by the Iraqis as the al-Hussein, could deliver a conventional or chemical warhead, possibly even a nuclear warhead if the Iraqis developed that capability. While the conventional war-headed Scud certainly warranted concern, a chemical Scud could cause grave mass casualties. Saddam had used chemical weapons before, and CENTCOM had little reason to doubt he would use them against Coalition forces or against civilians in Riyadh or major cities in Israel. So serious was the potential threat that CENTCOM outfitted all Coalition forces with cumbersome chemical weapons gear. Saudi and Israeli authorities issued gas masks to civilians. In addition to their usual kit of helmets and body armor, members of the media also carried chemical suits.

The Scud attacks were part of Saddam's gambit to quickly draw Israel into the war, the result of which he hoped would cause Arab states to withdraw from the Coalition. No Arab state aligned against Iraq, Saddam reasoned, could justify fighting a fellow Arab state alongside Israeli allies. While Schwarzkopf remained skeptical of the military effectiveness of Scuds and of the possible impact of Israeli retaliation, Bush and his advisors in Washington had not unreasonably convinced themselves that Israeli action would completely undermine DESERT STORM. As the seven Scuds headed toward Israel, the Israeli Air Force scrambled jets to deliver retaliatory strikes. In the White House, Bush, Secretary of State Baker, and Secretary of Defense Cheney quickly debated what to do upon learning of the Scud strikes, which hit Tel Aviv and Haifa. Initial reports indicated the missiles contained chemical warheads, which if true would mean the Israelis would assuredly respond with quick and lethal force. Within hours, however, Israeli authorities confirmed to the White House that the Scuds contained conventional warheads and had not caused any casualties. Israel requested US Army Patriot missile batteries to protect its cities from future Scud attacks, which Bush quickly approved. Israel exercised dramatic restraint after Bush assured Israeli Prime Minister Yitzak Shamir that the Israelis "couldn't do anything that we weren't accomplishing already."[22]

"Scud Thursday," as the Bush team called that hectic night, added a new dimension to the conflict. Showing rare strategic forethought, Saddam made sure not to fire Iraqi Scuds at Jerusalem so as not to draw the ire of Arabs for attacking the divided holy city occupied in part by 200,000 Palestinians. Contradicting this move, however, the Iraqi dictator ordered Scuds fired at Saudi Arabia and the Gulf States in addition to several more launches against Israel. Regardless of questionable Scud targets, the Scud's unreliable accuracy, and the effectiveness of Saddam's Scud attacks, the missiles were more than a mere nuisance for the Coalition. As a result, a reluctant Schwarzkopf had to take valuable assets away from primary missions dictated by the air campaign to track down and destroy as many of the mobile Scud launchers and static sites as possible. Thus began the Great Scud Hunt.

Pressured by Washington to invest maximum effort in the Scud Hunt, Schwarzkopf, who was largely unconvinced of the strategic importance of expending resources to hunt and kill these mostly ineffectual weapons, nevertheless ordered the Scuds destroyed. This proved much easier said than done. Locating the mobile "shoot and scoot" Scud launchers proved an extremely frustrating challenge. For one, no one seemed exactly sure how many mobile launchers the Iraqis had. Pre-war estimates placed the number at thirty-six mostly Soviet-made launchers, but that number did not account for those built by the Iraqis or purchased from Eastern European countries. The number of missiles also varied in American intelligence reports, ranging from 300 to as many as 700. The Iraqis moved the massive, multi-wheeled truck-launchers adeptly at night, quickly setting up for launch, firing, then driving away, moving like a thief on the lam, never staying in the same place twice. Iraqi Scud crews learned not to fire during the day, keeping their launchers hidden effectively in culverts, wadies, and under outcrops until dark. To further complicate finding and destroying launchers and missile stockpiles, the Iraqis also used decoys so alike in appearance that only through close inspection could one discern an actual Scud from a fake one. Moreover, the concentration of petroleum, oil, and lubricant (POL) trucks and other large trailered vehicles resulted in the destruction of numerous vehicles mistaken for Scud launchers. A post-war study found that although pilots claimed to have destroyed over sixty Scud launchers many of these purported kills were later found to be POL trucks.[23]

CENTCOM attacked the Scud problem with air assaults on static launch sites and missile production facilities. A squadron of F-15 Strike

Eagles remained on station to respond against mobile launchers, hoping to catch them in the open and destroy them. Results, however, were hard in coming. The Iraqis rarely used their static launch sites, bringing into question the expense of assets used in the effort to destroy them. The mobile launchers often escaped attack as well. As the Scud firings continued, Schwarzkopf tried to downplay their military effectiveness. While in a military sense technically if not tactically correct, Schwarzkopf, in the eyes of Bush and Secretary of Defense Cheney, seemed too dismissive of the broader strategic implications of the Scud attacks. The White House pressured CENTCOM to do more, and to do so quickly, to bring the Scud problem under control. At Cheney's direction, Schwarzkopf accepted Scud-related target lists developed by the Israeli defense ministry. Glosson's Black Hole group even proposed a three-day all-out offensive against the Scud threat, a proposal that by implication meant putting the overall air campaign on hold for three valuable days that DESERT STORM could ill-afford to sacrifice. Schwarzkopf accepted the Israeli target list out of courtesy but rejected Glosson's proposal. Eager to get Delta Force, Rangers, and other unique units into the war, the US Special Operations Command proposed using its forces to infiltrate Iraq's western desert to track down the mobile launchers. Commandos using specially equipped dune buggies, helicopters, and A-10 Warthogs crossed into Iraq to track down their elusive prey. An apprehensive Schwarzkopf rightly feared the potential friction of special operations inside Iraq, including the propaganda disaster that would erupt if a Delta Force unit, for example, were to be captured by the Iraqis or the risk to lives and equipment in mounting rescue missions if a special forces unit got in a tight spot. While the American and British special operations effort to catch Scuds destroyed several decoys and despite claims of knocking out dozens of actual Scuds and launchers, later assessments determined that the effort to destroy them had been ineffective. The "snake eaters," as they were known in military slang, still managed to disrupt mobile launches during the third, fourth, and fifth weeks of the war so much so that the Iraqis spent more time moving launchers to avoid detection than actually launching missiles, resulting in a dramatic decrease in missiles fired at Israel and Saudi Arabia.[24]

Built by Raytheon and operated by the US Army, the radar-guided Patriot missile defense system used to protect Israel, Saudi Arabia, and other military and political centers from Scud attacks proved almost as controversial as the Scuds themselves. Designed to defend air bases and military installations from medium-range ballistic missiles, the mobile Patriot SAM had been in the American arsenal since the late 1970s but

Figure 3   *An A-10A Thunderbolt takes part in a mission during Operation DESERT STORM. Photograph by Senior Airmen Chris Putnam.*
Source: United States Department of Defense, DefenseImagery.mil.

had never been tested in combat. Like a mobile Scud launcher, a Patriot SAM battery was mounted on a tractor-trailer rig and could be set up and turned operational in less than an hour. Radar guided the Patriot SAM to its target to either ideally destroy the incoming missile or at least to deflect it off target. With live television coverage of just about every missile warning in Israel and Saudi Arabia, the Patriot received a great deal of media and public attention, but its performance as a wonder weapon was greatly exaggerated. Speaking at Raytheon's Andover, Massachusetts, plant on February 15, 1991, President Bush praised the purported success rate of the Patriot, telling his audience that the Patriot batteries in Israel were "41 for 42: 42 Scuds engaged, 41 intercepted."[25] Its actual effectiveness was questionable, as initial claims of high success rates at knocking Scuds out of the sky came under intense scrutiny to reveal that the Patriot has been less than perfect if not a total disappointment. The Army later revealed the Patriot SAMs hit less than half of the Scuds fired into Israel, often with warheads surviving Patriot strikes to fall where they may and explode.[26]

Iraqi Scuds did occasionally cause significant damage and inflict casualties. On February 25, a Patriot battery malfunctioned and missed an inbound Scud, which by chance struck a US Army barracks at Dhahran in Saudi Arabia, killing twenty-eight service members and wounding ninety-seven others.[27] Another Scud hit a neighborhood in Tel Aviv, injuring over ninety people. Iraq fired eighty-eight Scud missiles during the war, including forty missiles at Israel that killed two Israelis and injured at least 200. Militarily, however, the Iraqi Scud campaign proved just as ineffective as the CENTCOM effort to eradicate the Scud threat. Still, Saddam's Scud attacks did have a political impact, as the attacks proved to be one of the more significant points of friction during the war. The Scud problem certainly threatened to widen the war and weaken the Coalition, and addressing the Scud problem irritated relations between Secretary of Defense Cheney and CENTCOM commander-in-chief General Schwarzkopf. The coming ground campaign redirected Coalition attention as the Scud threat subsided.

Al Khafji

As the Coalition continued its air campaign and dealt with the Scud problem, Saddam decided to test further Coalition resolve by ordering an incursion into Saudi Arabia on January 29. Saddam may have intended to draw the Coalition into a ground war before it was ready and inflict heavy casualties, hoping that the bloodshed would finally trigger the Vietnam syndrome to undermine public support for the war in the United States. Saddam was perfectly willing to sacrifice troops in this attempt to seize the initiative from Schwarzkopf and the Coalition.

On the night of January 29–30, two Iraqi armored battalions joined by a mechanized battalion departed from their positions in Kuwait, to head for the Saudi border. Their objective was Ras al Khafji, a small coastal resort town just over ten miles inside Saudi Arabia from the southernmost tip of Kuwait. Saudi authorities had evacuated the town after the Iraqi invasion of Kuwait, fearful of civilian casualties if Saddam decided to invade Saudi Arabia from Kuwait. As this force moved down Saudi Highway 95, several Iraqi patrol boats made their way along the coast, carrying landing parties to demonstrate south of Khafji to distract the town's defenders. A second, much larger force consisting of 60,000 Iraqi troops and over 200 tanks waited inside Kuwait at al Wafra. Once the initial force took Khafji, the second wave would invade Saudi Arabia from Wafra and its "forest" of oil wells. Saddam's bold move promised big dividends if it worked.

Only a handful of Saudi troops garrisoned Khafji, an insufficient force to hold the town against the Iraqi spear. American Marines patrolled the vast emptiness thirty-odd miles to the west of the coast. When Iraqi tanks approached the Kuwaiti border on January 28, Marine outposts reported the movement. A-10 Warthogs blunted the border crossing, destroying several tanks and other vehicles. Dismissing the Iraqi movements as mere probing, the Marines did not expect the assault that came on the next night. In a coordinated attack, Iraqi tanks moved across the border. A Marine outpost bore the brunt of the first shots fired and was just able to call in airstrikes to avert a complete disaster. But things for the Marines did not go as they had hoped. In the nighttime confusion, eleven Marines were killed by friendly fire both from fellow Marines on the ground and A-10s in the air. Still, close air support (CAS) allowed the Marines to beat a hasty withdrawal from this and surrounding outposts and bought elements of the 2nd Marine Division time to establish a defensive perimeter. Marines fired TOW missiles at Iraqi tanks while A-10s and other aircraft engaged Iraqi armor from the air to later retake the outposts. The fighting west of Khafji was the most intense the Marines had experienced since Vietnam.

The Iraqi force moving down the coast toward the town of Khafji, however, achieved its objective. Only the seaborne assault had failed, falling victim to British fighter-bombers and helicopters patrolling the coast. So sudden was the Iraqi movement, however, that Marines and Saudi troops quickly abandoned their outposts between the border and Khafji, falling back through the town. By the morning, the Iraqi advance force of some 800 troops held Khafji. To the surprise of the Americans, the Iraqis stayed put rather than pushing southward. Inside Khafji, two Marine reconnaissance teams decided to stay in the town, banking on Iraqi troops moving onward so that they could make their escape. With the Iraqi force in place, however, the Marines had to dig in and remain undetected. One team fortified itself on top of a building to better coordinate air attacks against the Iraqis in the town. Incredibly, the Iraqis had no idea the Marines were looking down upon them from a rooftop.

The air response had to this point been disjointed, as a mishmash of aircraft from carriers in the Persian Gulf and air bases in Saudi Arabia rolled in to deliver uncoordinated attacks. Air Force Lieutenant General Chuck Horner, however, rectified the situation by taking control of the air tasking order (ATO) to coordinate airstrikes against Iraqi forces in the town. Meanwhile, King Fahd, angered at Saddam's incursion into his kingdom, demanded that the Coalition eliminate Iraqi forces in Khafji and destroy the town, if necessary. Schwarzkopf felt otherwise, arguing that destroying an entire town over "a few Iraqis" was a waste of resources that would unnecessarily draw the ire of world opinion for wanton destruction of a town of no military value. Schwarzkopf, however, acquiesced to General Khalid's plan to retake Khafji. A joint force of Saudi and Qatari armored and mechanized units organized to attack on January 30, making two attempts to enter Khafji but withdrawing both times. With the Iraqis now isolated, however, time was on the side of Coalition forces. Relentless air strikes pounded the Iraqis in Khafji, who continued to resist despite great casualties. Coalition forces suffered losses as well. An Iraqi shoulder-fired SAM brought down an American C-130 gunship, killing all fourteen of its crew, and enemy fire killed several Saudi troops caught unaware, believing the battle to be over.

The final Coalition assault to retake Khafji occurred on January 31. By this point, Saudi forces had strengthened and reorganized, while their exhausted Iraqi counterparts had grown short of ammunition and determination and realized with increasing dread the extent of Coalition air superiority as their desperate calls for Iraqi air support went unanswered. By the night of January 31, Saudi forces controlled the town, forcing Iraqis who had not been killed or captured to withdraw to Kuwait. In addition to the Marines killed during the first night of the invasion and the Air Force crew lost in the C-130 incident, Saudi and Qatari forces lost nineteen killed and over thirty wounded in the intense fighting. The cost for Saddam's initiative, however, was much higher. With over 100 Iraqis killed, over 100 tanks and other armored vehicles destroyed, and dozens taken prisoner, Saddam got a taste of what awaited his forces once the ground war truly commenced.

As it stood, for Saddam the Battle of Khafji failed in every respect. Schwarzkopf tried to downplay Khafji, calling it a "mosquito on an elephant." Khafji, however, had been a tactical surprise to the Americans and revealed shortcomings in Coalition readiness to fight. American doctrine, tactics, and communications did not provide for integration with partner forces from other countries, as repeated hitches with Saudi forces in the Battle of Khafji revealed. Moreover, intelligence had failed to recognize Iraqi intentions and the American reaction to the incursion had been sloppy and uncoordinated. Friendly fire, known as "blue-on-blue" in military slang, remained a significant potential problem, as evidenced in the Khafji fight. Because the battle had largely involved only Marines and Air Force and Navy air assets, the Army, including Schwarzkopf, seemed dismissive of whatever lessons the Battle of Khafji might have offered. As a result, CENTCOM planners made no alterations to the ground campaign plan. Still, a sizable Iraqi armored force had been beaten back and the Marines had received their baptism by fire in the Persian Gulf.[28]

Peace Feelers and Ultimatums

The intensity of the air campaign and the Battle of Khafji led to several attempts to make peace before major ground operations commenced. Saddam entertained these overtures, looking for a way out that would leave him both in power and still powerful. Without President Bush's knowledge, Secretary of State Baker and the new Soviet Foreign Minister, Aleksandr Bessmertnykh, had issued a joint statement on January 29 offering a cease-fire if Saddam agreed to withdraw from Kuwait. The statement implied linkage with the Palestinian issue, a condition that violated Bush's bedrock commitment to an unconditional Iraqi withdrawal from Kuwait. Baker's initiative blindsided a "furious" Bush, who ordered his White House team into damage control mode to tactfully retract the statement without causing Baker, Bush's Secretary of State and good friend, too much embarrassment.[29]

Soviet President Gorbachev made yet another attempt to reach a settlement and stop the war before potentially costly ground operations got under way. On February 13, Gorbachev offered to hold talks in Moscow to settle the crisis and address other Middle Eastern issues, with a cease-fire in effect during the talks. Clearly trying to improve his tenuous position at home in the Soviet Union, Gorbachev had also been of great help in forging the Coalition against one of the Soviet Union's chief allies in the region. Yet, Bush could ill-afford any deal that allowed Saddam to claim the slightest hint of victory. For his part, Saddam poorly played such overtures that could have weakened the Coalition by making Bush appear the aggressor.

On February 15, the Iraqis announced they would withdraw from Kuwait in accordance with UN Security Council Resolution 660, but with the conditions that all Coalition forces would also withdraw from the Persian Gulf region, that the United States would pay for damages in Iraq, that all Iraqi debts would be cancelled, and that the Israeli-Palestinian issue would be linked to any settlement of Iraq's claims against Kuwait. Such an empty unrealistic proposal had no chance of gaining any traction among the Coalition countries, much less the United States. Bush rejected the proposal outright, calling it a "cruel hoax" while urging the Iraqi military and Iraqi people "to take matters in their own hands—to force Saddam Hussein, the dictator, to step aside" so that Iraq could "rejoin the family of peace-loving nations." Bush was unequivocal: "They must withdraw without condition. There must be full implementation of all the Security Council resolutions. And there will be no linkage to other problems in the area."[30]

On February 18, Iraqi Foreign Minister Aziz met with Gorbachev in Moscow, where Gorbachev offered another cease-fire plan. In exchange for withdrawing from Kuwait, Gorbachev proposed a guarantee of Iraqi sovereignty and the survival of Saddam's regime, cessation of all UN-mandated sanctions, and later discussions of the Palestinian question. Aziz took the plan back to Baghdad, while the Soviets sent it to the other four permanent members of the UN Security Council. Bush tactfully but firmly rejected the proposal and reiterated that Iraq must comply with all UN resolutions and that there would be no linkage to the Palestinian issue. Aziz nevertheless returned to Moscow on the February 21 to meet with a still hopeful Gorbachev. Aziz altered the plan to include a time-frame for implementation of a cease-fire, the exchange of POWs, Iraq's complete withdrawal from Kuwait, and the end of all UN resolutions. Significantly, the proposal did not include linkage to a broader Middle Eastern peace plan. Most importantly, however, it allowed Saddam to fight another day. In a lengthy phone conversation on February 22, Bush explained to Gorbachev that he could not agree to the terms. Iraq would have to comply with the UN resolutions and withdraw from Kuwait unconditionally.

To take the initiative from Gorbachev and regain control of the situation, Bush issued an ultimatum, demanding that Iraq begin an unconditional withdrawal from Kuwait by 1200 hours Washington time (2000 hours local time in Kuwait) on February 23, and be out of Kuwait City by February 25. If the Kuwaiti government was not restored by then, the ground war would begin. Just forty-five minutes before the noon deadline, Saddam requested a hearing before the UN to take place after the February 23 deadline so that he could make his case for a settlement of the crisis. Not giving up, Gorbachev phoned Bush at Camp David to inform him of Saddam's last-minute request, but Bush politely told his Soviet friend, "I can't let a deadline pass without action." With no sign of Iraqi forces moving out of Kuwait as the deadline passed, Bush ordered General Schwarzkopf to begin the ground war, and then asked the American people to "stop what you are doing and say a prayer for all the coalition forces, and especially for our men and women in uniform who this very moment are risking their lives for their country and for all of us."[31]

7

The Ground War

At 0400 hours local time in the Persian Gulf on February 24, Schwarzkopf ordered his main ground forces into Kuwait and southern Iraq in accordance with deadlines set by President Bush. Battlefield preparation had been progressing for several days, as the air campaign transitioned from focusing on command-and-control targets in Iraq to concentrating more on fielded forces in southern Iraq and Kuwait. Heavy bombing by B-52s had given way to pinpoint strikes, known as "tank plinking," by A-10s and other attack aircraft against individual tanks, pieces of artillery, and other heavy vehicles in place inside bunkers and other locations. Estimates placed Iraqi forces depleted by bombing and desertion at 220,000 troops, along with the loss of 1,700 tanks and 1,000 artillery pieces. The Coalition had over 575,000 troops in the KTO, complemented by over 3,700 tanks and 1,500 artillery pieces. Despite prevailing confidence among CENTCOM and field commanders, they expected significant casualties on both sides. The devastating combination of Coalition firepower and entrenched Iraqi defenses, which included oil pits, minefields, and ambush alleys, presented one of the most lethal battlefield environments in history.

Preparing for the Ground War

Battle damage assessment (BDA) nevertheless remained conflicted, as analysts attempted to interpret video and other evidence to measure bombing success in percentages rather than in practical terms, resulting in, for example, repeated strikes against the same bridge being assessed as 25 percent destroyed despite the fact that for all practical purposes the missing central span of the bridge made it impassable after the first air strike. Despite these issues, Schwarzkopf and his commanders were confident that they were ready to begin the ground campaign, designated as DESERT SABRE by CENTCOM planners. For Schwarzkopf, such issues with analysts had brought back unpleasant memories of similar tensions between analysts and practitioners in Vietnam.[1]

For the Iraqis, however, INSTANT THUNDER had been just short of devastating. Iraqi military leaders had expected the Coalition attack to begin with an air campaign lasting a week to ten days before the launch of a direct ground assault against Iraqi forces in Kuwait. Contesting Coalition air superiority had not been part of their plan. Instead, the Iraqis hoped the relatively brief air campaign would bring on the much anticipated ground war, in which the Iraqi military believed it could bloody American and Coalition forces so badly that the United States and European participants would lose their will to fight for Kuwait. The Iraqi experience in the Iran–Iraq War, combined with what they thought they knew about American experience in Vietnam and Lebanon, easily led to such a conclusion. That the air campaign lasted much longer than expected, however, dashed Iraqi hopes of an early ground phase.[2]

INSTANT THUNDER had been much more effective than Schwarzkopf perhaps realized. Iraqi ground forces in the KTO had suffered significant losses in personnel and equipment during the air campaign. Because of losses and desertions, many Iraqi units remained only 50 percent effective, resulting in an Iraqi force that had numbered over 500,000 before the start of the war now numbering closer to 300,000 unenthusiastic troops. Many of these soldiers in basic Iraqi infantry divisions were Shia conscripts, who had no spirit to fight and still less love for Saddam. That the air campaign had not destroyed more equipment could be attributed to the actual low number of PGMs used to target entrenched Iraqi tanks and artillery.

The air campaign had severely affected Iraqi logistics, especially to frontline defenses in Kuwait. American and Coalition air forces did not have to destroy Iraqi stockpiles that were in place, though these too were attacked. Instead, they destroyed Iraq's ability to get supplies to intended locations. Any truck caught on a highway or road in the KTO was literally an instant target. One Iraqi division commander commented after the war that his fleet of over eighty transport trucks had been reduced to less than ten before the ground war even began due to the intensity of the air campaign. When Schwarzkopf determined that it was time to initiate the ground war, his forces enjoyed superiority in "virtually every quantitative and qualitative category."[3]

American and Coalition forces were ready for the ground war. They had been gathering and training for weeks, in some cases months, for what lay ahead. Since the initial deployments American support and logistical units had worked feverishly to accommodate the increasingly large number of troops arriving daily at King Khalid Military City and other less permanent bases in Saudi Arabia. In addition to getting combat equipment, munitions, and fuel to Saudi Arabia, Army Major General William G. Pagonis and his logistics command had made sure that the thousands of tents, cots, blankets, generators, water purification units, kitchens, refrigerators, portable shower units and toilets, and a seemingly endless list of equipment to house, feed, and care for hundreds of thousands of troops while they prepared for war made it to Saudi Arabia. The Saudi government provided both money and facilities for water, fuel, ground and air transportation, and housing for American and Coalition forces. Just to support a force of 135,000 midway in the deployment phase required, per day, 1.5 million gallons of water, 95 tons of ice, over 350,000 gallons of fuel (all types), and facilities to do 40,000 bundles of laundry, among other daily needs.[4]

Once in Saudi Arabia, troops had found themselves in a desolate desert landscape surrounded by a foreign culture. Long days of work demanded activity for relaxation. Mobile recreation centers had appeared at various base camps and even at some forward deployed positions. These included equipment for indoor as well as outdoor physical activities. To help maintain morale, the military kept its troops in touch with home as much as possible. Email and other electronic communication had not yet become the norm, so troops in Saudi Arabia relied upon regular mail and occasional satellite phone calls with loved ones at home. Satellite television units brought the Armed Forces Network to TVs in recreation centers. Watching college and professional football, in particular, proved as it had in previous wars, a popular diversion. "Wolfmobiles" serving Wolfburger fast food gave troops a break from their daily ration of Meals, and Ready-to-Eat (MREs) and other preprepared meals. Of course, the Saudi government wisely prohibited any sort of alcohol on American and Coalition bases, though enterprising individuals assuredly found ways to subvert this restriction.[5]

Training in theater for the coming war had intensified as more forces arrived. Both XVIII Corps and VII Corps had practiced breaching entrenched defenses. Mockups of minefields, tank traps, trench networks, and fortifications derived from intelligence reports and information from the Iran–Iraq War had provided soldiers realistic environments in both form and scale. One tactic with which VII Corps had experimented was using plow-equipped tanks to simply bulldoze over trenches in the expectation that Iraqi troops would flee in panic. Use of the tactic by the 1st Infantry Division at the start of the ground war led to allegations that units buried thousands of Iraqi soldiers alive while gunning down fleeing troops. Investigations following the war concluded that several Iraqis were indeed killed using this technique but that thousands of Iraqis surrendered as a result of the mere threat of being buried in their trenches.[6]

While training to cut through conventional Iraqi defenses, American and Coalition forces had remained keenly aware of the threat posed by Iraqi chemical and biological weapons. While publically downplaying this potential threat, within CENTCOM Schwarzkopf and his commanders were deeply concerned that the Iraqis would wait until American and Coalition ground forces slowed to assault Iraqi defenses to unleash barrages of chemical-laced artillery shells on troops caught in the open in static conditions. Protecting against chemical attack presented a difficult challenge. Troops would not function for any length of time if they wore the hot, heavy, cumbersome chemical suits every day, all day long. As in previous wars, quick reaction to a chemical threat was by necessity the best approach. Even before American forces had been deployed, they practiced donning chemical gear. Every minute counted, so getting into one's gear as fast as possible became an individual art despite attempts to standardize the sequence for putting on the suit, mask, and additional equipment. The earlier the warning, the less likely it was that there would be casualties in a chemical attack. During the war, television viewers grew accustomed to military staff and reporters quickly changing into chemical suits when an alarm sounded. Troops had also practiced the quick injection of antidotes and first aid for comrades injured in such an attack. It was a major concern for all involved, one that fortunately, if not incredibly, did not materialize.

As the UN Security Council deadline had approached, American and Coalition forces had conducted several individual as well as combined maneuvers and live fire exercises. DESERT SHIELD/DESERT STORM was the first large-scale American-led campaign integrating so many coalition militaries since Vietnam, possibly even World War II. Resolving issues involving communications, weapons and ammunition needs, and command structure was a high priority for CENTCOM. These exercises had also helped artillerists, tank gunners, helicopter crews, and pilots providing CAS to both coordinate their fire and also get accustomed to the desert landscape, which offered few if any landmarks for navigation and ranging. Numerous helicopter crashes during night exercises due to the blurring of the lightless sky with the flat desert terrain had forced changes in flight regulations, such as limiting minimum flight altitudes and requiring low altitude alarms. Exercises had also given

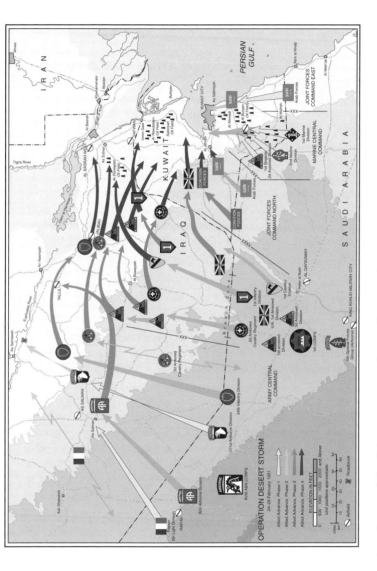

Map 2 *American and Coalition movements during the ground war.*
Source: United States Army Center of Military History.

troops the opportunity to calibrate night vision, radar, and thermal imaging equipment. It is easy to underestimate the level to which the late twentieth century American military relied upon technology, much of which had been designed during the Cold War for use in Western Europe. Adjusting this technology for use in desert warfare had required great effort.[7]

While the air campaign had continued, VII and XIII Corps had moved their respective units into their jump-off positions. Even at this late point, however, units and equipment had continued to arrive daily and did so through the end of the ground campaign. On January 23, advance teams had moved into Iraq to clear paths through minefields and marked rally points. Marine and Navy units had demonstrated near the Kuwaiti coast to keep Iraqi forces focused on the much anticipated Marine assault on Kuwait's beaches. Other Coalition units had kept Iraqi forces occupied along the Kuwaiti and Iraqi borders. Farther afield, along the Saudi border with Iraq, over 200,000 troops and their equipment had stood largely undetected and ready to conduct the great envelopment in accordance with Schwarzkopf's plan. CENTCOM's deception campaign, thus far, had worked.[8]

DESERT SABRE Begins

All three spears of the ground campaign penetrated Iraq and Kuwait. At the extreme northwest flank, XVIII Airborne Corps under US Army Lieutenant General Gary Luck advanced into Iraq, swinging toward the Euphrates River to prevent Iraqi forces, particularly Republican Guard units, from escaping across the river into central Iraq. Luck was an experienced commander and like many of his peers also a combat veteran of the Vietnam War. Before taking over XVIII Airborne Corps, Luck had commanded the 2nd Infantry Division as well as the US Army's Special Operations Command. On the far left, the French 6th Light Armored Division and the American 101st Airborne Division conducted a combined ground-air advance of over 100 miles into Iraq near Highway 8, blocking the road at key crossings and establishing a forward operating base (FOB), called COBRA, for the logistics caravans following behind to use as a supply depot for continuing operations. The airlift of the 101st Airborne's 1st Brigade involved over 300 helicopters, making it one of the largest helicopter lifts in history. The 6th Light Armored Division had a brief engagement at point ROCHAMBEAU, capturing over 2,500 Iraqis at the cost of two killed and some wounded. With the support of the

American 82nd Airborne Division, the French then secured As Salman just to the north of ROCHAMBEAU and west of COBRA to protect the very end of the Coalition's left flank.[9]

Major General Barry McCaffrey's 24th Mechanized Infantry Division of over 25,000 troops and hundreds of tanks and other vehicles smashed through Iraqi defenses in the middle of XVIII Airborne Corps' area of operations. Like President Bush, McCaffrey had also attended Phillips Academy before matriculating at West Point, where he was commissioned as a second lieutenant in 1964. After participating in the 1965 intervention in the Dominican Republic, McCaffrey had served on two tours of duty in Vietnam as an ARVN advisor and a company commander, earning two Distinguished Service Crosses and receiving three Purple Hearts along the way. McCaffrey brought a reputation as an aggressive, tough commander to the 24th Infantry Division. According to the ground plan, the 24th Division would drive deep into the Euphrates River Valley to block withdrawal routes of Republican Guard units, then turn east to link with units from VIII Corps. McCaffrey's force covered ground with amazing speed. With the assistance of night vision equipment and infrared markings on tanks and other vehicles to identify friend from foe, darkness did not slow the advance. By day's end, XVIII Corps had pushed as far as 170 miles into Iraq, meeting little resistance and taking thousands of eagerly surrendering Iraqi prisoners. These conscripts who had suffered weeks of bombardment during the air campaign had little fight left in them. The impact of the air campaign on Iraqi logistics was evident, as the POWs indicated that they had received little food and fresh water in the previous weeks. Luck's XVIII Corps had advanced much faster than expected, due in part to ingenious improvisation along the way to keep tanks fueled and troops at the very front well supplied and supported with artillery and air power.[10]

To the right of XVIII Corps, Lieutenant General Fred Franks' VII Corps advance began much earlier than planned because of the rapid progress made by Luck's corps. Franks, a 1959 graduate of West Point, had lost a leg to wounds he had received in the Cambodian incursion during the Vietnam War in 1970. Despite his injury, the Army had allowed the highly decorated combat veteran to remain on active duty. He had commanded the 1st Armored Division before taking over as commander of VII Corps in Germany in 1989. VII Corps' plan of attack included moving north deep into Iraq, then wheeling eastward toward Kuwait to trap Iraqi forces in Kuwait. In Franks' path, however, lay well-equipped and entrenched Republican Guard armored divisions. CENTCOM had outfitted VII Corps accordingly, giving it over 140,000 troops, over 1,500 tanks, 1,500 Bradley personnel carriers, and numerous other vehicles and aircraft, an astonishing 48,500 vehicles and aircraft of all types in total. The logistical chain alone had required enormous effort to keep VII Corps on the offensive. Each day, Franks' command required 5.6 million gallons of fuel, 3.3 million gallons of water, and over 6,000 tons of ammunition to stay on the offensive. The weather made things difficult for VII Corps, as a strong wind stirred up the fine desert sand, significantly reducing visibility to make keeping formation difficult. Low clouds and high winds also reduced CAS availability. To contend with both the Republican Guard and the weather was, for Franks, more than he had bargained for. His lack of progress indicated as much.[11]

VII Corps, nevertheless, pressed the attack. The 1st Armored Division spearheaded the assault on the corps' left flank, with the 3rd Armored Division on the right. Both would converge at Objective COLLINS near the town of al Busayyah, an Iraqi supply base located about eighty miles into Iraq. The 1st Infantry Division, the famed "Big Red One," led the main attack in VII Corps' center line, pushing forward some thirty miles and clearing twenty-four lanes across ten miles of Iraqi defenses for the British 1st Armoured Division's tanks to use without fear of mines. Along the way, the 1st Infantry Division engaged two Iraqi divisions in brief but intense fights, after which thousands of Iraqis surrendered. Unlike Luck's XVIII Airborne Corps' rapid deep advance, Franks' VII Corps did not cover as much ground. Defensive obstacles and concentrated Iraqi forces, and, according to critics, Frank's over-cautiousness, slowed progress. Franks ordered a halt at the thirty-mile mark to give his massive and now-dispersed force time to dress ranks before making the "Giant Wheel" turn eastward.[12]

To the far east and right of VII Corps, I MEF, along with forces from JFC North and JFC East, began its advance directly toward Kuwait City. JFC North, comprised of Egyptian, Saudi, and Kuwaiti forces, protected VII Corps' right flank and degraded Iraqi defenses inside Kuwait. JFC East pushed northward along the coast and provided fire support for naval vessels near the Kuwaiti Coast. I MEF undertook the difficult task of assaulting entrenched Iraqi units inside Kuwait, with the 1st Marine Division moving toward the al-Jabir airfield and the 2nd Marine Division, supported by the Army's Tiger Brigade, advancing on Mutla Pass, where both CENTCOM and the Iraqis expected the toughest fight. Marine Lieutenant General Walter Boomer, the commander of I MEF and also a combat veteran of the Vietnam War, knew his force had to make quick progress along the Mutla Pass toward Kuwait City to convince the Iraqis that his was the main Coalition assault, while providing cover for the envelopment. In any given sector, literally thousands of Iraqis surrendered to I MEF after the destruction of only a few tanks. Indeed, so many surrendered that dealing with POWs became a logistical problem. Many Coalition units simply took away the Iraqis' guns and sent them marching unescorted under a white flag toward the Saudi border. By day's end, I MEF controlled the airfield, had destroyed and captured over 100 Iraqi tanks, and taken over 10,000 Iraqis as POWs.[13]

The Iraqi Defense

Iraqi army commanders had fully expected a ground war, but not the one that quickly developed. Since the August 1990 invasion of Kuwait, the Iraqis had feverishly dug in along the Kuwaiti border and neutral zone area with Saudi Arabia, building in short order an impressive line of command bunkers, entrenchments, artillery emplacements, and anti-tank berms while camouflaging as much of their exposed equipment as possible to blend with the surrounding desert landscape. The Iraqi defense plan had been very much influenced by Iraq's experience in the Iran–Iraq War. Iraqi infantry in entrenched positions would face the initial onslaught of Schwarzkopf's offensive. Armored and mechanized units in reserve were positioned to quickly plug any breach in the first line. Republican Guard units were held in strategic reserve to counterattack the maneuver of the invading forces, hopefully to envelop them after being blunted by the first lines of defense. As in the Iran–Iraq War, mass frontal assaults characterized Iraqi expectations of blunting the Coalition offensive. The deployment of Iraqi forces revealed as much, as the Iraqi general staff concentrated mass in the KTO where they expected the primary Coalition push.

The Iraqi defense plan had several shortcomings, not the least of which was that it had completely underestimated Coalition capabilities in speed and maneuver. This assumption reflected the Iraqi tendency to view an enemy as the Iraqis viewed themselves. They did not have the capability to maneuver in the open desert where the absence of roads and their lack of navigation aids, such as GPS, presented difficulties that the Iraqis assumed were insurmountable. Schwarzkopf's "Great Wheel" across the Iraqi desert was to the Iraqis wholly unexpected.[14]

Going Deep

On February 25 Coalition forces continued their advance, and on February 26 engaged Republican Guard divisions. XVIII Corps continued its rapid pace, reaching all of its major objectives, including setting up blocking positions at the entrance to the Euphrates River Valley and capturing thousands of POWs, all at the expense of two KIA and two MIA. Franks' VIII Corps moved much more slowly, too much so for Schwarzkopf, who harried Franks to pick up the pace lest Iraqi forces escape from Kuwait intact. VII Corps would not reach point COLLINS until late in the evening of the 25th. The British 1st Armoured Division, under the command of Major General Rupert Smith, achieved its objectives will little resistance and was now ready to turn toward the Kuwaiti coast.

I MEF advanced within ten miles of Kuwait City, but not without tough fighting, made all the more difficult by lack of visibility from blowing sand and thick smoke from burning Kuwaiti oil wells. To slow the Coalition attack, Saddam had ordered Kuwaiti oil fields set alight, intentionally starting hundreds of oil fires across Kuwait that produced an eerie, apocalyptic darkness during mid-day. Putting out these over 600 oil fires took weeks, and it cost billions of dollars to extinguish the fires and then repair the damaged oil wells. Earlier, Saddam had ordered pipelines opened along the Kuwaiti coast, dumping over 125 million barrels of oil into the Persian Gulf, surpassing the Exxon *Valdez* oil disaster by ten times in volume of oil spilled and costing over $5 billion dollars to clean. The environmental impact was devastating. The Marines and the Army's Tiger Brigade, however, prevailed in several close quarter engagements with Iraqi armor, destroying dozens of Iraqi vehicles and in one instance capturing an entire Iraqi brigade and its commander.[15]

On February 26, the 101st and 82nd Airborne Divisions continued operations to block Highway 8 and secure communications and logistical lines back to COBRA. McCaffrey's 24th Infantry Division entered the Euphrates River Valley and moved toward Iraqi airfields at Jalibah and Tallil, as strong winds kicked up desert sand, resulting occasionally in zero visibility. Once in the valley, the 24th Infantry Division hit entrenched Iraqi units, including the Nebuchadnezzar Division of Saddam's Republican Guard, that put up strong resistance. Still, technology and mobility gave American forces a clear advantage, as thermal imaging and radar systems allowed tank and artillery crews to see Iraqi tanks and artillery in fixed positions, often before the Iraqis could detect the moving Americans. Firefinder weapons locator systems allowed artillerists to pinpoint Iraqi artillery positions immediately upon firing, enabling American artillery to respond with five to six shells for every Iraqi shot fired. In all, the 24th Infantry Division destroyed six entire Iraqi artillery battalions in the river valley. Although receiving tank fire,

Figure 4   *Oil well fires rage outside Kuwait City after being set on fire by Iraqi forces. Photograph by Tech SGT David McCloud.*
Source: United States Department of Defense, DefenseImagery.mil.

which was the most intense of the war, American tanks responded with deadly accuracy, using thermal imaging to target and destroy Iraqi tanks. The Soviet-built T-55s and T-72s had turrets so heavy that only gravity held them in place on the tank chassis. Direct hits on the turret literally "popped" the top off of the tank, resulting in hundreds of "pop-tops" scattered across the Iraqi desert.[16]

In the VII Corps area, the American 1st Armored Division took al Busayyah in a sandstorm by noon on February 26, destroying an Iraqi division and capturing over one hundred tons of ammunition. Later in the day, the 1st Armored struck the Tawakalna Division of the Republican Guard, destroying over thirty Iraqi tanks. Meanwhile, the American 3rd Armored Division finally reached COLLINS, having first to fight its way through elements of the Tawakalna Division. The fighting intensified as the 2nd Armored Calvary Regiment moved ahead of the 1st Infantry Division east of COLLINS. Franks had cautioned his advance armor units not to get entangled with numerically superior Republican Guard units but as the 2nd Cavalry advanced, contact with the Tawakalna Division became unavoidable. Near longitudinal map line 70 Easting, the 2nd Armored Cavalry struck the Tawakalna Division's T-72 tanks, many still in fixed defensive positions. Unlike previous engagements where hundreds of Iraqis surrendered after only a few tanks had been destroyed, the Tawakalna kept fighting. In the intense battle lasting over four hours, 2nd Cavalry destroyed at least twenty-nine tanks and numerous other vehicles, while taking over 1,300 Iraqis prisoner. The 2nd Cavalry kept fighting as it advanced to map line 73 Easting. The intense engagement had been neither planned nor anticipated and had been conducted mostly on the initiative of the field-grade officers of the 2nd Cavalry. American armor had defeated their Republican Guard counterparts with lethal skill and efficiency. With the battle won, the 1st Infantry Division and the 2nd Armored Cavalry Regiment continued their advance eastward.[17]

In Kuwait City, the 1st Marine Division raced toward Kuwait International Airport, while the 2nd Marine Division and Tiger Brigade secured Mutla Ridge. By holding this comparatively short ridge, the Marines could control the intersection of two major highways going in and out of Kuwait City, but the ridge was not taken without first engaging and destroying several Iraqi tanks and armored vehicles and clearing extensive minefields. The extent of the deception campaign became apparent, as many Iraqi tanks, artillery pieces, and other weapons faced seaward. As the Marines and Tiger Brigade approached, Iraqi commanders frantically tried to reposition tanks and vehicles from their otherwise superbly fortified positions to face westward. The main hindrance slowing I MEF's advance into Kuwait was, ironically, the thousands of Iraqi POWs that surrendered *en masse*. In some cases, Iraqi soldiers surrendered to journalists, who themselves had either become lost or had unknowingly advanced ahead of the Coalition attack. Meanwhile, JFC-East entered Kuwait City.[18]

Iraqis retreated pell-mell from Kuwait City, taking any vehicle they could find, loading them with ill-gotten loot and causing a mammoth traffic jam on the main highway connecting Kuwait City and Basra through Mutla Pass in Iraq. Coalition aircraft quickly spotted their exposed and defenseless quarry. By dropping mines on the highway in front of and behind the fleeing Iraqis, Coalition air forces created in essence a "kill box." Then began a relentless "turkey shoot," as aircraft after aircraft dropped all sorts of ordnance on the Iraqis, so much so that pilots actually had to wait their turn before releasing their loads on the mass of vehicles. Tanks later joined what appeared to be a slaughter. Over 2,000 vehicles were destroyed. Media analysts quickly dubbed the road the "Highway of Death," a name that certainly fit the images of charred corpses and vehicles that subsequently appeared on television and in newspapers. Later, military investigators determined that most Iraqis had abandoned their vehicles at the first sign of incoming Coalition aircraft and had escaped unharmed. Nevertheless, while a violent if not questionable act, the military defended its attack against what it considered as "retreating" Iraqi forces. In Washington, however, Bush and his advisors were keenly aware of the negative fallout such images could produce. Bush did not want what appeared to be senseless slaughter to mar his certain victory over Saddam.[19]

By February 27, Schwarzkopf sensed that the end of the war was near. McCaffrey and the 24th Infantry Division approached the key city of Basra in eastern Iraq, engaging elements of the Republican Guard's Hammurabi Division along the way. Intense fighting along Highway 8, where the 24th Infantry and 101st Airborne blocked Iraqi forces, resembled that on the Highway of Death, as hundreds of burning vehicles littered the road. VII Corps also hit Republican Guard divisions whenever possible, including during a major engagement on February 27 in what became known as the Battle of Medina Ridge. The largest tank battle of the war took place at Medina Ridge, where the 2nd Brigade of the 1st Armored Division confronted the entrenched 2nd Brigade of the Medina Division. The Iraqis had hoped to take advantage of the shallow downward slope of the ridge, but they had dug in too far away so that the guns of their T-72s could not reach the American tanks on the ridgeline. The Iraqi plan was to surprise the American armor from its camouflaged positions and destroy as many American tanks as possible on the crest of the ridge, then drive the Americans back into the wadi behind the ridge, where Iraqi artillery had pre-sighted a field of fire to destroy the American tanks. Incredibly, the Iraqi artillery never realized that the Medina Division's tanks were being decimated by American fire and nonetheless fired several timed barrages into the empty wadi far behind the American tank lines. For the Americans with their M1 Abrams tanks and thermal imaging capability, the Iraqi tanks at a range of 3,000 meters were just at the outer edge of their gunnery capability. The 2nd Brigade's commander, Colonel Montgomery Meigs, nonetheless cleared his tanks to fire. Over 300 American tanks supported in the air by several Apache attack helicopters with Hellfire missiles, opened fire on targets the naked eye could barely see but that appeared as bright hotspots on their thermal imaging screens. The 2nd Brigade kept advancing toward the entrenched Iraqi tanks, firing at a steady and deadly pace. In some cases, a single American tank knocked out two or three Iraqi tanks before the Iraqis could get off a single and often ineffective shot.

The fight with the Medina Division was, nevertheless, not easy. The rapid advance toward the Iraqi line caused the 2nd Brigade's line to get out of kilter within its only battalions and the 1st and 3rd Brigades of the 1st Armored Division. Meigs ordered his force to pull back several hundred meters to realign, and then to renew the advance. The 1st and 3rd Brigades carried on with the fight, which lasted into the late afternoon. American firepower destroyed over seventy Iraqi tanks, and hundreds of armored personnel carriers and other vehicles at the cost of one soldier killed and four M1 Abrams disabled by Iraqi fire. Considering the intensity and rate of incoming as well as outgoing fire, the low American losses were remarkable. The Medina Division still had units intact and thus remained a threat, but the awesome power associated with the elite Iraqi armor had been all but destroyed.[20]

Still, with the door to Basra not completely shut, many Republican Guard units escaped across the Tigris and Euphrates Rivers into central Iraq. The ground campaign had unfolded so quickly that the expected movement of Republican Guard divisions southward to block the advance on Kuwait did not materialize. Instead, Saddam wisely decided to get as much of his elite force out of harm's way as quickly as possible. Saudi-led forces had by now occupied Kuwait City, while the 1st and 2nd Marine Divisions had secured positions around the Kuwaiti capital. Aware of the power of images, especially in the Middle East, CENTCOM made a conscious choice to ensure Arab forces rolled into Kuwait before other Coalition units (especially American units), which followed close behind.[21]

From the Iraqi military's perspective, the flaws of both its defensive plan and its limited tactical and operational capability rose too quickly to the surface. According to interrogations of captured Iraqi officers, frontline forces had no idea that they were about to be attacked, much less that two American corps would swing wide through the desert in a grand flanking maneuver. The Iraqi expectation that the ground fighting would consist of brief bursts of combat followed by extended periods of regrouping and repositioning, as had been the case in the Iran–Iraq War, did not materialize. Faced instead with remarkable speed, firepower, and maneuver, as well as with imagination, the Iraqi military machine crumbled before the Coalition onslaught. The Iraqi forces that stood their ground, as compared to the bulk that deserted and melted away, fought well, but without creative junior officers who would seize the initiative, they were doomed.[22]

War Termination

In Washington, Bush and his White House team followed the unfolding ground campaign closely. By February 26, it became clear that things were going extremely well; by the 27th, it looked like the war would end within days. Schwarzkopf declared as much at the "Mother of All Briefings" in Riyadh at 2100 hours (local time) on the night of the 27th, telling reporters "we have accomplished our mission" before delightfully going into a lengthy multi-slide presentation explaining the ground campaign plan until that point in the operation. The briefing irritated the air planners in the Black Hole, who felt Schwarzkopf had all but ignored the enormous and effective air campaign that had made the ground campaign possible, exposing again the still-existent rifts among the services despite Goldwater–Nichols. With the announcement made in Riyadh, however, that Kuwait was now in Coalition hands, Bush concurred with Powell and Cheney that the Coalition, rather than Saddam, should set the time and conditions for a cease-fire to go into effect. After consultation with Schwarzkopf and major Coalition partners, the Bush team agreed that the war would end at midnight local time in Washington on February 28, thus at 0800 hours local time in the Persian Gulf. Doing so at that specific time would end the ground war exactly 100 hours after it had begun on February 24, a public relations ploy that bothered Schwarzkopf not one bit.[23]

Bush delivered a live televised address from the White House at 2100 hours local time on February 25 to announce the cease-fire. Proudly declaring that "Kuwait is liberated," Bush made it clear that "it is up to Iraq whether this suspension on the part of the Coalition becomes part of a permanent cease-fire." Bush laid out the terms for the cease-fire, including full compliance with all UN Security Council resolutions and Iraq's agreement to pay restitution for damages "its aggression had caused." Additionally, Bush demanded that Iraq release all POWs, detained foreign nationals, and Kuwaiti citizens, as well as "the remains of all who have fallen." Bush warned Saddam that any violation of these terms or initiation of hostilities by Iraq to break the cease-fire would lead to the resumption of military operations by the Coalition. Incredibly, after having for so many months denied Iraq's multiple attempts to link its dispute with Kuwait to a broader Middle Eastern settlement, Bush then told the world that the United States stood ready to "assist and support the countries of the region and be a catalyst for peace" in the region. Secretary of State Baker, Bush declared, would visit the Middle East to "begin a new round of consultations" in hopes of "securing a potentially historic peace." Bush demanded Iraqi representatives meet with Schwarzkopf within forty-eight hours to sign a formal cease-fire agreement.[24]

Several hours remained, however, before the Coalition would suspend hostilities, time that Schwarzkopf did not waste. He ordered all units to engage and destroy Iraqi tanks, other vehicles, and artillery to leave Saddam's military machine in as much disarray as possible. Coalition forces followed the order to the letter, not letting up until 0800 hours the morning of February 28. Things remained largely quiet the next day, but on March 2 a mixed Iraqi force, including units of the Hammurabi Division of the Republican Guard, attempted to break through the lines of the 24th Infantry Division near Highway 8. McCaffrey moved elements of the 24th Infantry Division to block the Hammurabi Division's attempt to escape along a causeway near the Rumaila oil field. Two isolated but minor Iraqi attacks unleashed a fury of American firepower that destroyed over 300 Iraqi vehicles and numerous other pieces of equipment. Three thousand more Iraqis joined their comrades as POWs of the Coalition, while McCaffrey's 24th Infantry Division did not lose a single soldier.

This action was not without its critics. Some alleged that McCaffrey had overreacted to minor incidents in his orders in moving to seal off the causeway with such a massive disproportionate response against Iraqi forces that were clearly in retreat if not disarray. The Iraqis were not

Figure 5   *A view of Iraqi armored personnel carriers, tanks, and trucks destroyed on a road in the Euphrates River Valley. Photograph by Staff SGT Dean Wagner.*
Source: Department of Defense, DefenseImagery.mil.

seeking to fight an American mechanized division at this stage. They were instead trying to get out of the area to reach Basra and safety. McCaffrey used artillery, tank, and air assaults to bracket the Iraqi force on the causeway. Most fled their burning vehicles to escape into the marshes, but many were not so fortunate. Allegations surfaced that McCaffrey had committed a war crime by conducting such an assault after the implementation of a cease-fire. After the war, the Army investigated the incident and concluded McCaffrey had reacted appropriately. Subsequent investigations by the Department of Defense found no evidence of war crimes. Years later in 2000, the journalist Seymour Hersh, who had broken the My Lai story in 1969, published in the *New Yorker* a scathing indictment of McCaffrey, accusing the then retired general of war crimes. Hersh quoted his own interviews with soldiers on the scene who had claimed that the Iraqis were not a threat and that they had received no significant Iraqi fire to warrant McCaffrey's response. McCaffrey vehemently denied the allegations and accused Hersh of grandstanding in the hope of finding another My Lai-like scoop and of denigrating McCaffrey just before the retired general's scheduled testimony before Congress as President Bill Clinton's new Drug Czar (as the director of the Office of National Drug Control Policy was known). Both Powell and Clinton publically defended McCaffrey.[25]

To Schwarzkopf, the imperative of a formal cease-fire was now all the more important to prevent similar incidents and needless casualties. Schwarzkopf decided to hold a meeting with his Iraqi counterparts at Safwan airfield, just south of Basra, along the front line of the Coalition advance. Powell and Schwarzkopf had discussed using the battleship *Missouri*, on station in the Persian Gulf, for a surrender ceremony to match the one on the deck of the same vessel that had ended the war with Japan in September 1945, but had reconsidered their decision after realizing the logistical nightmare involved in organizing what would in essence be a public relations stunt. As an alternative, Schwarzkopf chose Safwan, just inside the Iraqi border, under the assumption that Franks' VII Corps held the airfield. In reality, VII Corps did not. The airfield was instead occupied by a small Iraqi garrison. This, combined with Schwarzkopf's frustration with Franks' slowness during the first day of the ground war, sent the CENTCOM commander's blood boiling in one his infamous rages. Elements of the 1st Infantry Division promptly surrounded the airfield and invited the Iraqis to depart, which they quickly did.[26]

Schwarzkopf orchestrated every detail of the meeting. He had fresh M1 Abrams tanks and Bradley personnel carriers deployed in fighting positions around the airfield and near the tent in which the meeting would take place. Apache attack helicopters and other aircraft were to circle overhead, with dozens more parked in neat but nonetheless intimidating rows on the tarmac. Schwarzkopf clearly wanted the Iraqis to "be in the right frame of mind" when they arrived at Safwan. He and Powell had already worked out the details of the cease-fire agreement. With the Vietnam MIA issue at the forefront of their minds as veterans of the American war in Vietnam, the two generals had made the return of POWs and the remains of military personnel the top priority on their list of conditions. They also wanted the locations of all Iraqi NBC sites and a clear demarcation line to separate the two forces to prevent accidental shootings and other incidents. Saudi General Prince Khalid, who would also participate in the meeting, wanted the Iraqis to affirm Saudi and Kuwaiti sovereignty as a symbolic gesture to not only both countries but also the rest of the Arab world, one that would cause Saddam to lose even more face among his Arab brethren. Military representatives of other Coalition countries would also attend. Lieutenant General Sultan Hashim Ahmad, the deputy chief of staff for Iraq's Defense Ministry, and Lieutenant General Salah Abud Mahmud, the commander of what was left of Iraq's III Corps, would represent Iraq. Neither Schwarzkopf nor Khalid intended to shake hands with the Iraqis and before the meeting agreed not to do so.

The meeting was set for 1100 hours on the morning of March 3. Schwarzkopf flew from Kuwait City International Airport to Safwan aboard Franks' command Black Hawk helicopter. Along the way, he saw the destructive results of his war to liberate Kuwait. Burned out hulks that had once been Iraqi tanks littered the landscape. Wrecked vehicles of all types still smoldered on the Highway of Death. What ignited Schwarzkopf's anger, though, was the site of burning oil wells and the thick acrid smoke that darkened the skies. Schwarzkopf recalled: "By the time we set down at Safwan, I was just plain mad." The site had been prepared to the letter of Schwarzkopf's instructions, including dozens of Apache and Black Hawk helicopters parked in line along the runway. Tanks and other vehicles, with their crews at the ready, surrounded the entire airfield. Coming from Basra under a white flag, the Iraqis transferred to American Humvees, which took the Iraqi generals intentionally past the display of American firepower. Schwarzkopf doubted that the Iraqi leadership in Baghdad fully realized the extent of the destruction that the Coalition had wrought on Iraq's military machine.

Tension filled the air in the large tent used for the meeting. Schwarzkopf, Khalid, and an interpreter sat on one side of the rectangular table, across from Generals Ahmad and Mahmud and their interpreter. The Iraqis quickly agreed to Schwarzkopf's list of demands, though they balked at repatriating Kuwaiti nationals taken at the time of the invasion, claiming that these people had been of Iraqi descent and wished to return to Iraq. The Iraqis reluctantly agreed, however, to allow anyone who approached the International Red Cross to freely return to Kuwait. They also bristled at the idea of a demarcation line, going to some length to make certain the line was neither permanent nor intended to serve as a border. Remarkably, Schwarzkopf conceded to the Iraqi request to fly helicopters so that they could assess damage to roads, bridges, and other infrastructure, but the American commander refused to allow flight of any other aircraft. In hindsight, this concession proved to be a grave mistake, as the Iraqis used helicopter gunships to brutally suppress rebellions that erupted in Basra and other areas following the cease-fire. Iraqi helicopter gunships contributed to the slaughter of over 20,000 Shia in southern Iraq as they did to the killing of thousands of Kurds in the north after the war. The decision had been made in part to hasten disengagement and not get American forces bogged down in an

Figure 6   *General H. Norman Schwarzkopf, CENTCOM commander, and Lieutenant-General Prince Khalid, commander of Joint Forces in Saudi Arabia, sit across the table from their Iraqi counterparts at Safwan.*
Source: Department of Defense, DefenseImagery.mil.

extended occupation. As a result, those American forces still in Kuwait could do nothing as Saddam's Republican Guard crushed the Shia rebellion in Basra. Schwarzkopf later wrote, "In the following weeks, we discovered what the son of a bitch really had in mind," but defended the decision, citing the far greater potential impact of the twenty-four Iraqi divisions that had not been in the KTO as opposed to the damage done by dozens of helicopters upon the insurgents.

Schwarzkopf then asked the Iraqis for an accounting of all Coalition POWS, to which they responded with a prepared list: seventeen Americans, two Italians, twelve British, one Kuwaiti, and nine Saudis were held by the Iraqis. Schwarzkopf quickly began listing a number of Coalition MIAs, at which point General Ahmad interrupted, demanding the number of POWs held by Coalition forces. Schwarzkopf told Ahmad that over 60,000 Iraqis were in Coalition hands. According to Schwarzkopf, Ahmad's face went "completely pale," as he had not realized the enormity of his army's defeat. With that, the meeting concluded.[27]

The liberation of Kuwait had cost Coalition forces 240 combat dead, including 147 Americans killed in action (among them the twenty-eight Americans who perished in the Scud strike on the barracks at Dhahran and thirty-five killed in blue-on-blue incidents). Another 235 Americans had died from non-hostile causes. The Coalition wounded included 467 Americans and 318 from other Coalition countries, again including many injured in blue-on-blue incidents. By far the worst accident occurred when a Saudi Royal Air Force C-130 carrying over ninety troops from Senegal crashed while trying to land in Saudi Arabia after the war on March 21, 1991. Smoke from burning Kuwaiti oil wells had caused the crash.[28]

The damage done to Saddam's military had been tremendous, but not complete. In addition to 3,800 tanks, 1,450 armored personnel carriers, and 2,900 artillery pieces destroyed or captured, an estimated 25,000 Iraqi soldiers had perished in the war. Some estimates place the number as high as 50,000. CENTCOM, under Schwarzkopf's direction, had refused to carry out any sort of "body count" system during the war, fearing that such a practice would be too analogous to similar practices during the Vietnam War. As many as 60,000 Iraqis had been wounded. Coalition forces had actually taken over 85,000 Iraqis as POWs during the war. Only seven of forty-three Iraqi divisions remained operational at war's end. Though badly mauled, the Iraqi dictator survived his strategic miscalculation to stay in power for another twelve years.[29]

8

Aftermath and Legacies

In response to a May 1991 Gallup Poll question on whether liberating Kuwait "was worth a war," 72 percent (down from a high of 80 percent the week of February 28–March 3, 1991) of Americans polled said "yes."[1] To many observers, the Persian Gulf War had been a stunning exhibition of modern combat arms, with low casualties and the political objective achieved in a shockingly short period, considering the size of the forces and the scale of the territory involved. Modern military technology impressed analysts and captured the public's imagination, leading some to claim that a historic "revolution in military affairs," or RMA, was underway.[2]

Equally stunning had been the survival of the American-led Coalition, which had held together through seven months of negotiations, resolutions, deployments, posturing, rogue initiatives, deadlines, Scuds, and war, among other trials and tribulations. For the United States in particular, many hoped the ghosts of Vietnam had been finally exorcised. Many Americans rediscovered a patriotic affection for the military and neoconservatives re-envisioned the possibilities for American military power to shape the post-Cold War world. Others were not so quick to join the victorious euphoria, criticizing Bush for fighting an unnecessary war and aggravating the already unstable situation in the Middle East rather than creating an opportunity for a lasting settlement in the volatile region, and for jeopardizing the global economy. Most significantly, Saddam survived the war and the subsequent rebellions and attempts from within his own circle to overthrow him. Unfortunately, the world had not heard the last of Saddam Hussein.

Post-War Tensions

The Gulf War may have ended with the cease-fire on March 4, but the conflict with Saddam and Iraq continued for another twenty years. President Bush made a calculated strategic choice in leaving Saddam in power, a choice for which Bush would be much criticized in subsequent years. Iraqi intransigence continued, as Saddam half-heartedly cooperated with UNSCOM observers sent to Iraq to ensure compliance with UN Security Council demands, as outlined in the Safwan cease-fire agreement and Security Council Resolution 687, the "mother of all resolutions." The longest-ever resolution produced by the UN Security Council, Resolution 687 formalized the conditions outlined in the cease-fire and added numerous other sanctions, inspections, and other demands with which Iraq had to comply. To keep Saddam's military machine in check, Resolution 687 forced Iraq to disclose all NBC and ballistic missile manufacturing facilities and weapons stockpiles, and also provided for their UN-supervised destruction. Furthermore, Iraq would also have to pay for damages incurred by Kuwait during the invasion and occupation as well as for damage caused by the environmental warfare Saddam had unleashed on Kuwait and the Persian Gulf. Iraqi oil revenues went into a special UN fund to pay for these damages, with the remainder going toward food and reconstruction costs in Iraq in what later became known as the "oil for food" program. To some extent, controlling these monies curtailed Saddam's attempts to use revenue to reconstitute Iraq's NBC programs as well as to rebuild his military.[3]

Saddam nevertheless made enforcing Resolution 687 and subsequent Security Council resolutions difficult. Making a good show of outwardly meeting the conditions mandated by the Security Council, behind the scenes Saddam misled UN observers at every opportunity to get his chemical and biological programs up and running again. He placed his greatest deceptive efforts in masking the Iraqi nuclear program, bedeviling UN investigators for years. Saddam frequently demanded that the Security Council end its sanctions against Iraq, but his double-handed attitude toward UN authorities kept him in the hot seat with the UN and the United States. Combined with his brutal crackdown on rebels in the south of his country and his violent suppression of yet another Kurdish uprising in northern Iraq, the United States, along with Great Britain and France, maintained air assets in the Persian Gulf region to enforce UN-established "no-fly" zones in southern and northern Iraq and to deliver the occasional air strike when Saddam stepped too far out of line. Retaliatory strikes by American Tomahawk cruise missiles also tried to keep Saddam under control.

The "no-fly" zones had originally resulted from Saddam's violent attacks against rebels inspired by Iraq's defeat in the Gulf War to challenge Saddam's rule. The Kurds, believing they had President Bush's blessing and support, rose up in the hope of getting out from under Saddam's thumb to finally claim their independence. In several Kurdish cities, from early March to mid-April 1991, rebels staged a well-organized and well-planned revolt, even taking brief control of the Kirkuk oil fields. So successful was the Kurdish revolt that to put it down Saddam had to mount what amounted to an invasion of the Kurdish region. While the UN "no-fly" zone above the 36th parallel prevented Iraqi aircraft from attacking the Kurds, it did little to stop Saddam's ground forces from moving into the region to deliver swift retribution. Frantic refugees flooded major border stations, trying desperately to escape into Turkey and Iran, creating a desperate humanitarian crisis. In Operation PROVIDE COMFORT, the United States and other Coalition governments used military forces and other agencies to establish safe havens and refugee camps to protect Kurds fleeing from the Iraqi onslaught. In the end, the Kurds felt bitterly betrayed by the United States, which had encouraged the rebellion only to leave them at Saddam's mercy.

In southern Iraq, Shias also answered President Bush's invitation to rebel against Saddam and the Sunni-dominated Ba'ath Party. Yet, as it did with the Kurds in northern Iraq, the US government left the southern Shias in Najaf and Karbala on their own. Using helicopters as allowed by the Safwan cease-fire agreement, Saddam's forces violently suppressed the uprising. A "no-fly" zone established in 1992 south of the 32nd parallel was too little too late, but it did prevent further Iraqi military action in the region. Saddam undertook what in essence was an ethnic cleansing policy in southern Iraq to punish the rebellious Shia. Under the guise of exploring for petroleum deposits, Saddam ordered the Qurna Marshes between the Tigris and Euphrates Rivers drained, eradicating thousands of square miles of fertile land worked predominantly by the so-called Marsh Arabs, most of whom were Shias. Draining the marshes "uprooted and displaced" over half a million Marsh Arabs. With their farms now baking in the desert heat, these refugees scattered across Iraq in search of work to support their families. As Saddam had hoped, draining the marshes undercut whatever rebellious fight the Shias had left. As he had in setting Kuwaiti oil fields alight in 1991, Saddam had again used the environment as a strategic tool, this time to maintain domestic order through the forced relocation of a people.[4]

Critics at the time and later with the benefit of hindsight questioned Bush's decision not to remove Saddam from power. For Bush, Powell,

Schwarzkopf, and others involved in the decision, removing Saddam had never been a serious objective of the war, nor had such an objective been authorized by the UN Security Council in any of its several resolutions dealing with the Persian Gulf crisis. It is also unlikely that the Coalition, particularly the participation of the Arab States, would have survived a drive to Baghdad, and more than a few countries worried that the precedent of regime change, if done in Iraq, would encourage the United States to apply the same to other countries in the not too distant future. The impracticalities of overthrowing Saddam alone argued against such a move. As Schwarzkopf later put it, "I'm not sure that even with a full-scale invasion we could have ever found Saddam in this large armed camp that is Iraq."

Of course, if the residents of Baghdad, for example, had taken action against Saddam, neither Bush nor anyone else on his team would have objected. Others speculated that letting the war last just another two weeks could have weakened Saddam's hold on power enough to cause his regime to crumble from within. Occupying southern Iraq, instead of withdrawing to Kuwait at the end of the war, some speculated, could have proffered the same result. Still, enough uncertainties both presented themselves and remained unrevealed throughout the conflict to dissuade taking the extra step of removing Saddam and his Ba'ath regime from power. Militarily, the Coalition did not have the forces in place for a drive to Baghdad, despite the surprising ease with which it had ousted Iraqi forces from Kuwait. Even though the expected 10,000 Coalition casualties in the war did not materialize, facing the surviving Republican Guard divisions in a fight to the death near Baghdad had given Bush and his team pause in considering such an option. Moreover, Bush had to consider the potential power vacuum in Iraq and the instability that could be caused in the region by taking out Saddam, especially in Iraq's role as a balance against the state-sponsored Islamic extremism of Iran. Secretary of Defense Cheney alluded to the challenges of removing Saddam in a speech in 1992: "I think we got it right, both when we decided to expel him from Kuwait, but also when the president made the decision that we'd achieved our objectives and we were not going to go get bogged down in the problems of trying to take over and govern Iraq." At the time in 1991, the notion of one state exercising regime change against another during the transition from the Cold War to a new world order was simply not possible. That, along with Cheney's view on removing Saddam and governing Iraq, would change a decade later.[5]

During the 1990s, Saddam's ceaseless testing of American will irritated his overseers to no end. His intransigence forced the United States,

Great Britain, and France to maintain an active and expensive military presence in Turkey, Kuwait, and the Persian Gulf to enforce the "no-fly" zones conducted through Operations NORTHERN WATCH and SOUTHERN WATCH. Both operations remained active until the American invasion of Iraq in 2003. Saddam occasionally pressed too far and received an "appropriate" slap on the wrist from the US military to get the Iraqi dictator temporarily back in line. A foiled Iraqi assassination plot against George H. W. Bush during his visit to Kuwait in 1993, for example, convinced President Bill Clinton to respond by having the US Navy unleash twenty-three Tomahawk cruise missiles against targets in and around Baghdad, including the Iraqi intelligence agency's headquarters. Saddam continued to obstruct UNSCOM inspections of suspected NBC sites, which in part led to the US Congress appropriating over $100 million in 1998 to support rebel groups in Iraq to overthrow Saddam. Saddam used the Iraqi Liberation Act to cut off UNSCOM's inspection program. Clinton and British Prime Minister Tony Blair resolved to punish Iraq for this act and for its numerous violations of UN inspection resolutions since 1991. Over the course of four days in December 1998, Operation DESERT FOX launched American and British warplanes to destroy several Iraqi air defense sites and other military targets while dropping hundreds of bombs on suspected NBC sites that UNSCOM inspectors had not been able to visit. Over 400 cruise missiles were used in the attack, surpassing the 317 that had been used against Iraq in the entire Gulf War. Fearing retaliation against Kurds in northern Iraq, several British and American Special Forces teams were deployed among Kurdish settlements to deter Saddam from attacking the Kurds. DESERT FOX disrupted Saddam's regime, almost to the point of collapse. The Iraqi dictator responded with hundreds of arrests and executions. Clinton was criticized for timing the attacks to distract media attention from his troubles in the Monica Lewinsky scandal and congressional consideration of his impeachment. Arab leaders also complained about the ferocity of the strikes, questioning whether the true objective of the attacks was to punish Saddam or cause his overthrow. If it was the latter, they worried about the destabilizing "then what" if Saddam did fall from power.[6]

Operation IRAQI FREEDOM

After multiple Iraqi violations of the "no-fly" zones, obstruction of UN inspectors, and other affronts to UN authority throughout the 1990s into the early 2000s, President George W. Bush, the son of President George H. W. Bush, ordered the invasion of Iraq and the overthrow of the Iraqi dictator and his Ba'athist regime in 2003. Using as catalysts Iraq's purported support of terrorism following the September 11, 2011, attacks by Al Qaeda on the World Trade Center in New York City and on the Pentagon in Washington, DC, and fears that Saddam was close to having an operational nuclear weapon, the younger Bush apparently fulfilled what had been a top priority upon his election to the presidency in 2000—to rid the world of Saddam once and for all.

Operation IRAQI FREEDOM, as the George W. Bush administration called the invasion, followed very closely CENTCOM's 1990 alternative plan to drive all the way to Baghdad in a dual push northward, though in this case it involved a much smaller force than that of DESERT STORM and was made up of mostly American and British forces with the support of a smaller coalition that significantly included no Arab countries. Beginning on March 20, 2003, American and British forces invaded Iraq from Kuwait, using a joint air–ground campaign based on speed, maneuver, and the decisive defeat of Iraqi forces, particularly the Republican Guard. The US Air Force argued for an INSTANT THUNDER-like pre-ground phase air campaign, but CENTCOM command Army General Tommy Franks opted for a simultaneous combined offensive. A pre-invasion air campaign would have little effect on an Iraqi military machine that in 2003 was dispersed across Iraq to maintain domestic order rather than being concentrated in southern Iraq and Kuwait, as it had been in 1991. Moreover, an extended air campaign would have given time for Saddam to mass his forces and prepare defenses for an anticipated assault on Baghdad.

Franks' plan was a bold one. Baghdad lay some 300 miles from Kuwait. Innumerable tributaries of the Euphrates and Tigris rivers required either capturing bridges intact or building one's own as the advance moved northward. Speed and surprise were key to American success. Franks had a force in 2003 that was much lighter and more lethal than its DESERT STORM counterpart of 1991. Precision weapons had improved dramatically since the early 1990s, as had night vision and thermal imaging capabilities. Mature GPS systems, Internet communications, and satellite capabilities also gave Franks' force an advantage over that of Schwarzkopf's, who had only been able to use these resources when they were in their comparative infancy. American planners had also learned from their Gulf War experience, as well as from more recent air campaigns in the former Yugoslavia, that destroying infrastructure, such as electrical grids and water treatment plants, even bridges, created a rash of unintended consequences, not the least of which were bad press and expensive post-war rebuilding costs. In 2003, the air offensive focused on military targets, a tactic that also minimized collateral damage.

From Kuwait, the 3rd Infantry Division and I MEF drove north to Karbala and Nasiriyah, then split apart, with the 3rd Infantry Division speeding through the desert along the western side of the Euphrates River while I MEF drove northward to Kut and Numaniyah before turning toward Baghdad. The 82nd and 101st Airborne Divisions secured key bridges along the way. Units from the 7th Marine Regiment and the Royal Marines took Um Qasr to make safe the Rumaila oil fields, while the British 1st Armoured Division took control of Basra to secure southern Iraq and the Shatt al-Arab waterway. American and British air forces, along with naval vessels firing Tomahawk cruise missiles from the Persian Gulf, struck strategic and tactical targets to help clear the way for advancing ground forces and hopefully decapitate the Iraqi government and military command structure in Baghdad. Franks had hoped to use the American 4th Infantry Division to invade Iraq from southern Turkey, but the Turkish government rejected American requests for staging the invasion from within its border.

As in 1991, women played an important role in combat operations during the 2003 invasion. They were captured and killed in battle, raising again the debate over women in combat. The media, too, again played a major role, though in 2003 with fewer shackles as the military allowed reporters to "embed" themselves in various units throughout the entire invasion. In the Gulf War, Schwarzkopf and CENTCOM had tightly controlled the media through their daily press briefings. In 1991, few reporters had been allowed contact with fielded troops and even then interviews had been conducted in semi-artificial environments under the watchful gaze of military civil affairs officers. Censorship had run high compared to previous American wars, especially Vietnam, where the media had more or less had a free hand. In 2003, the media had more freedom and less censorship than their colleagues in 1991, but it came at a price. Access to the battlefront resulted in dozens of reporters being killed or wounded during intense firefights. Antagonism between the media and the American military increased as the insurgency continued into 2004 and beyond. The military believed that reporters focused on the bad at the expense of the good that was happening in Iraq. Their relationship remains contentious.[7]

The 2003 invasion was fast and decisive but not without its foibles. Military planners did not expect the walkover of 1991 to be repeated in 2003. Planned logistical links with rapidly advancing forces sometimes delayed the advance because of simple traffic congestion caused by thousands of support vehicles crawling at a snail's pace along hundreds of miles of desert highways. Far from the expected liberation celebrations, American forces met instead suspicious Iraqis who remembered all too vividly their abandonment by the United States in 1991. Iraqi forces, especially the Republican Guard, fought harder, sometimes to the death. Un-uniformed fighters, called the fedayeen, waited for the bulk of the invasion force to pass, then attacked with fanatical ferocity the long and exposed logistical train of vehicles. These attacks completely surprised American planners, as the fedayeen became the backbone of the Iraqi insurgency against American occupation.

Despite these setbacks, American forces took Baghdad by April 9. Saddam fled into hiding. The Iraqis were finally free from Saddam's harsh rule, but the hardest work remained. Aboard the carrier *Abraham Lincoln* on April 15, President George W. Bush dramatically declared the war over, despite the growing insurgency, which Secretary of Defense Donald Rumsfeld dismissed as mere "looting." In its most controversial move, the George W. Bush administration decided to disband the Iraqi military, forcing hundreds of thousands of now unemployed former soldiers onto the streets. Many of these joined the fedayeen.

American losses included 139 KIA, including one woman—Army PFC Lori Ann Piestewa—while British forces lost at least thirty-three KIA. Estimates placed Iraqi military losses at over 9,000 KIA and as many as 7,000 civilians killed in the invasion. The war, however, was not over, as fighting continued for several more years, costing the lives of over 4,400 American, 179 British, and over 100 other coalition military personnel and tens of thousands more Iraqi insurgents and civilians. Former Secretary of Defense Dick Cheney played a major role in the decision to invade Iraq as George W. Bush's vice president, while former Chairman of the Joint Chiefs of Staff Colin Powell reluctantly and controversially supported the invasion as Bush's secretary of state. American Special Forces killed Saddam's sons Uday and Quesay in July 2003 and finally captured Saddam near his hometown of Tikrit in December 2003. A court of the new Iraqi government tried the former Iraqi dictator for various crimes against the Iraqi people, convicted him, and ordered his execution by hanging in December 2006. The last American troops left Iraq in December 2011, leaving only a token security force and other personnel for the American Embassy in Baghdad. Some observers now call the long conflict between the United States and Iraq the Twenty Years' War.[8]

Kicking the Vietnam Syndrome

While the American conflict with Iraq may indeed be a Twenty Year War, the Gulf War of 1991 nevertheless warrants consideration in its own right. While praising the professionalism, capability, and courage of the American military, President George H. W. Bush had declared to the American armed forces in March 1991 that "The specter of Vietnam has been buried forever in the desert sands of the Arabian Peninsula."[9] The Vietnam syndrome, Bush had told a gathering of veterans' organizations, had been "kicked," and as president he had wanted the welcome home of the troops who had served in the Persian Gulf to serve as "long overdue" symbolic thanks to veterans of the Vietnam War.[10] Many Americans had indeed wanted to put the Vietnam experience behind them or at least place it in some sort of livable perspective. The Gulf War, with its quick victory, low casualties, and apparent just cause, had seemed to do just that.[11]

While the public had been wary of sending American forces into harm's way in the Persian Gulf during the fall of 1990, once Operation DESERT STORM had begun, the American people had overwhelmingly supported their field forces. To follow the strong affirmation of 80 percent of the American public that the United States had been right to go to war against Iraq, nine out of ten Americans had believed their military "was doing a good job."[12] Unlike the years of strong antimilitary feelings following the Vietnam War, after the war in the Persian Gulf 89 percent of Americans polled had expressed "confidence" in the United States military as an institution, an approval rating higher than that of any institution in American society, outpacing Congress, churches, and even banks. As president, Bush's overall approval rating had hit a record high of 89 percent, with 92 percent approving his handling of the war, only to fall away by the November 1992 presidential election, which he lost to Arkansas Governor and Democrat Bill Clinton. Victory in war did not translate to electoral victory, as a stagnant recessed economy contributed to the defeat of a successful wartime president. Also unlike Vietnam, where American commander General William Westmoreland had been an extremely polarizing figure, military leaders enjoyed immense popularity after the Gulf War. Schwarzkopf had the highest approval rating at 88 percent, followed closely by Powell at 87 percent.[13]

During the war, the "yellow ribbon syndrome" had taken hold across the United States, as throughout the conflict Americans had shown their support for the troops by tying yellow ribbons around trees and utility poles, as well as by displaying American flags and bumper stickers declaring "Support the Troops." Celebrities had sung the American national anthem to patriotic crowds at the Super Bowl and other sporting events. Great crowds had greeted returning troops at airports, military bases, and other venues. Major cities, such as San Diego, Chicago, and Denver, had held parades, often including veterans from other wars, especially those of the Vietnam War. It had not been uncommon for a small town to stage a parade to honor the one or two veterans of the Gulf War returning home from their victorious war. A National Victory Celebration parade costing over $12 million had taken place on June 8, 1991, on Constitution Avenue in Washington, DC, led by "Stormin' Norman" himself, who had exchanged a dramatic and emotional salute with President Bush. This patriotic exhibition had been followed by a traditional ticker-tape parade for returning service members in New York City on June 10, 1991.[14]

While the American people had gone to great lengths to symbolically make up for poor treatment of returning veterans of the Vietnam War and to "kick" the Vietnam syndrome through parades and other events for

Figure 7   *An M1 Abrams tank from the 24th Infantry Division proceeds along the parade route during the National Victory Celebration parade in Washington, DC. Photograph by Michael E. Buchanan.*
Source: Department of Defense, DefenseImagery.mil.

veterans of the Gulf War, the ghosts of Vietnam did not disappear completely. Throughout the 1990s, the Vietnam syndrome surfaced again and again, often in crises resulting in American casualties, such as in Somalia in 1993, or when uncertain national interests were at stake, such as in the former Yugoslavia. Ironically, the very success of the conflict with Iraq reinforced the American aversion to casualties, as Americans now expected war to be "clean." Anti-war protests, though not nearly on the scale of those during the latter years of the Vietnam War, had occurred on college campuses and elsewhere during the Gulf War—as they did during the several subsequent instances when the United States used military force, especially during the 2003 invasion of Iraq. Perhaps the most important surviving legacy of the Vietnam War, however, was the American public's intolerance for fighting messy wars, such as insurgencies and guerrilla wars. A relatively bloodless war with clear and just objectives against a conventional enemy was more suited to American tastes, which may explain in part the American public's support of the Gulf War, once Coalition military operations began in January 1991, compared to its lack of support for military action in Somalia and post-2003 Iraq. Questions concerning presidential authority to send American military forces into hostile action without a constitutional declaration of war, too, remain controversial, as the great congressional debate before the January 15, 1991 deadline resulted in authorization to use force but did not resolve the long-standing conflict between Congress and the president over war-making authority.[15]

Post-War Challenges for the American Military

Other issues arose from the Gulf War that both challenged the American military and provided it opportunities for reconciliation and social progress in the post-Cold War era. Over 40,000 women, for example, had served in the US Armed Forces in the Persian Gulf. Deployed to Saudi Arabia, where women exist in a completely different if not restricted culture than the comparatively equal one that women enjoy in the United States or Western Europe, military women had faced numerous cultural challenges. Saudi soldiers had balked at American female officers giving orders to male soldiers. Military women had been generally restricted in their access to and behavior in public places, sometimes even having to wear black veils and robes to conform to cultural norms for Saudi women. Despite these differences, women had played a critical part in their military roles, which had often been the same as those of their male counterparts. They had served as truck drivers, mechanics, pilots, navigators, engineers, logisticians, radio and communications specialists, air traffic controllers, weapons specialists, law enforcement personnel, chaplains, and in numerous other military occupations. In addition to perhaps more traditional roles as doctors, nurses, and medics, in the Gulf War women had commanded units from the platoon to the brigade level. While technically excluded from combat, women had nonetheless found themselves in harm's way as pilots, truck drivers, gunners, police, medical personnel, and while carrying out other duties. Five American military women had been killed in action and twenty-one had been wounded during the Gulf War. Four women Marines had been awarded the Combat Action Ribbon for exchanging fire with Iraqi troops. The fears concerning possible capture, which became all too real for Rhonda Cornum and Melissa Rathbun-Nealy, had weighed heavily during the build-up and of course during the war. Women in theater had been briefed on what they might face if captured by the Iraqis—torture, physical abuse, rape, and probably death. Army PFC Karen Perkins, who had enlisted less than a year before being deployed to Saudi Arabia in October 1990, had told an Army historian in January 1991 that if she realized she was going to be captured she would kill herself. Several other women had indicated they would take the same action. They had accepted the possibility of being in combat and not surprisingly believed women should be legally allowed to be in combat, but capture presented an entirely different set of concerns. The high-profile service of women in the conflict drew attention to the controversy surrounding whether women should perform combat roles. While the war resulted in an expansion of combat-related duties for women, the intense debate over the issue remains controversial.[16]

Gulf War Syndrome is another controversial legacy of the conflict. After the war, thousands of military personnel who had seen service in the Persian Gulf complained of tiredness and headaches as well as suffering from largely unexplained illnesses. In part because of its negligence in dealing with the illnesses suffered by veterans exposed to Agent Orange and other chemical pesticides during the Vietnam War, the United States government in the large proactively approached the challenges presented by Gulf War Syndrome. Numerous government studies from 1993 through the early 2000s were unable to pinpoint an exact cause of the maladies suffered by thousands of Gulf War veterans, but theories on the causes range from possible exposure to chemical weapons, to exposure to depleted uranium used in several types of ammunition, to poisoning from the potent vaccination cocktails designed to protect personnel from disease, to exposure to biological agents. Currently, the Department of Defense and the Department of Veterans Affairs provide care and benefits to veterans suffering from variations of Gulf War Syndrome, and the congressionally-mandated Research Advisory Committee on Gulf War Veterans' Illnesses continues to investigate the issue.[17]

Assessing the Gulf War

The Gulf War had offered many things that had impressed observers. Militarily, the costly and sometimes controversial procurement of several Cold War-era weapons and other systems, from aircraft to missiles to GPS, had appeared vindicated. Despite some systems being more than twenty years old by 1990–91, with some much older, many had never before been used in battle. With the exception of the Patriot SAM defense system, which was later much improved, these untried weapons, tanks, personnel carriers, aircraft, missiles, and other equipment had performed quite well on the whole. Moreover, the AVF had also performed well, showing the benefits of its training, equipment, and professionalism in conducting the American military's first division-level operations since the Korean War. Intelligence, too, had given the Coalition an unprecedented military advantage, as the disparity between the American military intelligence community, the best in the world, and the almost blind, were it not for CNN, Iraqis had been unique in modern warfare. Also, airpower advocates in particular had reveled in the success of the air campaign, while the Army had validated its armored mobility. Moreover, the successful war had confirmed the ability of a unified regional CINC to conduct large-scale military operations under the auspices of the Goldwater–Nichols Act of 1986.[18]

The overall conditions under which the Gulf War had been fought in many ways ensured success, leading one observer to declare that the Gulf War's "relevance is in the fact that it occurred at all." The Soviet Union's decline had made conducting such a war possible—had it occurred some years before, major American military operations would not have been politically or militarily likely due to the Soviet threat to Western Europe and Soviet interests in the Middle East. Nor could Saddam have dared to make an attempt to take control of Middle Eastern oil reserves. The flux of the international system due in part to the decline of the Soviet Union and the easing of Cold War tensions in Eastern Europe had made it advantageous for many countries to join the American-led Coalition without fear of repercussions from the Soviet Union. The post-Cold War situation had also allowed for unprecedented unity among the permanent members of the UN Security Council, a fact that had allowed the United States to lead the Coalition in the name of the UN rather than act unilaterally. Despite brief intense fighting, these conditions had allowed the Coalition to face a strategically incompetent enemy that was economically, diplomatically, and militarily isolated.[19]

The Coalition may have been the most crucial key to the overall success of the campaign. Largely pieced together by President Bush and Secretary of State Baker, the Coalition had held together despite high odds against its doing so. Differing national, cultural, religious, and economic interests could have derailed the Coalition at any time. The threat of Israeli participation in the war in response to Saddam's intimidating but ultimately ineffective Scud attacks, too, could have not only broken apart the Coalition but could also have widened the war across the Middle East.

Other observers had not been so enthralled with the stunning victory. Critics had charged that the apparent success of American military technology would only serve to intensify the military's reliance upon that technology. Whereas in the Vietnam War the reliance upon technology, information, and analysis had arguably contributed to the defeat of American forces in Southeast Asia, in the Gulf War such technological wonders had contributed to victory. Yet, while the Pentagon had proclaimed the Gulf War to be a harbinger of future wars, complete with technology and the Powell Doctrine as its talismans, some had argued that the post-Cold War world would not accommodate DESERT STORM-style conflict. "Technological Utopianism" was dangerous, analysts like Andrew Bacevich had declared, because presidents would now turn to the military option under such low risk–high yield conditions. Techno-war made it easier to go to war. Such beliefs had also made the Powell Doctrine irrelevant, as one no longer needed massive overwhelming force to achieve limited political objectives. Thus, for example, when Somali bandits ambushed American forces attempting to capture Somali warlord Mohamed Farrah Aidid in Mogadishu in 1993 and a suicide attack via a rubber motor boat killed seventeen sailors and Marines aboard the destroyer USS *Cole* while anchored in Aden, technology was of little use.[20]

Observers had also questioned the contention that the Gulf War had validated the Goldwater–Nichols Act and the success of the "jointness" movement. Operationally, the services had performed jointly like never before, a direct credit to Goldwater–Nichols. Despite that achievement, the ground campaign had failed to destroy the Republican Guard, revealing a strategic disconnect among battlefield commanders, Schwarzkopf, and political leaders in Washington that saved Saddam's lifeline to remaining in power. In Washington, the war changed little for the services as each continued to put its own interests before those of the others in procurement and budgetary matters, resulting in waste, inefficiency, and redundancy, all of which had long plagued the American defense establishment since the early days of the Cold War. In CENTCOM, critics had argued, the war had belonged to Schwarzkopf and the Army. Post-war studies by the Army lauded its own prowess while downplaying the finely planned pre-ground phase air campaign. Moreover, American intelligence had overestimated the strength and fighting capability of the Iraqi military, grossly so, resulting in an expensive use of overwhelming force that ultimately did not stabilize the region. The Battle of Khafji had been a prime indicator of lack of will among Iraqi forces, but Schwarzkopf and CENTCOM had ignored what the Air Force and Marines concluded from the battle—Coalition air superiority had prevented Iraqi forces from moving, and if they could not move, they could not and likely would not put up a tough fight. Both the macro-level of the war and the micro-level of Khafji had given plenty cause to question American intelligence estimates. Additionally, where Powell had earlier wondered why Saddam used such a large force to take Kuwait in August 1990, critics after the war wondered why Powell had used such a large force to oust Saddam from Kuwait in 1991.[21]

Despite the success in the war, maintaining a Cold War-sized military in the post-Cold War world was difficult for Congress and President Bush, then President Clinton, to justify. With this in mind even while fighting the war, each service had played up its role in the conflict while subtly downplaying that of the others. The Navy had the most difficult time promoting its role as key to success in the Gulf War, while the Air Force and Army jockeyed for the title of "most indispensable to victory." Downsizing forced reorganization, with the Air Force moving to the Air Expeditionary Group model, the Army remaking itself into a lighter and more lethal force of twelve divisions versus its Cold War strength of eighteen, the Navy facing the loss of three carrier groups, and the Marine Corps embracing its Marine Expeditionary Force rapid deployment scheme.[22]

Observers had also speculated what if anything could be learned from the Gulf War. The conflict had been such an aberration, some claimed, that little could be gleaned despite the rush of the armed services to produce "lessons learned" from their triumph. Many of these lessons were "self-evident platitudes" that offered nothing new, such as the value of domestic and international legitimacy in the support of use of force, the wonder of PGMs, and the great advantage of American technology, information, and intelligence. The same could be said for weaknesses in the American military machine, such as limited air and sealift capability, slow and disconnected BDA, and the constant problem of friendly fire. To all of the praise for the M1 Abrams tank, various attack helicopters, and stealth aircraft, critics countered that the lack of sustained Iraqi resistance in the form of return fire and maneuver had not truly tested these and other weapons system and equipment. The use of airpower had been massive and effective, but ultimately airpower had not lived up to its strategic billing—it could destroy targets and degrade personnel, but could it cause a government to collapse? Defenders of the air campaign and airpower in general argue that such a question misses the point. The air campaign in the Gulf War had been designed as an integrated component of a campaign to achieve a political objective—the liberation of Kuwait. Still, "victory through airpower" remained elusive. Moreover, the extremely brief war had not fully tested the AVF, nor had it tested the patience and will of the American people. These tests came, however, in the post-9/11 wars in Afghanistan and Iraq. The Gulf War had offered nothing new in learning how to fight a self-sufficient enemy, how to fight a Third World country supported by an industrialized ally, or how to build logistical support from scratch, as Iraq had not been self-sufficient—and had had no Soviet Union or China unlike Vietnam—and the US had already built King Khalid Military City in Saudi Arabia long before the Iraqi invasion of Kuwait. Nor had the Gulf War taught the American military how to fight a competent military foe, as the much-vaunted Iraqi military had turned out to be a paper tiger, commanded by one of the most incompetent and overblown military minds of the twentieth century. For American forces in the Iraq War from 2004 to 2011, the 1990–91 war in the Persian Gulf offered little guidance—nothing on fighting a protracted insurgency, nothing on fighting in population areas, and nothing on how to deal with mounting American casualties.[23]

A Revolution in Military Affairs?

Was the Gulf War, then, an RMA, a transformation realized from innovations in technological, political, and social "landscape" that alters the way one nation-state wars on another? The technological aspect of RMA tempts an affirmative conclusion, though as Thomas A Keaney and

Eliot A. Cohen note, "Technology alone does not a revolution make."[24] The advent of PGMs, satellite imagery, and other technology in the 1970s had led Soviet military leaders to conclude that the destructive capability and decisive potential of conventional weapons was approaching that of nuclear weapons, so much so that Marshal Nikolai V. Ogarkov speculated that war would change dramatically in the very near future and that the United States and the Soviet Union were in the midst of an RMA. The Gulf War, according to proponents of RMA, confirmed that an RMA had indeed occurred. The center of this RMA, however, has been too narrowly focused on the technological wizardry of new weapons and capabilities rather than on a more accurate concentration on the RMA as a "triumph of concepts and doctrine."[25]

The American military that fought the Gulf War had the benefit of not only almost twenty years of technological innovation, but also the great advantage of revolutionary doctrinal change over the same period. The AVF, AirLand Battle, Goldwater–Nichols, and other non-technological changes had certainly contributed to victory in the Gulf War, even though these innovations had been geared exclusively toward a particular enemy—the Soviet Union—rather than the comparatively inferior Iraq. The Gulf War victory, then, may have been more about doctrinal innovation, righting the problems of Vietnam, and, according to Stephen Biddle, force deployment, and how technology interacted with these developments rather than about technology alone.[26]

That this RMA for the United States was due to war with Iraq rather than against the Soviet Union led, according to MacGregor Knox and Williamson Murray, to an "overdetermined" victory in the Gulf War. The world saw up close, in the Gulf War, the fruition of the American RMA, exposing to the world American military technological and fighting prowess. Now that the world knew what the United States could do with its military, the RMA, according to Knox and Murray, had ended, as peer competitors and others began "adaptation, innovation, and strategic and diplomatic realignments aimed at redressing the imbalance so graphically demonstrated" by the Gulf War.[27] The temptation to nevertheless view the Gulf War as a sign of unheralded American power with unfettered technological capabilities to "strike anywhere with force, precision, and relative safety, its enemies electronically confused into submission with little of warfare's normal collateral destruction" persisted through the 1990s. The danger, Steven Metz and James Kievit warned, lay in being overcome by "what American military force could do" rather than in developing a comprehensive national security strategy that determined "what it *should* do."[28]

The issue, then, became whether American military and political leaders realized the RMA in conventional capability had perhaps passed and that a new paradigm shift was in the offing after the Gulf War that has resulted in the current so-called information technology RMA. Or, more accurately perhaps, there has been indeed a single RMA in process since the end of the Vietnam War that was affirmed through the Gulf War, and is still evolving today, as Keith Shimko suggests.[29] The defense establishment seemed to miss the RMA in conventional capability and instead hailed the dawn of a new American way of war, one that promised through technology and network-centric operations an American military decades ahead of its nearest peer competitor (be that China or Russia, for the answer depends upon whom one asks). As the nature of threats against the United States has both increased and broadened to include both state and non-state actors offering symmetrical and asymmetrical challenges to American national security, the American defense establishment has, some critics charge, remained too reliant upon technology rather than focusing on how to effectively use that technology to destroy an enemy.[30] In other words, the substitution of technology for strategy does not a strategy make. According to military historian Brian McAllister Linn, by 2001 "sloganeering replaced substance" in how the United States approached war. Catchy phrases, such as "precision engagement," "shaping the battlespace," and "dominant maneuver," were derived from the Gulf War experience but lacked substantive doctrine and meaning. This resulted, according to Linn, in "doctrinal floundering," especially in the Army.[31]

The social aspect of RMA was also exposed in the Gulf War. Jeremy Black notes that the American reliance upon the AVF, a professional volunteer fighting force, has made controversial what for the World War II generations had been the norm. In their "limited militarism," Americans, if not most peoples of Western nations, are content to let these voluntary warriors fight their wars rather than rely upon outdated notions of "fighting to the end in defense of home and hearth." History, too, plays a role, as memory in American culture dictates that a defeated enemy state accepts defeat, though such was not the case in the American Civil War, the Gulf War, and the Iraq War. As Black suggests, an RMA based upon technological innovation alone does not account for these other social and cultural factors. The RMA debate is ongoing, as it should be if one accepts that the science and art of war is constantly evolving, changing, and developing as if it were a living thing.[32]

War Termination

Perhaps the sharpest criticism and most valuable lesson of the Gulf War centered upon the way the war ended and the difficulty of war termination. Critics charged that the Bush team had no plan for ending the war beyond a clear-cut Iraqi withdrawal from Kuwait. Plans for a long-term settlement to address the causes of the war, assure Saddam's defeat, and secure stability in the Persian Gulf region did not exist. Victory on the battlefield does not translate neatly into peace, as the United States discovered in Iraq in 1991 and again in Iraq in 2003. The United States had encouraged the Kurds and the Shias to rebel, then left them to be slaughtered by Saddam's intact Republican Guard. Saddam's regime did not crumble, as the Bush team assumed it would after having been so weakened by the Gulf War. The failure to destroy the Republican Guard allowed Saddam to use his loyal elite force to both slaughter the Kurds and Shias and to defend his regime. When American forces rumbled through southern Iraq in 2003, the Shias did not welcome them as liberators—their memory proved longer than that of the Americans.[33]

As Bush and his advisors in Washington made the decision to end the war after 100 hours of ground action, they did not have a complete or accurate picture of the battlefield. Nor did Schwarzkopf, for that matter, as his subordinates in the field had not achieved all of their assigned military objectives when the war came to a close and had not informed CENTCOM of their failure to do so as the cease-fire went into effect. The failure surrounding Safwan is a case in point, as was the ill-informed announcement by Schwarzkopf on February 27, 1991, that "the gate is closed." The gate was not closed, nevertheless Bush decided to end the war. Critics claim that Bush should have allowed Schwarzkopf to continue operations until Iraq surrendered unconditionally. Instead, by unilaterally ending the war at an arbitrary 100 hours into the ground phase of DESERT STORM, Bush allowed Saddam to survive, and survive with enough of his military machine intact to re-secure his hold on Iraq and live to fight another day. Indeed, Saddam claimed victory in 1991—he should never have been a position to do so. In the end, expelling Saddam's military forces from Kuwait was a military objective rather than a political one. The political objective should have been to create stability in the Persian Gulf region. Defense analyst Jeffrey Record highlighted this shortcoming of the war: "The Gulf War was a magnificent victory barren of any significant diplomatic gains .... Accordingly, future historians may regard the war as a complete failure."[34]

The Iraqis, however, certainly did their part to make war appear so one-sided. They had underestimated the effectiveness and destructive capability of American and Coalition airpower and had ill-conceived perceptions that led to deluded conclusions about the strategic and operational limitations of American and Coalition imagination in planning and carrying out a ground campaign. They completely misinterpreted the American will to fight. In their defense, the Iraqis had few strategic choices. The obvious and most advantageous long-term choice was simply to not fight for Kuwait. Having called the bluff, however, the hundreds of thousands of Iraqi soldiers who did not desert remained in their positions to fight. The decision to fight, though, exposed their lack of tactical, operational, and strategic ability. If ever there was a case in which military capability drove tactical choice, perhaps Iraq's decision to fight the way it did could be it. Realizing this, the Iraqi high command chose to use Iraqi forces in the only way that they could be used—in static entrenched defensive positions with no expectation of maneuver. When forced to maneuver by American and Coalition ground forces, they were destroyed. That they did manage to save such a large portion of their fielded force, including the Republican Guard, from complete annihilation, though, begs some credit to the Iraqi high command. Saving those forces, too, gave Saddam the force he needed to brutally crush the post-war Shia and Kurdish rebellions.[35]

An Imperfect War

A victorious President Bush had told the US Congress after the war, "Now, we can see a new world coming into view. A world in which there is the very real prospect of a new world order."[36] That much hoped-for world, one that could put behind the unprecedented tensions of the Cold War and embraced collective security, peace, and economic prosperity under the multilateral leadership of a sole superpower, the United States, did not, unfortunately, come to pass. The end of the Cold War ended an international order in which confrontation between the Soviet Union and the United States largely overshadowed and contained regional tensions and long-simmering ethnic hostility. The removal of that controlling lid allowed these tensions to boil over. Few should have been surprised by the increase in civil wars, regional rivalry, and ethnic struggles, because these conflicts had already increased and become more brazen as the Cold War dynamic evolved in the 1970s and 1980s. The Iran–Iraq War and Saddam's invasion of Kuwait, among other conflicts, testified to this trend continuing beyond the Cold War. By the 1990s, these conflicts presented the greatest threat to global political and economic stability, as the world order may have been new but the tradition of using war as the continuation of politics by other means remained. Now, in the post-9/11 world, warfare includes much greater use of asymmetrical means, such as terrorism, the threat of NBC warfare by non-state actors, and other types of "small wars" where even the most advanced and powerful military in world history potentially can have limited if not minimal impact.

Like World War II before it, the Gulf War may well indeed have been an aberration, in this case a perfect "storm" of circumstances, technology, leadership, and context that allowed for one of the most unique, one-sided conflicts in modern history but that nevertheless offered grave testament to the challenges of post-conflict resolution. It may well have banished the ghosts of Vietnam by bringing together, as Harry Summers suggests, the Clausewitzian trinity of people, government, and military in 1991 that had eluded the United States from 1965 through 1973.[37] At the very least, however, if it offers any consistency with conflict before and since, the Gulf War was an imperfect war.

Chronology

1916	British- and French-supported Arab Revolt against Ottoman rule begins
1920	New state of Iraq becomes British-mandated territory
1921	Great Britain establishes Kingdom of Iraq
1922	Treaty of Uqair establishes Kuwait's borders with Saudi Arabia and Iraq
1932	Great Britain gives Kingdom of Iraq its independence
1958	
July 14	Republic of Iraq established after overthrow of King
1961	Great Britain grants Kingdom of Kuwait independence
1968	Ba'athists overthrow Abdul Rahman Arif and take power in Iraq
1969	Nixon "Twin Pillars" Doctrine establishes Iran and Saudi Arabia as the "pillars" of US policy in the Middle East
1979	
January 16	Shah of Iran overthrown by Islamic Revolution forces loyal to Ayatollah Khomeini
July 17	Saddam Hussein becomes President of Republic of Iraq
December 27	Soviet Union invades Afghanistan
1980	
January	Carter Doctrine states United Sates will protect Persian Gulf region, with force if necessary
September	Iran–Iraq War begins
1988	
August 20	Cease-fire ends fighting in Iran–Iraq War
1990	
July 10	Kuwaiti and Iraqi representatives meet in Jeddah without reaching agreement

July 25	US Ambassador April Glaspie meets personally with Saddam
July 15	Saddam orders Iraqi forces to mass near Kuwaiti border
August 2	Iraqi forces invade Kuwait
August 2	UN Security Council passes Resolution 660, condemning the Iraqi invasion and demanding Iraq withdraw from Kuwait
August 6	UN Security Council passes Resolution 661, establishing embargo against Iraq
August 8	Saddam announces annexation of Kuwait at the 19th Province of the Republic of Iraq
August 8	DESERT SHIELD to protect Saudi Arabia from possible Iraqi invasion begins
August 10	Twelve of the Arab League's twenty members vote to support UN Resolution 661 and participate in US-led Coalition to enforce embargo against Iraq
August 12	United States rejects Iraqi offer to withdraw from Kuwait in exchange for Syrian withdrawal from Lebanon and Israeli withdrawal from occupied territories
August 16	Naval blockade of Iraq begins
August 25	UN Security Council votes to allow use force to maintain embargo against Iraq
October 14	Soviet Union fails to negotiate Iraqi withdrawal from Kuwait
November 8	President Bush announces deployment of 200,000 additional American troops to Middle East to give Coalition forces "offensive option"
November 29	UN Security Council passes Resolution 678, authorizing military action to force Iraq to withdraw from Kuwait and sets January 15, 1991, as the deadline for Iraqi withdrawal
December 6	Saddam releases all foreign hostages
1991	
January 9	U.S. Secretary of State James Baker meets with Iraqi Foreign Minister Tariq Aziz in Geneva but reach no agreement
January 12	Congressional debate to support military action against Iraq concludes with Senate voting 52-47 and the House voting 250-183 to grant President Bush authority to use military force
January 15	UN deadline for Iraqi withdrawal from Kuwait passes with no Iraqi action
January 17	DESERT STORM begins with air and missile attacks against Baghdad and Iraqi forces along Saudi and Kuwaiti borders
January 18	Iraq launches SCUD missile attacks against Israel

January 25	Saddam orders Iraqi forces to open oil pipelines near Persian Gulf, dumping thousands of barrels of crude oil into the gulf
January 30	Battle of Khafji
February 15	President Bush rejects Iraqi proposal for conditional withdrawal from Kuwait
February 22	President Bush sets deadline of 2000 hours local time February 23 for Iraqi withdrawal from Kuwait—failure to comply will initiate ground war
February 24	Ground phase of DESERT STORM begins
February 26	Saddam announces Iraqi forces will withdraw from Kuwait
February 27	Iraq accepts UN Security Council resolutions
March 3	Coalition and Iraqi commanders agree to cease-fire at Safwan
March 7	Protests against Saddam breakout in several Iraqi cities
March 14	Emir of Kuwait returns to Kuwait City
April 2	Iraqi forces suppress Kurdish uprisings
April 2	UN Security Council passes Resolution 687, ending military action against Iraq and removing sanctions so long as Iraq accepts and abides punitive conditions
April 6	Iraq agrees to conditions outlined in UN Security Council Resolution 687
1992	
August 27	US and Coalition forces begin Operation SOUTHERN WATCH to enforce UN-sanctioned no-fly zone over southern Iraq; SOUTHERN WATCH ends in 2003 with US invasion of Iraq
1997	
January 1	US and Coalition forces begin Operation NORTHERN WATCH to enforce UN-sanctioned no-fly zone over northern Iraq; NORTHERN WATCH ends in 2003 with US invasion of Iraq
2003	
March 20– April 30	US and British forces invade and occupy Iraq as part of the War on Terror in response to terrorist attacks against the United States on September 11, 2001
December 13	US forces capture Saddam near Tikrit
2006	
November 5	Iraqi court convicts Saddam of crimes against humanity and sentences the former Iraqi leader to death by hanging
December 30	Iraqi authorities execute Saddam at an Iraqi Army base near Baghdad
2011	
October 21	President Barack Obama orders complete withdrawal of remaining American forces in Iraq by end of 2011

Notes

Preface

1. For simplicity, "Gulf War" rather than "Persian Gulf War" will be used throughout.

1 Inventing the Middle East and Iraq

1. Vernon O. Egger, *A History of the Muslim World to 1405: The Making of a Civilization* (Upper Saddle River, NJ: Prentice Hall, 2004), 62–171; Terry H. Anderson, *Bush's Wars* (New York: Oxford University Press, 2011), 3–6; Vali Nasr, *The Shia Revival: How Conflicts within Islam Will Reshape the Future* (New York: Norton, 2006), 31–63, 185–250.
2. Clayton R. Koppes, "Captain Mahan, General Gordon, and the Origins of the Term 'Middle East,'" *Middle Eastern Studies* 12: 1 (January 1976): 95–98; Roger Adelson, *London and the Invention of the Middle East: Money, Power, and War, 1902–1922* (New Haven: Yale University Press, 1995), 22–23.
3. David Fromkin, *A Peace to End All Peace: Creating the Modern Middle East, 1914–1922* (New York: Henry Holt and Company, 1989), 146–49.
4. Ibid., 173–78.
5. Ibid., 168–72, 184.
6. See T.E. Lawrence, *Revolt in the Desert* (Garden City, NY: Doubleday, Doran, and Company, 1928) and *Seven Pillars of Wisdom: A Triumph* (Garden City, NY: Doubleday, Doran, and Company, 1935); and James Barr, *Setting the Desert on Fire: T.E. Lawrence and Britain's Secret War in Arabia, 1916–1918* (New York: W.W. Norton, 2008).
7. Fromkin, *A Peace to End All Peace*, 188–96.
8. Michael B. Oren, *Power, Faith, and Fantasy: America in the Middle East, 1776 to the Present* (New York: Norton, 2007), 355–66. See also Jonathan Schneer, *The Balfour Declaration: The Origins of the Arab-Israeli Conflict* (New York: Random House, 2010).

9. Schneer, *The Balfour Declaration*, 365–73; Fromkin, *A Peace to End All Peace*, 403, *passim*.

10. Christopher Catherwood, *Churchill's Folly: How Winston Churchill Created Modern Iraq* (New York: Carroll and Graf, 2004), 140–43; Anderson, *Bush's Wars*, 12. See also Charles Townshend, *When God Made Hell: The British Invasion of Mesopotamia and the Creation of Iraq, 1914–1921* (London: Faber and Faber, 2010).

11. Erik J. Dahl, "Naval Innovation: From Cola to Oil," *Joint Forces Quarterly* (Winter 2000–2001): 50–57; Courtney Hunt, *The History of Modern Iraq* (Westport, Connecticut: Greenwood Press, 2005), 64–65.

12. Hala Fattah, with Frank Caso, *A Brief History of Iraq* (New York: Checkmark Books, 2009), 170–71.

13. See Sean McMeekin, *The Berlin-Baghdad Express: The Ottoman Empire and Germany's Bid for World Power* (Cambridge: Harvard University Press, 2010).

14. Anderson, *Bush's Wars*, 8–9; J. E. Peterson, "Britain and the Gulf: At the Periphery of Empire," in Lawrence G. Potter, ed., *The Persian Gulf in History* (New York: Palgrave Macmillan, 2009), 277–94.

15. Fattah, *A Brief History of Iraq*, 174–75.

16. Reeva S. Simon, *Iraq between the Two World Wars: The Creation and Implementation of a Nationalist Ideology* (New York: Columbia University Press, 1986); Hunt, *The History of Modern Iraq*, 70.

17. Fattah, *A Brief History of Iraq*, 176–77; Hunt, *The History of Modern Iraq*, 70–71; Simon, *Iraq between the Two World Wars*, 145–65; see also Robert Lyman, *Iraq 1941: The Battles for Basra, Habbaniya, Fallujah, and Baghdad* (New York: Osprey, 2005).

18. Charles Tripp, *A History of Iraq*, 3rd ed. (Cambridge: Cambridge University Press, 2007), 111–19; Hunt, *The History of Modern Iraq*, 74.

19. Kenneth M. Pollack, *Arabs at War: Military Effectiveness, 1948–1991* (Lincoln: University of Nebraska Press, 2002), 149–55.

20. Tripp, *A History of Iraq*, 115–23; Charles Tripp, "Iraq and the 1948 War: Mirror of Iraq's Disorder," in Eugene L. Rogan and Avi Shlaim, *The War for Palestine: Rewriting the History of 1948* (Cambridge: Cambridge University Press, 2001), 125–50; Pollack, *Arabs at War*, 148–55.

21. Oren, *Power, Faith, and Fantasy*, 491; Ilan Pappé, *The Making of the Arab-Israeli Conflict, 1947–1951* (London: I.B. Tauris, 2006), 25–26.

22. Memorandum of Conversation, by Counselor of Embassy in Iraq (Ireland), August 20, 1953, *Foreign Relations of the United States, 1952–1954, Vol. IX, The Near and Middle East, Part 2* (Washington, DC: Government Printing Office, 1986), 2352–54.

23. Elie Podeh, *The Quest for Hegemony in the Arab World: The Struggle over the Baghdad Pact* (New York: Brill, 1995), 61–63.

24. Ibid., 118–25; Geoff Simons, *Iraq: From Sumer to Saddam* (New York: St. Martin's Press, 1994), 210–14; Pact of Mutual Cooperation between Iraq

and Turkey, February 23, 1955, in United Nations, *Treaty Series*, Vol. 233 (1956), 199–217. The Baghdad Pact became known as the Central Treaty Organization and remained in effect until 1979; Iraq withdrew from the alliance in 1959.

25. Oren, *Power, Faith, and Fantasy*, 508–14.
26. Special National Intelligence Estimate, Nasser and the Middle East Situation, July 31, 1956, *Foreign Relations of the United States, 1955–1957, Volume VXI: Suez Crisis, July 26–December 31, 1956* (Washington, DC: Government Printing Office), 78–93; Oren, *Power, Faith, and Fantasy*, 514–16; Vernon O. Egger, *A History of the Muslim World since 1260: The Making of a Global Community* (Upper Saddle River, NJ: Pearson Prentice Hall, 2008), 439–41. See also David A. Nichols, *Eisenhower 1956: The President's Year of Crisis—Suez and the Brink of War* (New York: Simon and Schuster, 2011).
27. Oren, *Power, Faith, and Fantasy*, 510–12. See also Stephen Kinzer, *All the Shah's Men: An American Coup and the Roots of Middle East Terror* (Hoboken, NJ: John Wiley and Sons, 2004).
28. Simons, *Iraq*, 216–17; Kinzer, *All the Shah's Men*, 211–15.

2   Republican Iraq and the Rise of Saddam Hussein

1. Charles Tripp, *A History of Iraq*, 3rd ed. (Cambridge: Cambridge University Press, 2007), 140–41.
2. Paper Prepared by the National Security Council Planning Board, Issues Arising Out of the Situation in the Near East, July 29, 1958, *Foreign Relations of the United States, 1958–1960, Volume XII: Near East Region; Iraq; Iran; Arabian Peninsula* (Washington, DC: Government Printing Office, 1993), 114–24; Geoff Simons, *Iraq: From Sumer to Saddam* (New York: St. Martin's Press, 1994), 217–19.
3. Tripp, *A History of Iraq*, 146–48; Simons, *Iraq*, 221–22.
4. Courtney Hunt, *The History of Modern Iraq* (Westport, Connecticut: Greenwood Press, 2005), 79–80; Tripp, *A History of Iraq*, 15–53; Terry H. Anderson, *Bush's Wars* (New York: Oxford University Press, 2011), 16.
5. Anderson, *Bush's Wars*, 19–20; Roger Hilsman, *George Bush vs. Saddam Hussein: Military Success! Political Failure?* (Novato, CA: Lyford Books, 1992), 7–9.
6. Anderson, *Bush's Wars*, 15–16.
7. Tripp, *A History of Iraq*, 160–61.
8. Simons, *Iraq*, 223–25; Tripp, *A History of Iraq*, 159–60; Anderson, *Bush's Wars*, 16.
9. Anderson, *Bush's Wars*, 17.
10. Kenneth M. Pollack, *Arabs at War: Military Effectiveness, 1948–1991* (Lincoln, NE: University of Nebraska Press, 2002), 167; Anderson, *Bush's Wars*, 18. See also Michael B. Oren, *Six Days of War: June 1967 and*

the Making of the Modern Middle East (New York: Oxford University Press, 2002).

11. Tripp, *A History of Iraq*, 178–85.

12. Hilsman, *George Bush vs. Saddam Hussein*, 10–13.

13. Hunt, *The History of Modern Iraq*, 85–87; Tripp, *A History of Iraq*, 186–206.

14. Pollack, *Arabs at War*, 166–76.

15. Simons, *Iraq*, 245–49.

16. Ibid., 246–50.

17. Rob Johnson, *The Iran-Iraq War* (New York: Palgrave Macmillan, 2011), 92; Anderson, *Bush's Wars*, 26–27.

18. William R. Polk, *Understanding Iraq* (New York: Harper Collins, 2005), 125–28; Simons, *Iraq*, 253–54; Tripp, *A History of Iraq*, 215–18.

19. Stephen C. Pelletiere, *The Iran-Iraq War: Chaos in a Vacuum* (Westport, CT: Praeger, 1992), 13–15.

20. Ibid., 16–18.

21. Dilip Hiro, *The Longest War: The Iran-Iraq Military Conflict* (New York: Routledge, 1991), 34–36.

22. Stephen Kinzer, "Inside Iran's Fury: Scholars Trace the Nation's Antagonism to Its History of Domination by Foreign Powers," *Smithsonian* 29: 7 (October 2008): 60–70; Hiro, *The Longest War*, 38.

23. Johnson, *The Iran-Iraq War*, 44–45; Hal Brands, "Why Did Saddam Invade Iran? New Evidence on Motives, Complexity, and the Israel Facto," *Journal of Military History* 75 (July 2011): 861–85.

24. Sharam Chubin, "Reflections on the Gulf War," *Survival* (July–August 1986): 308, quoted in Hiro, *The Longest War*, 39.

25. Hiro, *The Longest War*, 37–39; Johnson, *The Iran-Iraq War*, 43.

26. Pelletiere, *The Iran-Iraq War*, 43–45; Hiro, *The Longest War*, 38.

27. Efraim Karsh, *The Iran-Iraq War, 1980–1988* (Oxford: Osprey, 2002), 16–21; Hiro, *The Longest War*, 297, 299.

28. The State of the Union: Addressed Delivered before a Joint Session of Congress, January 23, 1980, *Public Papers of the Presidents of the United States: Jimmy Carter, 1980–81, Book I* (Washington, DC: Government Printing Office, 1981), 197.

29. Presidential Directive/NSC 63, 15 January 1981, Jimmy Carter Library and Museum, http://www.jimmycarterlibrary.gov/documents/pddirectives/pd63.pdf, accessed June 8, 2011; Zbigniew Brzezinski, *Power and Principal: Memoirs of the National Security Advisor, 1977–1981* (New York: Farrar, Straus, and Giroux, 1983), 443–45; Janet A. McDonnell, *After Desert Storm: The U.S. Army and the Reconstruction of Kuwait* (Washington, DC: Department of the Army, 1999), 5.

30. Polk, *Understanding Iraq*, 131–30; Karsh, *The Iran-Iraq War*, 50–51.

31. Karsh, *The Iran-Iraq War*, 53–55.

32. Johnson, *The Iran-Iraq War*, 192–93.

33. Karsh, *The Iran-Iraq War*, 89; Hiro, *The Longest War*, 250–51.
34. Steve A. Yetiv, *The Persian Gulf Crisis* (Westport, CT: Greenwood Press, 1997), 5–8; Pelletiere, *The Iran-Iraq War*, 151–53.

3   The Iraqi Invasion of Kuwait

1. Lawrence Freedman and Efraim Karsh, *The Gulf Conflict, 1990–1991: Diplomacy and War in the New World Order* (Princeton: Princeton University Press, 1993), 45–47.
2. Terry H. Anderson, *Bush's Wars* (New York: Oxford University Press, 2011), 33; Freedman and Karsh, *The Gulf Conflict*, 47–49.
3. Alastair Finlan, *The Gulf War 1991* (Oxford: Osprey, 2003), 25–26.
4. Freedman and Karsh, *The Gulf Conflict*, 50–51; Finlan, *The Gulf War 1991*, 26.
5. "Confrontation in the Gulf: Excerpts from Iraqi Document on Meeting with U.S. Envoy," *New York Times* (September 23, 1990): A19.
6. Position Paper: Heightened Tensions between Iraq–Kuwait–UAE, July 25, 1990, Digital National Security Archive.
7. Bob Woodward, *The Commanders* (New York: Simon and Schuster, 1991), 212–13; Freedman and Karsh, *The Gulf Conflict*, 48–49, 108–09.
8. Colin Powell, with Joseph E. Perisco, *My American Journey* (New York: Random House, 1995), 464–66.
9. Woodward, *The Commanders*, 54–55.
10. Ibid., 205–21.
11. Finlan, *The Gulf War 1991*, 26; Freedman and Karsh, *The Gulf Conflict*, 58–61.
12. Finlan, *The Gulf War 1991*, 26; Freedman and Karsh, *The Gulf Conflict*, 67.
13. Rodney P. Carlisle, *Persian Gulf War* (New York: Facts on File, 2003), 102–03.
14. Ibid., 46–47; Jean P. Sasson, *The Rape of Kuwait: The True Story of Iraqi Atrocities against a Civilian Population* (New York: Knightsbridge Publishing, 1991).
15. Statement by Deputy Press Secretary Popaduik on the Iraqi Invasion of Kuwait, August 1, 1990, *Public Papers of the Presidents of the United States: George Bush, 1990, Book II—July 1 to December 31, 1990* (Washington, DC: Government Printing Office, 1991), 1082; Statement by Deputy Press Secretary Popaduik on the Iraqi Invasion of Kuwait, August 2, 1990, *Public Papers of the Presidents of the United States: George Bush, Book II*, 1083; Security Council resolution condemning Iraq's invasion of Kuwait, demanding the immediate and unconditional withdrawal of Iraqi forces and calling for negotiations for a peaceful resolution of their differences, S/RES/660 (1990), 2 August 1990, United Nations Department of Public Information, *The United Nations and the Iraq-Kuwait Conflict, 1990–1996* (New York: United Nations Department

of Public Information, 1996), 167; Security Council resolution imposing mandatory economic sanctions against Iraq and establishing a committee to monitor those sanctions, S/RES/661 (1990), 6 August 1990, The United Nations Department of Public Information, *The United Nations and the Iraq-Kuwait Conflict*, 168–69. Both Cuba and Yemen abstained in the vote on Resolution 661, resulting in a 13-0 vote in favor of the resolution.

16. Remarks and a Question-and-Answer Session with Reporters in Aspen, Colorado, Following a Meeting with Prime Minister Margaret Thatcher of the United Kingdom, August 2, 1990, *Public Papers of the Presidents of the United States: George Bush, Book II*, 1085–88; Remarks and Exchange with Reporters on the Iraqi Invasion of Kuwait, August 5, 1990, *Public Papers of the Presidents of the United States: George Bush, Book II*, 1100–02.

17. Joe Hyams, *Flight of the Avenger: George Bush at War* (New York: Harcourt, Brace, Jovanovich, 1991).

18. Timothy Naftali, *George H. W. Bush* (New York: Henry Holt, 2007), 5–64.

19. The Gang of Eight included Vice President Dan Quayle, Secretary of State James Baker, White House Chief of Staff John Sununu, National Security Advisor Brent Scowcroft, Secretary of Defense Dick Cheney, Chairman of the Joint Chiefs of Staff Colin Powell, Undersecretary of Defense Robert Gates, and to make eight, President Bush himself.

20. Steve A. Yetiv, *The Persian Gulf Crisis* (Westport, CT: Greenwood Press, 1997), 10–13.

21. Anderson, *Bush's Wars*, 77–81.

22. Remarks and an Exchange with Reporters on the Iraqi Invasion of Kuwait, August 5, 1990, *Public Papers of the Presidents of the United States: George Bush, Book II*, 1100–02.

23. Yetiv, *The Persian Gulf Crisis*, 13–15; Carlisle, *Persian Gulf War*, 50–51.

24. Address to the Nation Announcing the Deployment of United States Armed Forces to Saudi Arabia, August 8, 1990, *Public Papers of the Presidents of the United States: George Bush, Book II*, 1107–09.

25. Colin Powell, with Joseph E. Perisco, *My American Journey* (New York: Random House, 1995), 466–67.

26. Woodward, *The Commanders*, 219–21.

27. Frank N. Schubert and Theresa L. Kraus, General Editors, *The Whirlwind War: The United States Army in Operations DESERT SHIELD and DESERT STORM* (Washington, DC: US Army Center of Military History, 1995), 48–50; Finlan, *The Gulf War 1991*, 2.

28. Finlan, *The Gulf War 1991*, 29.

29. See, for example, Andrew Krepinevich, *The Army and Vietnam* (Baltimore: Johns Hopkins University Press, 1986); Guenter Lewy, *America in Vietnam* (New York: Oxford University Press, 1978); Bernard Rostker, *"I Want You!": The Evolution of the All-Volunteer Force* (Santa Monica, CA: RAND, 2006).

30. See, for example, David R. Segal, *Recruiting for Uncle Sam: Citizenship and Military Manpower Policy* (Lawrence: University Press of Kansas, 1989).

31. United States Department of the Army, FM 100-5 Operations (Washington, DC: Department of the Army, 1986); Schubert and Kraus, *The Whirlwind War*, 25–28; Brian McAllister Linn, *The Echo of Battle: The Army's Way of War* (Cambridge: Harvard University Press, 2007), 209–11. See also Douglas W. Skinner, *AirLand Battle Doctrine* (Alexandria, VA: Center for Naval Analyses, 1988).

32. Carl von Clausewitz, *On War*, edited and translated by Michael Howard and Peter Paret; introductory essays by Peter Paret, Michael Howard, and Bernard Brodie; commentary by Bernard Brodie (Princeton: Princeton University Press, 1975); Powell, *My American Journey*, 207–08; Hew Strachan, *Clausewitz's on War: A Biography* (New York: Atlantic Monthly Press, 2007), 1–3.

33. Strachan, *Clausewitz's on War*, 17–19; MacGregor Knox and Williamson Murray, *The Dynamics of Military Revolution, 1300–2050* (Cambridge: Cambridge University Press, 2001), 190–92.

34. Linn, *The Echo of Battle*, 5–9.

35. Richard W. Stewart, ed., *American Military History*, Volume II, 2nd ed. (Washington, DC: US Army Center of Military History, 2010), 406; James R. Locher, *Victory on the Potomac: The Goldwater–Nichols Act Unifies the Pentagon* (College Station, TX: Texas A&M University Press, 2002).

36. Adrian R. Lewis, *The American Culture of War* (New York: Routledge, 2007), 310–15.

37. These unified joint commands included Pacific Command (PACOM), Atlantic Command (LANTCOM), European Command (EUCOM), Southern Command (SOUTHCOM), and Central Command (CENTCOM), plus Space Command (SPACECOM), Special Operations Command (SOCOM), and Transportation Command (TRANSCOM). Strategic Air Command (SAC) and Forces Command (FORSCOM) remained as specified commands.

38. Woodward, *The Commanders*, 209; Roger Cohen and Claudio Gatti, *In the Eye of the Storm: The Life of General H. Norman Schwarzkopf* (New York: Farrar, Straus, and Giroux, 1991), 41–178.

39. Schubert and Kraus, *The Whirlwind War*, 43–44.

40. Ibid., 252–69.

41. Casper W. Weinberger, "The Uses of Military Power" (Washington, DC: National Press Club, November 28, 1984).

42. Colin L. Powell, "U.S. Forces: Challenges Ahead," *Foreign Affairs* (Winter 1992/93): 32–45; Heiko Meiertöns, *The Doctrines of U.S. Security Policy: An Evaluation under International Law* (Cambridge: Cambridge University Press, 2010), 174–76; Strachan, *Clausewitz's on War*, 178.

43. Lewis, *The American Culture of War*, 309–10; Kenneth J. Campbell, "Once Burned, Twice Cautious: Explaining the Weinberger-Powell Doctrine," *Armed Forces & Society* 24: 3 (Spring 1998): 357–74.

4   Building DESERT SHIELD

1. Gary R. Hess, *Presidential Decisions for War: Korea, Vietnam, and the Persian Gulf* (Baltimore: Johns Hopkins University Press, 2001), 162.
2. Lawrence Freedman and Efraim Karsh, *The Gulf Conflict, 1990–1991: Diplomacy and War in the New World Order* (Princeton: Princeton University Press, 1993), 114–18.
3. Hess, *Presidential Decisions for War*, 170.
4. Freedman and Karsh, *The Gulf Conflict, 1990–1991*, 120–25.
5. Rodney P. Carlisle, *Persian Gulf War* (New York: Facts on File, 2003), 57.
6. See James Baker, *The Politics of Diplomacy: Revolution, War and Peace, 1989–1992* (New York: Putnam, 1995), for Baker's recounting of his role as Secretary of State during the Persian Gulf Crisis.
7. Carlisle, *Persian Gulf War*, 57–58.
8. Baker, *The Politics of Diplomacy*, 287–99.
9. Carlisle, *Persian Gulf War*, 58–60.
10. Security Council resolution deciding that the annexation of Kuwait by Iraq under any form is considered null and void, S/RES/662 (1990), 9 August 1990, United Nations Department of Public Information, *The United Nations and the Iraq-Kuwait Conflict, 1990–1996* (New York: United Nations Department of Public Information, 1996), 169.
11. Hess, *Presidential Decisions for War*, 170–72; Security Council resolution demanding that Iraq permit the departure of third-State nationals from Kuwait and Iraq, S/RES/664 (1990), 18 August 1990, United Nations Department of Public Information, *The United Nations and the Iraq-Kuwait Conflict*, 171; Remarks at the Annual Conference of the Veterans of Foreign Wars in Baltimore, Maryland, 20 August 1990, George Bush Presidential Library and Museum, Public Papers, 1990, http://bushlibrary.tamu.edu/research/public_papers.php?id=2171& year=1990&month=8, accessed June 20, 2011.
12. Freedman and Karsh, *The Gulf Conflict*, 160–61.
13. Security Council resolution expanding the sanctions against Iraq and authorizing maritime forces to take "commensurate" measures to ensure strict compliance, S/RES/665 (1990), 25 August 1990, United Nations Department of Public Information, *The United Nations and the Iraq-Kuwait Conflict*, 171–72; Freedman and Karsh, *The Gulf Conflict*, 146–50, 175–79; Hess, *Presidential Decisions for War*, 176–77.
14. Freedman and Karsh, *The Gulf Conflict*, 157–59, 166–72; Mark Grossman, *Encyclopedia of the Persian Gulf War* (Oxford: ABC-CLIO, 1995), 171.
15. Hess, *Presidential Decisions for War*, 175.

16. Freedman and Karsh, *The Gulf Conflict*, 156–57, 172–75.
17. Ibid., 161–62.
18. Ibid., 180–88.
19. Ibid., *The Gulf Conflict*, 189–98.

5   Moving to the Offensive

1. Rodney P. Carlisle, *Persian Gulf War* (New York: Facts on File, 2003), 58–61.
2. See *Dellums v. Bush*, 752 F. Supp. 1141 (1990).
3. Gary R. Hess, *Presidential Decisions for War: Korea, Vietnam, and the Persian Gulf* (Baltimore: Johns Hopkins University Press, 2001), 174, 177–80.
4. James Baker, *The Politics of Diplomacy: Revolution, War and Peace, 1989–1992* (New York: Putnam, 1995), 325–26.
5. Ibid., 326.
6. Hess, *Presidential Decisions for War*, 181–83; Lawrence Freedman and Efraim Karsh, *The Gulf Conflict, 1990–1991: Diplomacy and War in the New World Order* (Princeton: Princeton University Press, 1993), 232–34; Baker, *The Politics of Diplomacy*, 326–28; Security Council resolution authorizing Member States cooperating with the Government of Kuwait to use "all necessary means to uphold and implement" the Council's resolutions on the situation unless Iraq fully complies with those resolutions on or before 15 January 1991, S/RES/678 (1990), 29 November 1990, *The United Nations and the Iraq-Kuwait Conflict*, 178.
7. The President's News Conference, November 11, 1990, George Bush Presidential Library and Museum, Public Papers, 1990, http://bushlibrary.tamu.edu/research/public_papers.php?id=2516&year=1990&month=11, accessed June 20, 2011.
8. Baker, *The Politics of Diplomacy*, 346.
9. Freedman and Karsh, *The Gulf Conflict*, 234–39.
10. Ibid., 241–42; Hess, *Presidential Decisions for War*, 186–87.
11. Hess, *Presidential Decisions for War*, 188; Baker, *The Politics of Diplomacy*, 347–54.
12. Ibid., 356.
13. For the full text of the letter, see Statement by Press Secretary Fitzwater on President Bush's Letter to President Saddam Hussein of Iraq, January 12, 1991, Bush Papers, 1991, George Bush Presidential Library and Museum, http://bushlibrary.tamu.edu/research/public_papers.php?id=2617&year=1991&month=1, accessed June 20, 2011.
14. Baker, *The Politics of Diplomacy*, 357–65; Hess, *Presidential Decisions for War*, 189–90.
15. George Bush and Brent Scowcroft, *A World Transformed* (New York: Random House, 1998), 443.

16. The President's News Conference on the Persian Gulf Crisis, January 9, 1990, Bush Papers, 1990, George Bush Presidential Library and Museum, http://bushlibrary.tamu.edu/research/public_papers.php?id=2605&year=1991&month=1, accessed June 28, 2011.

17. Colin Powell, with Joseph Persico, *My American Journey* (New York: Ballantine, 1995), 502.

18. Letter to Congressional Leaders on the Persian Gulf Crisis, August 8, 1991, Bush Papers, 1991, George Bush Presidential Library and Museum, http://bushlibrary.tamu.edu/research/public_papers.php?id=2599&year=1991&month=1, accessed June 23, 2011.

19. The President's News Conference on the Persian Gulf Crisis, January 9, 1991, Bush Papers, 1991, George Bush Presidential Library and Museum, http://bushlibrary.tamu.edu/research/public_papers.php?id=2605&year=1991&month=1, accessed June 28, 2011.

20. "Build-up to War: American Opinion on Events in the Persian Gulf, January 1991," *The Gallup Poll Monthly*, No. 304 (January 1991): 2–35.

21. For a discussion of this testimony and Kuwait propaganda effort in the United States, see John R. McArthur, *Second Front: Censorship and Propaganda in the 1991 Gulf War* (New York: Hill and Wang, 1992).

22. Hess, *Presidential Decisions for War*, 184.

23. Ibid., 191.

24. Ibid.

25. "Give the Sanctions Time to Work," House of Representatives, January 10, 1991, *Congressional Record*, 102nd Congress (1991–1992), H116, http://thomas.loc.gov/, accessed June 10, 2011.

26. "The Persian Gulf Crisis," House of Representatives, January 10, 1991, *Congressional Record*, 102nd Congress (1991–1992), H124, http://thomas.loc.gov/, accessed June 10, 2011.

27. "There's No Need to Rush to War," House of Representatives, January 10, 1991, *Congressional Record*, 102nd Congress (1991–1992), H174, http://thomas.loc.gov/, accessed June 10, 2011.

28. "It's Time for Congress to Force a Pause in America's Slide toward War," House of Representatives, January 10, 1991, *Congressional Record*, 102nd Congress (1991–1992), H116, http://thomas.loc.gov/, accessed June 10, 2011.

29. "The Situation in the Middle East," House of Representatives, January 10, 1991, *Congressional Record*, 102nd Congress (1991–1992), H244, http://thomas.loc.gov/, accessed June 10, 2011.

30. "Why I Will Vote with the President's Resolution on the Persian Gulf," House of Representatives, January 10, 1991, *Congressional Record*, 102nd Congress (1991–1992), H179, http://thomas.loc.gov/, accessed June 10, 2011.

31. Hess, *Presidential Decisions for War*, 192–93.

32. "The Persian Gulf," Senate, January 10, 1991, *Congressional Record*, 102nd Congress (1991–1992), S101, http://thomas.loc/gov, accessed June 12, 2011.
33. Ibid., S103, http://thomas.loc/gov, accessed June 12, 2011.
34. "Authorizing Use of U.S. Armed Forces Pursuant to U.N. Resolution," Senate, January 12, 1991, *Congressional Record*, 102nd Congress (1991–1992), S396, http://thomas.loc/gov, accessed June 12, 2011.
35. "War Means Death and Destruction," Senate, January 10, 1991, *Congressional Record*, 102nd Congress (1991–1992), S113, http://thomas.loc/gov, accessed June 12, 2011.
36. Ibid., S141, http://thomas.loc/gov, accessed June 12, 2011.
37. "Authorizing Use of U.S. Armed Forces Pursuant to U.N. Resolution," Senate, January 12, 1991, *Congressional Record*, 102nd Congress (1991–1992), S391, http://thomas.loc/gov, accessed June 12, 2011.
38. "The Situation in the Middle East," House of Representatives, January 12, 1991, *Congressional Record*, 102nd Congress (1991–1992), H484–85, http://thomas.loc/gov, accessed June 12, 2011.
39. "Authorizing Use of U.S. Armed Forces Pursuant to U.N. Resolution," Senate, January 12, 1991, *Congressional Record*, 102nd Congress (1991–1992), S403, http://thomas.loc/gov, accessed June 12, 2011.
40. "To Authorize the Use of United States Armed Forces Pursuant to United Nations Security Council Resolution 678," H.J. Res. 77 and S.J. Res. 2, August 12, 1990, 102nd Congress (1991–1992), http://thomas.loc/gov, accessed June 12, 2011.
41. "The President's News Conference," January 12, 1991, Bush Papers, 1991, George Bush Presidential Library and Museum, http://bushlibrary.tamu.edu/research/public_papers.php?id=2616&year=1991&month=01, accessed June 28, 2011.
42. Bush and Scowcroft, *A World Transformed*, 446.
43. Freedman and Karsh, *The Gulf Conflict*, 268–70.
44. Statement by the Secretary-General to the press on 15 January 1991, S/22091, 17 January 1991, *The United Nations and the Iraq-Kuwait Conflict*, 179–80.
45. Freedman and Karsh, *The Gulf Conflict*, 270–74.
46. Bob Woodward, *The Commanders* (New York: Simon and Schuster, 1991), 247–53.
47. John A. Warden III, *The Air Campaign: Planning for Combat* (San Jose: toExcel, 1998), 144–47.
48. Woodward, *The Commanders*, 253; Alastair Finlan, *The Gulf War 1991* (Oxford: Osprey, 2003), 31–32.
49. Robert H. Scales, Jr., *Certain Victory: The US Army in the Gulf War* (Washington, DC: Office of the Chief of Staff, US Army, 1993), 112, 125.
50. Frank N. Schubert and Theresa L. Kraus, General Editors, *The Whirlwind War: The United States Army in Operations DESERT SHIELD and*

DESERT STORM (Washington, DC: US Army Center of Military History, 1995), 101–2; Scales, *Certain Victory*, 119.

51. Scales, *Certain Victory*, 115–19.
52. Ibid., 123–24; Carl von Clausewitz, *On War*, edited and translated by Michael Howard and Peter Paret (Princeton: Princeton University Press, 1989), 119.
53. Thomas A. Keaney and Eliot A. Cohen, *The Gulf War Air Power Survey: Summary Report* (Washington, DC: Government Printing Office, 1993), 4–6.
54. Woodward, *The Commanders*, 304–07.
55. Finlan, *The Gulf War 1991*, 49–50. See, for example, Mark Grossman, *Encyclopedia of the Persian Gulf War* (Oxford: ABC-CLIO, 1995), 71–75, for a list of countries and their contributions to the Coalition.
56. See Michael B. Ballard, *Vicksburg: The Campaign That Opened the Mississippi River* (Chapel Hill: University of North Carolina Press, 2010) and Ken Ford, *Gazala 1942: Rommel's Greatest Victory* (Oxford: Osprey, 2008).
57. Scales, *Certain Victory*, 135–39.

6 INSTANT THUNDER

1. "Statement on Allied Military Action in the Gulf," January 16, 1991, Bush Papers, 1991, George Bush Presidential Library and Museum, http://bushlibrary.tamu.edu/research/public_papers.php?id=2624&year=1991&month=01, accessed June 30, 2011; Rodney P. Carlisle, *Persian Gulf War* (New York: Facts on File, 2003), 65.
2. Lawrence Freedman and Efraim Karsh, *The Gulf Conflict, 1990–1991: Diplomacy and War in the New World Order* (Princeton: Princeton University Press, 1993), 299–300; Bob Woodward, *The Commanders* (New York: Simon and Schuster), 370; George H.W. Bush and Brent Scowcroft, *A World Transformed* (New York: Knopf, 1998), 450.
3. "Address to the Nation Announcing Allied Military Action in the Persian Gulf," January 16, 1991, Bush Papers, 1991, George Bush Presidential Library and Museum, http://bushlibrary.tamu.edu/research/public_papers.php?id=2625&year=1991&month=01, accessed June 30, 2011.
4. "Address to the Nation Announcing Allied Military Action in the Persian Gulf," January 16, 1991, Bush Papers, 1991, George Bush Presidential Library and Museum, http://bushlibrary.tamu.edu/research/public_papers.php?id=2625&year=1991&month=01, accessed June 30, 2011.
5. "Responding to Iraqi Aggression in the Gulf," National Security Council Directive 54, January 15, 1991, Bush Presidential Library and Museum, http://bushlibrary.tamu.edu/research/pdfs/nsd/nsd54.pdf, accessed June 29, 2011.

6. "Responding to Iraqi Aggression in the Gulf," National Security Council Directive 54, January 15, 1991, Bush Presidential Library and Museum, http://bushlibrary.tamu.edu/research/pdfs/nsd/nsd54.pdf, accessed June 29, 2011.

7. Saddam Hussein, "Address to Iraqi People," January 20, 1991, in Steven A. Yetiv, *The Persian Gulf Crisis* (Westport, CT: Greenwood, 1997), 175–77.

8. Alastair Finlan, *The Gulf War 1991* (Oxford: Osprey, 2003), 34–35; Freedman and Karsh, *The Gulf Conflict*, 300–01; Carlisle, *Persian Gulf War*, 66.

9. Carlisle, *Persian Gulf War*, 68; Freedman and Karsh, *The Gulf Conflict 1991*, 321.

10. Freedman and Karsh, *The Gulf Conflict 1991*, 319–21; Carlisle, *Persian Gulf War*, 68.

11. Freedman and Karsh, *The Gulf Conflict 1991*, 321–22.

12. Finlan, *The Gulf War 1991*, 85; Freedman and Karsh, *The Gulf Conflict 1991*, 324–35.

13. Carlisle, *Persian Gulf War*, 72; Freedman and Karsh, *The Gulf Conflict 1991*, 326–28.

14. Carlisle, *Persian Gulf War*, 72; Bush and Scowcroft, *A World Transformed*, 457–59.

15. Rick Atkinson, *Crusade: The Untold Story of the Persian Gulf War* (Boston: Houghton Mifflin, 1993), 100–02.

16. "Remains Identified as Navy Captain Michael Scott Speicher," U.S. Department of Defense Press Release No. 571–09 (August 2, 2009), http://www.defense.gov/releases/release.aspx?releasedid=12862, accessed September 3, 3011.

17. Michael R. Gordon and Bernard E. Trainor, *The Generals' War: The Inside Story of the Conflict in the Gulf* (Boston: Little Brown, 1995), 249–6; Darrel D. Whitcomb, *Combat Search and Rescue in Desert Storm* (Maxwell Air Force Base, Alabama: Air University Press, 2006), 245–72.

18. Rick Atkinson, *Crusade: The Untold Story of the Persian Gulf War* (Boston: Houghton Mifflin, 1993), 126–39, 357–60, *passim*.

19. Rhonda Cornum is in 2011 a brigadier general in the United States Army. Elaine Sciolino, "Female POW Is Abused, Kindling Debate," *New York Times* (June 29, 1992), http://www.nytimes.com/1992/06/29/us/female-pow-is-abused-kindling-debate.html?pagewanted=all&src=pm, accessed October 2, 2011; see also Rhonda Cornum, with Peter Copeland, *She Went to War: The Rhonda Cornum Story* (New York: Presidio Press, 1993). For the experience of Bravo Two Zero, see among others Michael Asher, *The Real Bravo Two Zero* (London: Cassell/Orion, 2002). For an accounting of American POWs in the Gulf War, see Department of Defense Prisoner of War/Missing Personnel Office, "Desert Storm Captives/Unaccounted-for," http://www.dtic.mil/dpmo/gulf_war/documents/IRAQI05B.pdf, accessed October 24, 2011.

20. Finlan, *The Gulf War 1991*, 37–38; Carlisle, *Persian Gulf War*, 66, 74–75.

21. Kenneth M. Pollack, *Arabs at War: Military Effectiveness, 1948–1991* (Lincoln, NE: University of Nebraska Press, 2002), 241–43.

22. Bush and Scowcroft, *A World Transformed*, 452–55.

23. Defense Intelligence Assessment, "Mobile Short-Range Ballistic Missile Targeting in Operation DESERT STORM," November 1991, National Security Archive, http://www.gwu.edu/~ nsarchiv/NSAEBB/NSAEBB39/document8.pdf, accessed June 10, 2011; Gordon and Trainor, *The Generals' War*, 230.

24. Ibid., 241–47.

25. "Remarks to Raytheon Missile Systems Plant Employees in Andover, Massachusetts," February 15, 1991, Bush Papers, 1991, Bush Presidential Library and Museum, http://bushlibrary.tamu.edu/research/public_papers.php?id=2711&year=1991&month=2, accessed June 10, 2011.

26. Gordon and Trainor, *The Generals' War*, 239.

27. General Accounting Office, "Patriot Missile Defense: Software Problem Led to System Failure at Dhahran, Saudi Arabia," Report to the Chairman, Subcommittee on Investigations and Oversight, Committee on Science, Space, and Technology, House of Representatives, February 1992 (Washington, DC: Government Printing Office, 1992), http://archive.gao.gov/t2pbat6/145960.pdf, accessed June 8, 2011.

28. Gordon and Trainor, *The Generals' War*, 267–88; Freedman and Karsh, *The Gulf Conflict*, 364–67; H. Norman Schwarzkopf, with Peter Petre, *It Doesn't Take a Hero* (New York: Bantam Books, 1992), 424–27. See also David J. Morris, *Storm on the Horizon: Khafji—The Battle That Changed the Course of the Gulf War* (New York: Presidio Press, 2005).

29. Bush and Scowcroft, *A World Transformed*, 460–61; Baker, *The Politics of Diplomacy*, 392–95.

30. "Remarks to the American Association for the Advancement of Science," February 15, 1991, Bush Papers, 1991, Bush Presidential Library and Museum, http://bushlibrary.tamu.edu/research/public_papers.php?id=2709&year=1991&month=2, accessed June 30, 2011; Bush and Scowcroft, *A World Transformed*, 470–71.

31. Bush and Scowcroft, *A World Transformed*, 474–83; Freedman and Karsh, *The Gulf Conflict*, 380–85; "Address to the Nation Announcing Allied Military Ground Action the Persian Gulf," January 23, 1991, Bush Papers, 1991, Bush Presidential Library and Museum, http://bushlibrary.tamu.edu/research/public_papers.php?id=2734&year=1991&month=2, accessed June 30, 2011.

7   The Ground War

1. H. Norman Schwarzkopf, with Peter Petre, *It Doesn't Take a Hero* (New York: Bantam Books, 1992), 430–32.

2. Kenneth M. Pollack, *Arabs at War: Military Effectiveness, 1948–1991* (Lincoln, NE: University of Nebraska Press, 2002), 246.
3. Ibid., 246–47.
4. Frank N. Schubert and Theresa L. Kraus, General Editors, *The Whirlwind War: The United States Army in Operations DESERT SHIELD and DESERT STORM* (Washington, DC: U.S. Army Center of Military History, 1995), 55–67.
5. Ibid., 95–97.
6. Ibid., 146; Patrick Day Sloyan, "Buried Alive: U.S. Tanks Used Plows to Kill Thousands in Gulf War Trenches," *Newsday* (September 12, 1991): 1; John Simpson, *The Wars against Saddam: Taking the Hard Road to Baghdad* (Basingstoke: Palgrave Macmillan, 2004), 186–87.
7. Schubert and Kraus, *The Whirlwind War*, 147–51.
8. Rodney P. Carlisle, *Persian Gulf War* (New York: Facts on File, 2003), 87–88.
9. United States Army Center of Military History, *War in the Persian Gulf: Operations DESERT SHEILD and DESERT STORM, August 1990–March 1991* (Washington, DC: Center of Military History, 2010), 35–38.
10. Schubert and Krause, *The Whirlwind War*, 175–77.
11. Robert H. Scales, Jr., *et al.*, *Certain Victory: The US Army in the Gulf War* (Washington, DC: Office of the Chief of Staff, US Army, 1993), 247; Schubert and Kraus, *The Whirlwind War*, 177.
12. Alastair Finlan, *The Gulf War 1991* (Oxford: Osprey, 2003), 57–59; Schubert and Kraus, *The Whirlwind War*, 178–79.
13. Ibid., 181–82.
14. Pollack, *Arabs at War*, 238–39.
15. Finlan, *The Gulf War 1991*, 62; *War in the Persian Gulf*, 44–48, Carlisle, *Persian Gulf War*, 102–03.
16. *War in the Persian Gulf*, 50.
17. Schubert and Kraus, *The Whirlwind War*, 189–92; Michael R. Gordon and Bernard E. Trainor, *The Generals' War: The Inside Story of the Conflict in the Gulf* (Boston: Little Brown, 1995), 390–93.
18. Schubert and Kraus, *The Whirlwind War*, 192–93.
19. Carlisle, *Persian Gulf War*, 101; Gordon and Trainor, *The Generals' War*, 404.
20. Scales, *Certain Victory*, 291–300.
21. George H.W. Bush and Brent Scowcroft, *A World Transformed* (New York: Knopf, 1998), 483–84; Gordon and Trainor, *The Generals' War*, 400–402.
22. Pollack, *Arabs at War*, 256–58; Interrogation of Major Samir Ali Khadar, Commander, 2nd Battalion, 843rd Brigade, 45th Infantry Division, February 27, 1991, Forward Operation Base COBRA, interviewed by Major Robert K. Wright, Jr., U.S. Army Center of Military History, Catalog Number DSIT-002.

23. Schwarzkopf, *It Doesn't Take a Hero*, 467–71; Colin Powell, with Joseph Persico, *My American Journey* (New York: Ballantine, 1995), 520–23; Bush and Scowcroft, *A World Transformed*, 484–85.

24. "Address to the Nation on the Suspension of Allied Offensive Combat Operations in the Persian Gulf," February 27, 1991, Bush Papers, 1991, Bush Presidential Library and Museum, http://bushlibrary.tamu.edu/research/public_papers.php?id=2746&year=1991&month=2, accessed June 23, 2011.

25. Seymour Hersh, "Overwhelming Force," *The New Yorker* 76: 12 (May 22, 2000): 48–82; Daniel Forbes, "Gulf War Crimes?" Salon.com (May 15, 2000), http://www.salon.com/2000/05/15/hersh_4, accessed October 12, 2011; Gordon and Trainor, *The Generals' War*, 435–38.

26. Schwarzkopf, *It Doesn't Take a Hero*, 478.

27. Ibid., 481–91; Thomas E. Ricks, *Fiasco: The American Military Adventure in Iraq* (New York: Penguin, 2006), 4–6.

28. Table 8: Persian Gulf War Casualty Summary—DESERT SHIELD/DESERT STORM, in *American War and Military Operations Casualties: Lists and Statistics* (Washington, DC: Congressional Research Service, 2005), http://www.history.navy.mil/library/online/americanwarcasualty.htm#t8, accessed October 9, 2011; "92 Senegalese Soldiers Die in Saudi Arabia Air Crash," *New York Times* (March 22, 1991), http://www.nytimes.com/1991/03/22/world/after-the-war-92-senegalese-soldiers-die-in-saudi-arabia-air-crash.html, accessed October 2, 2011.

29. Freedman and Karsh, *The Gulf Conflict*, 407–9.

8   Aftermath and Legacies

1. Frank N. Schubert and Theresa L. Kraus, General Editors, *The Whirlwind War: The United States Army in Operations DESERT SHIELD and DESERT STORM* (Washington, DC: U.S. Army Center of Military History, 1995), 225–26; "Americans Remain Opposed to Lifting Sanctions against Iraq," *The Gallup Poll Monthly*, No. 309 (June 1991): 50.

2. Colin S. Gray, *Strategy for Chaos: Revolutions in Military Affairs and the Evidence of History* (London: Frank Cass, 2004).

3. UN Security Council Resolution 687, S/RES/687 (1991), 3 April 1991, United Nations Department of Public Information, *The United Nations and the Iraq-Kuwait Conflict, 1990–1996* (New York: United Nations Department of Public Information, 1996), 193–98.

4. Hassan Partow, *The Mesopotamia Marshlands: Demise of an Ecosystem* (Geneva: United Nations Environment Programme, 2001), 33–34, http://www.grid.unep.ch/activities/sustainable/tigris/mesopotamia.pdf, accessed October 3, 2011; Robert Fisk, *The Great War for Civilization: The Conquest of the Middle East* (New York: Viking, 2005), 842–47.

5. Fouad Ajami, "The Guns of August 1990: The Last 20 Years Would Have Been Very Different Had American Forces Taken That Open Road to Baghdad the First Time Around," *Wall Street Journal* (August 23, 2010): 15; George H.W. Bush and Brent Scowcroft, *A World Transformed* (New York: Knopf, 1998), 488–89; Colin Powell, with Joseph Persico, *My American Journey* (New York: Ballantine, 1995), 526–27; H. Norman Schwarzkopf, with Peter Petre, *It Doesn't Take a Hero* (New York: Bantam Books, 1992), 497–98; Charles Pope, "Cheney Changed His View on Iraq," *Seattle Post Intelligencer* (September 28, 2004), http://www.seattlepi.com/national/article/Cheney-changed-his-view-on-Iraq-1155325.php, accessed February 28, 2012; Mark Strauss, "Attacking Iraq," *Foreign Policy* No. 129 (March–April 2002): 14–19.

6. Steven A. Yetiv, *The Persian Gulf Crisis* (Westport, CT: Greenwood, 1997), 106–10; Terry H. Anderson, *Bush's Wars* (New York: Oxford, 2011), 43–45; Thomas E. Ricks, *Fiasco: The American Military Adventure in Iraq* (New York: Penguin, 2006), 18–22.

7. See, for example, Susan L. Carruthers, *The Media at War*, 2nd ed. (New York: Palgrave Macmillan, 2011).

8. For histories and examination of the Iraq War, see Williamson Murray and Robert H. Scales, Jr., *The Iraq War: A Military History* (Cambridge: Harvard University Press, 2003); John Keegan, *The Iraq War* (New York: Knopf, 2004); Michael R. Gordon and Bernard E. Trainor, *Cobra II: The Inside Story of the Invasion and Occupation of Iraq* (New York: Pantheon, 2006); Ricks, *Fiasco*; and Terry H. Anderson, *Bush's Wars* (New York: Oxford University Press, 2011); "Last Convoy of Troops Leaves Iraq, Marking War's End," *New York Times* (December 19, 2011): A6; Bret Stephens, "The Twenty Years' War: Defeating Saddam Took Nineteen Years Too Long," *Wall Street Journal* (August 23, 2010): 13.

9. "Radio Address to the United States Armed Forces Stationed in the Persian Gulf Region," March 3, 1991, Bush Papers, 1991, Bush Presidential Library and Museum, http://bushlibrary.tamu.edu/research/public_papers.php?id=2758&year=1991&month=3, accessed July 11, 2011.

10. "Remarks to Veterans' Service Organizations," March 4, 1991, Bush Papers, 1991, Bush Presidential Library and Museum, http://bushlibrary.tamu.edu/research/public_papers.php?id=2759&year=1991&month=3, accessed July 11, 2011.

11. Yetiv, *The Persian Gulf Crisis*, 126–27.

12. "The Persian Gulf War, February 1991: American Opinion on Events in the Persian Gulf," *The Gallup Poll Monthly*, No. 305 (February 1991): 10; "Build Up to War: American Opinion on Events in the Persian Gulf," *The Gallup Poll Monthly*, No. 304 (January 1991): 19.

13. "Victory's Aftermath: American Confidence Soars," *The Gallup Poll Monthly*, No. 306 (March 1991): 18.

14. "National Victory Celebration Parade," June 8, 1991, C-SPAN, http://www.c-spanvideo.org/program/18328-1, accessed July 12, 2011.

15. Michael J. Mazarr, Don M. Snider, and James A. Blackwell, Jr., *Desert Storm: The Gulf War and What We Learned* (Boulder, CO: Westview Press, 1993), 170.

16. United States Department of Defense, *Conduct of the Persian Gulf War: Final Report to Congress* (Washington, DC: Department of Defense, 1992), 740–42; Schubert and Kraus, *The Whirlwind War*, 209–15; Yetiv, *The Persian Gulf Crisis*, 128; Women in Combat: Interview with PFC Karen Perkins, SPC Vicky Craig, SGT Dorothy McNeill, SPC Tammy Marshall, and SSG Stephanie Quick, Interviewed by SSG LaDonna Kirkland, January 25, 1991, U.S. Army Center of Military History, Oral History Catalog No. DIST-AE-064.

17. United States Department of Veterans Affairs, "Gulf War Veterans' Illnesses," http://www.publichealth.va.gov/exposures/gulfwar/index.asp, accessed July 16, 2011; Alastair Finlan, *The Gulf War 1991* (Oxford: Osprey, 2003), 88; Yetiv, *The Persian Gulf Crisis*, 116–18; Rodney P. Carlisle, *Persian Gulf War* (New York: Facts on File, 2003), 120.

18. Robert H. Scales, Jr., *et al.*, *Certain Victory: The US Army in the Gulf War* (Washington, DC: Office of the Chief of Staff, US Army, 1993), 3, 380–84; Thomas A. Keaney and Eliot A. Cohen, *Revolution in Warfare? Air Power in the Persian Gulf* (Annapolis: Naval Institute Press, 1995), 209–26.

19. Bruce W. Watson, ed., "Lessons Learned and Lessons for the Future," in *Military Lessons of the Gulf War* (London: Greenhill Books, 1991), 213–14.

20. Andrew J. Bacevich, " 'Splendid Little War': America's Persian Gulf Adventure Ten Years on," in Andrew J. Bacevich and Efraim Inbar, eds., *The Gulf War of 1991 Reconsidered* (London: Frank Cass, 2003), 151–61.

21. Murray and Scales, *The Iraq War*, 7–13; Michael R. Gordon and Bernard E. Trainor, *The General's War: The Inside Story of the Conflict in the Gulf* (Boston: Little Brown, 1995), 472–73.

22. Jeffrey Record, *Hollow Victory: A Contrary View of the Gulf War* (Washington, DC: Brassey's, 1993), 134, 149; Yetiv, *The Persian Gulf Crisis*, 128–29; Watson, "Lessons Learned and Lessons for the Future," 218.

23. Record, *Hollow Victory*, 134–47; Gordon and Trainor, *The Generals' War*, 474; Benjamin S. Lambeth, *The Transformation of American Air Power* (Ithaca: Cornell University Press, 2000), 264–68.

24. Thomas A. Keaney and Eliot A. Cohen, *Revolution in Warfare? Air Power in the Persian Gulf War* (Annapolis: Naval Institute Press, 1995), 201.

25. MacGregor Knox and Williamson Murray, *The Dynamics of Military Revolution, 1300–2050* (Cambridge: Cambridge University Press, 2001), 189.

26. Stephen Biddle, *Military Power: Explaining Victory and Defeat in Modern Battle* (Princeton: Princeton University Press, 2004), 132–49.

27. Knox and Murray, *The Dynamics of Military Revolution*, 189–90.

28. Steven Metz and James Kietvit, *Strategy and the Revolution in Military Affairs: From Theory to Policy* (Carlisle Barracks: United States Army

War College, Strategic Studies Institute, 1995), 9, 40, http://www.strategicstudiesinstitute.army.mil/pubs/display.cfm?pubID=236, accessed October 15, 2011. Italics in the original.

29. See Keith L. Shimko, *The Iraq Wars and America's Military Revolution* (Cambridge: Cambridge University Press, 2010).

30. See, for example, Max Boot, *War Made New: Weapons, Warriors, and the Making of the Modern World* (New York: Gotham, 2007); Dima Adamsky, *The Culture of Military Innovation: The Impact of Cultural Factors on the Revolution in Military Affairs in Russia, the US, and Israel* (Stanford: Stanford University Press, 2010).

31. Brian McAllister Linn, *The Echo of Battle: The Army's Way of War* (Cambridge: Harvard University Press, 2007), 226–29.

32. Jeremy Black, *Rethinking Military History* (New York: Routledge, 2004), 148, 236.

33. Ricks, *Fiasco*, 5–6.

34. Thomas G. Mahnken, "A Squandered Opportunity? The Decision to End the Gulf War," in Andrew Bacevich and Efraim Inbar, eds., *The Gulf War of 1991 Reconsidered* (London: Frank Cass, 2003), 121–45; Record, *Hollow Victory*, 159.

35. Pollack, *Arabs at War*, 260–66.

36. "Address before a Joint Session of the Congress on the Cessation of the Persian Gulf Conflict," Bush Papers, 1991, Bush Presidential Library and Museum, http://bushlibrary.tamu.edu/research/public_papers.php?id=2767&year=1991&month=3, accessed July 10, 2011.

37. See Harry G. Summers, *On Strategy II: A Critical Analysis of the Gulf War* (New York: Dell, 1992).

Glossary and Acronyms

A-6	Two-crew attack aircraft designed and built by Grumman Aerospace in 1960 and acquired by the US Navy and Marine Corps in 1963, retired from service in 1997
A-10	Single-seat aircraft used for close air support and ground attack. Known as the Thunderbolt or Warthog, the A-10 was designed and built by Fairchild Republic in 1972 and acquired by the US Air Force in 1977
AAA	Anti-aircraft artillery, also called AA or Triple A
AH-1	Two-crew attack helicopter known as the Cobra, designed and built by Bell Helicopter. First flown in 1965 and acquired by the US military in 1967
AH-64A	Two-crew attack helicopter known as the Apache, designed by Hughes Helicopters and built by Boeing and McDonnell Douglas. First flown in 1985 and acquired by the US military in 1986
AJAX	Operational name for the 1953 American-backed coup against the government of Iranian Prime Minister Mohammad Mossadegh
Arab League	Also known as the League of Arab States. Formed in 1945, the Arab League includes Iraq, Kuwait, Egypt, Saudi Arabia, Jordan, and Syria, among several other Arab nations across North Africa and the Middle East
ATO	Air tasking order
AVF	All-volunteer force
AWACS	Airborne Warning and Control System. Introduced in 1977, AWACS is an airborne radar system that distinguishes enemy and friendly aircraft. In the US Air Force, AWACS is often used both to describe both the system and Boeing E-3 Sentry aircraft upon which AWACS is mounted and operated
B-52	Long-range jet bomber built by Boeing, known as the Stratofortress. The B-52 first flew in 1952 and served

	as the backbone of Strategic Air Command (SAC) since its acquisition by the US Air Force in 1955
Ba'ath Party	Arab nationalist political party founded in Syria in 1946 that came to prominence in Iraq in the late 1950s before becoming the leading party in Iraq in the 1960s; party of Saddam Hussein
BDA	Battle Damage Assessment
Bradley Fighting Vehicle	Armored, tracked vehicle developed by United Defense for the US Army and first used in 1981
CAS	Close air support
CENTO	Central Treaty Organization, originally the Middle East Treaty Organization (METO), formed in 1955
CIA	Central Intelligence Agency
CINC	Commander-in-chief
CNN	Cable News Network, launched in 1982 by media entrepreneur Ted Turner as the world's first twenty-four-hour television news network
Collateral damage	Unintended damage from military attack on legitimate enemy forces or targets
CSAR	Combat search and rescue
DESERT SABRE	Operational name for the ground phase of DESERT STORM
DESERT SHIELD	Operational name for defensive deployment to defend Saudi Arabia from possible Iraqi attack
DESERT STORM	Operational name for American-led Coalition offensive to force Iraqi military forces from Kuwait
DIA	Defense Intelligence Agency
Dumb bomb	Air-delivered conventional bomb that has no guidance system
F-1 Mirage	Single-engine attack fighter, developed by Dassault in 1966 and used by several countries, including France, Spain, and Iraq
F-4 Wild Weasel	Fighter-bomber equipped to destroy radar and SAMs
F-5	Twin-engine jet fighter, first built by Northrop 1959, with several subsequent variations; used by the US Navy and other countries, including Iran and Saudi Arabia
F-111 Aardvark	Single-engine fighter-bomber, developed by General Dynamics in 1964 and added to the United States Air Force fleet in 1967
F-117A Nighthawk	Multipurpose jet fighter, developed by Lockheed Martin and first flown in 1981; first USAF aircraft with radar-evading "stealth" capability

F-14A Tomcat	Twin-engined jet fighter, developed by Grumman and first flown in 1970; served as primary US Navy fighter aircraft from 1974 through the early 2000s
F-15E	Strike Eagle Twin-engine jet fighter, developed by McDonnell Douglas and first flown in 1972; common to the USAF as well as the Saudi and Israeli air forces
F-16	Fighting Falcon Single-engine jet multi-purpose fighter, developed by General Dynamics and first flown in 1974; common to the USAF, as well as numerous other air forces, including that of Israel, Egypt, Turkey, Jordan, and Bahrain
FOB	Forward operating base
GCFCG	Gulf Crisis Financial Coordination Group
GDP	Gross domestic product
GPS	Global Positioning System
Gulf War Syndrome	Range of illnesses, diseases, and other health issues associated with service in the Gulf War, possible due to exposure to chemical weapons, pesticides, depleted uranium, or inoculations
HARMs	High-speed anti-radiation missiles, used by F-4 Wild Weasels to destroy anti-aircraft defense networks
HMMWV	High mobility multipurpose wheeled vehicle, known as the Humvee or Hummer, first produced in 1984
ICP	Iraqi Communist Party
INSTANT THUNDER	Operational name for DESERT STORM air campaign
IPC	Iraq Petroleum Company
JFACC	Joint Force Air Component Commander
JFC	Joint Forces Command
JSTARS	Joint Surveillance Target Attack Radar System, primary airborne command-and-control system of the USAF, developed by Northrop Grumman using a Boeing 707 airframe
KIA	Killed-in-action
KTO	Kuwait Theater of Operations
LGB	Laser-guided bomb
M1 Abrams	American main battle tank, first used in 1970, developed by Chrysler Defense
MEDO	Middle East Defense Organization
MEF	Marine Expeditionary Force, consists of a Marine division, air wing, and supporting units
METT-T	Mission, enemy, terrain, troops and time

MH-53 Pave Low	Search and rescue helicopter, first built by Sikorsky in 1967; used by the US Air Force
MI-5	British intelligence, military branch
MIA	Missing-in-action
MiG-29	Soviet-made jet fighter first flown in 1977 that became the mainstay of the Soviet Air Force to face American F-15 and F-16 fighter aircraft
MRE	Meal, Ready-to-Eat
NATO	North Atlantic Treaty Organization
NBC	Nuclear, biological, and chemical weapons
NCRC	National Council of the Revolutionary Command
NRC	National Revolutionary Council
NORTHERN WATCH	Operational name for enforcement of UN-mandated no-fly zone over northern Iraq
NSD	National Security Directive
OPEC	Oil Producing and Exporting Countries
Patriot	Raytheon Patriot mobile missile defense system
PFC	Private first class
PGMs	Precision-guided munitions
PLO	Palestinian Liberation Organization
PME	Professional military education
POL	Petroleum, oil, lubricants
POW	Prisoner of war
RAF	Royal Air Force
RCC	Revolutionary Command Council
RDF	Rapid Deployment Force
RMA	Revolution in military affairs
SAC	Strategic Air Command
SAM	Surface-to-air missile
SAS	British Special Air Service
Scud	Surface-to-surface missile, launched from either fixed sites or mobile launchers
Smart bomb	Military term for a radar or laser guided bomb
Sortie	An individual air mission
SOUTHERN WATCH	Operational name for enforcement of UN-mandated no-fly zone over southern Iraq
SSM	Surface-to-surface missile
T-54 tank	Soviet-made main battle tank, first produced in 1947, later produced in Poland and Czechoslovakia
T-55 tank	Soviet-made main battle tank, first produced in 1950, later produced in Poland and Czechoslovakia
T-62 tanks	Soviet-made main battle tank, first produced in 1961
T-72 tank	Soviet-made main battle tank, first produced in 1970

Tomahawk	American-made long-range cruise missile, launched from ships and submarines, also known as a TLAM—Tomahawk Land Attack Missile
Tornado	Multipurpose jet fighter, first produced by Panavia in 1974, common to the British, Canadian, Saudi, German, and Italian air forces
TOW	Tube-launched optically tracked wire-command guided anti-tank missile
UAE	United Arab Emirates
UAR	United Arab Republic
UH-1H	Vietnam-era utility helicopter, known as a Huey
UH-60A Black Hawk	Utility helicopter
UN	United Nations
UNSCOM	United Nations Special Commission, established in 1991 to monitor Iraqi compliance with UN Security Council resolutions stemming from the Iraqi invasion of Kuwait and the Gulf War
USAF	United States Air Force
USCENTCOM or CENTCOM	United States Central Command
Vietnam Syndrome	Term used in public discourse referring to the impact of the Vietnam War on American domestic politics, military affairs, and foreign relations
VX	Chemical nerve agent, banned by international protocol in the 1990s
WIA	Wounded-in-action
WMD	Weapons of mass destruction

Select Bibliography

Adamsky, Dina. *The Culture of Military Innovation: The Impact of Cultural Factors on the Revolution in Military Affairs in Russia, the US, and Israel.* Stanford: Stanford University Press, 2010.

Amos, Deborah. *Lines in the Sand: Desert Storm and the Remaking of the Arab World.* New York: Simon and Schuster, 1992.

Anderson, Terry H. *Bush's Wars.* New York: Oxford University Press, 2011.

Atkinson, Rick. *Crusade: The Untold Story of the Persian Gulf War.* Boston: Houghton Mifflin, 1993.

Bacevich, Andrew J., and Efraim Inbar, eds. *The Gulf War of 1991 Reconsidered.* London: Frank Cass, 2003.

Baker, James A. *The Politics of Diplomacy: Revolution, War, and Peace, 1989–1992.* New York: Putnam, 1992.

Bennett, W. Lance. *Taken by Storm: The Media, Public Opinion, and US Foreign Policy in the Gulf War.* Chicago: University of Chicago Press, 1994.

Bin, Alberto, Richard Hill, and Archer Jones. *Desert Storm: A Forgotten War.* Westport, CT: Greenwood, 1998.

Blair, Arthur H. *At War in the Gulf: A Chronology.* College Station, TX: Texas A&M University Press, 1992.

Bloom, Saul, John Miller, James Warner, and Philippa Winkler, eds. *Hidden Casualties: Environmental, Health, and Political Consequences of the Persian Gulf War.* Berkeley, CA: North Atlantic Books, 1994.

Bourque, Stephen A. *Jayhawk!: The VII Corps in the Persian Gulf War.* Washington, DC: US Army Center of Military History, 2002.

Bush, George H.W., and Brent Scowcroft. A *World Transformed.* New York: Knopf, 1998.

Carlisle, Rodney P. *Persian Gulf War.* New York: Facts on File, 2003.

Carruthers, Susan L. *The Media at War*, 2nd ed. New York: Palgrave Macmillan, 2011.

Catherwood, Christopher. *Churchill's Folly: How Winston Churchill Created Modern Iraq.* New York: Carroll and Graf, 2004.

Clancy, Tom, and Fred Franks, Jr. *Into the Storm: A Study in Command.* New York: G. P. Putnam's Sons, 1997.

Cohen, Roger, and Claudia Gatti. *In the Eye of the Storm: The Life of General H. Norman Schwarzkopf.* New York: Farrar, Straus, and Giroux, 1991.

Cordingley, Patrick. *In the Eye of the Storm: Commanding Desert Rats in the Gulf War.* London: Hodder & Stoughton, 1996.

Cornum, Rhonda, with Peter Copeland. *She Went to War: The Rhonda Cornum Story.* New York: Presidio Press, 1993.

Davis, Richard G. *Decisive Force: Strategic Bombing in the Gulf War.* Washington, DC: US Air Force History and Museums Program, 1996.

Davis, Richard G. *Strategic Air Power in Desert Storm.* Washington, DC: Air Force History and Museums Program, 1995.

Denton, Robert E. *The Media and the Persian Gulf War.* New York: Praeger, 1993.

Dunnigan, James F., and Austin Bay. *From Shield to Storm: High-Tech Weapons, Military Strategy, and Coalition Warfare in the Persian Gulf.* New York: William Morrow, 1992.

El-Baz, Farouk, and R.M. Makharita. *The Gulf War and the Environment.* Lausanne, Switzerland: Gordon and Breach, 1994.

Fattah, Hala, with Frank Caso. *A Brief History of Iraq.* New York: Checkmark Books, 2009.

Fialka, John J. *Hotel Warriors: Covering the Gulf War.* Washington, DC: Woodrow Wilson Center Press, 1991.

Finlan, Alastair. *The Gulf War, 1991.* Oxford: Osprey, 2003.

Fisk, Robert. *The Great War for Civilization: The Conquest of the Middle East.* New York: Viking, 2005.

Freedman, Lawrence, and Efraim Karsh. *The Gulf Conflict, 1990–1991: Diplomacy and War in the New World Order.* Princeton: Princeton University Press, 1993.

Freidman, Norman. *Desert Victory: The War for Kuwait.* Annapolis: Naval Institute Press, 1992.

Fromkin, David. *A Peace to End All Peace: Creating the Modern Middle East, 1914–1921.* New York: Henry Holt, 1989.

Gehring, Stephen P. *From the Fulda Gap to Kuwait: US Army, Europe and the Gulf War.* Washington, DC: Government Printing Office, 1998.

Gordon, Michael R., and Bernard E. Trainor. *The General's War: The Inside Story of the Conflict in the Gulf.* Boston: Little Brown, 1995.

Greenberg, Bradley S., and Walter Gantz, eds. *Desert Storm and the Mass Media.* Cresskill, NJ: Hampton Press, 1993.

Grossman, Mark. *Encyclopedia of the Persian Gulf War.* Santa Barbara: ABC-CLIO, 1995.

Hahn, Peter L. *Missions Accomplished? The United States and Iraq since World War I.* New York: Oxford University Press, 2012.

Hallion, Richard P. *Stormover Iraq: Air Power and the Gulf War.* Washington, DC: Smithsonian Institution Press, 1992.

Hawley, T.M. *Against the Fires of Hell: The Environmental Disaster of the Gulf War.* New York: Harcourt Brace Jovanovich, 1992.

Head, William, and Earl H. Tilford, Jr., eds. *The Eagle in the Desert: Looking Back on US Involvement in the Persian Gulf.* Westport, CT: Praeger, 1996.

Hess, Gary R. *Presidential Decisions for Going to War: Korea, Vietnam, and the Persian Gulf.* Baltimore: Johns Hopkins University Press, 2001.

Hilsman, Roger. *George Bush vs. Saddam Hussein: Military Success! Political Failure?* Novato, CA: Lyford Books, 1992.

Hiro, Dilip. *Desert Shield to Desert Storm: The Second Gulf War.* New York: Routledge, 1992.

Hunt, Courtney. *The History of Modern Iraq.* Westport, CT: Greenwood Press, 2005.

Johnson, Rob. *The Iran-Iraq War.* New York: Palgrave Macmillan, 2011.

Karsh, Efraim. *The Iran-Iraq War, 1980–1988.* Oxford: Osprey, 2002.

Keaney, Thomas A., and Eliot A. Cohen. *Gulf War Air Power Survey: Summary Report.* Washington, DC: Government Printing Office, 1993.

Khadduri, Majid, and Edmund Ghareeb. *War in the Gulf, 1990–1991: The Iraqi-Kuwait Conflict and Its Implications.* New York: Oxford University Press, 1997.

Khalid bin Sultan, Prince, with Patrick Seale. *Desert Warrior: A Personal View of the Gulf War by the Joint Forces Commander.* New York: HarperCollins, 1995.

Knox, MacGregor, and Williamson Murray. *The Dynamics of Military Revolution, 1300–2050.* Cambridge: Cambridge University Press, 2001.

Lambeth, Benjamin S. *The Transformation of American Air Power.* Ithaca: Cornell University Press, 2000.

Linn, Brian McAllister. *The Echo of Battle: The Army's Way of War.* Cambridge: Harvard University Press, 2007.

Lowery, Richard. *The Gulf War Chronicles: A Military History of the First War with Iraq.* Lincoln, NE: iUniverse, 2003.

Marolda, Edward J., and Robert J. Schneller. *Shield and Sword: The US Navy in the Persian Gulf War.* Washington, DC: Naval Historical Center, 1998.

Mazzar, Michael J., Don M. Snider, and James Blackwell, Jr. *Desert Storm: The Gulf War and What We Learned.* Boulder, CO: Westview, 1993.

McArthur, John R. *Second Front: Censorship and Propaganda in the 1991 Gulf War.* New York: Hill and Wang, 1992.

McDonnell, Janet A. *After Desert Storm: The US Army and the Reconstruction of Kuwait.* Washington, DC: Department of the Army, 1999.

Menarchik, Douglas. *Powerlift—Getting to Desert Storm: Strategic Transportation and Strategy in the New World Order.* Westport, CT: Praeger, 1993.

Moore, Molly. *A Woman at War: Storming Kuwait with the US Marines.* New York: Scribner Associates Inc., 1993.

Morrin, Jean, and Richard H. Gimblett. *Operation Friction 1990–1991: The Canadian Forces in the Persian Gulf.* Toronto: Dundurn Press, 1997.

Morris, David J. *Storm on the Horizon: Khafji—the Battle That Changed the Course of the Gulf War.* New York: Presidio Press, 2005.

Morrison, David E. *Television and the Gulf War*. London: John Libbey, 1992.

Mueller, John. *Policy and Opinion in the Gulf War*. Chicago: University of Chicago Press, 1994.

Nye, Joseph S., and Roger K. Smith, eds. *After the Storm: Lessons from the Gulf War*. Lanham, MD: Aspen Institute and Madison Books, 1992.

Oren, Michael B. *Power, Faith, and Fantasy: America in the Middle East, 1776 to the Present*. New York: Norton, 2007.

Pagonis, William G. *Moving Mountains: Lessons in Leadership and Logistics from the Gulf War*. Boston: Harvard Business School Press, 1992.

Palmer, Michael A. *Guardians of the Gulf: A History of America's Expanding Role in the Persian Gulf, 1833–1992*. New York: Free Press, 1992.

Pape, Robert A. *Bombing to Win: Air Power and Coercion in War*. Ithaca, NY: Cornell University Press, 1995.

Pelletiere, Stephen C. *The Iran-Iraq War: Chaos in a Vacuum*. Westport, CT: Praeger, 1992.

Polk, William R. *Understanding Iraq*. New York: Harper Collins, 2005.

Pollack, Kenneth. *Arabs at War: Military Effectiveness, 1948–1991*. Lincoln, NE: University of Nebraska Press, 2002.

Potter, Lawrence G., ed. *The Persian Gulf in History*. New York: Palgrave Macmillan, 2009.

Powell, Colin, with Joseph Persico. *My American Journey*. New York: Ballantine, 1995.

Quilter, Charles J. *With the I Marine Expeditionary Force in Desert Shield and Desert Storm*. Washington, DC: History and Museums Division, Headquarters, US Marine Corps, 1993.

Record, Jeffrey. *Hollow Victory: A Contrary View of the Gulf War*. Washington, DC: Brassey's, 1993.

Reynolds, Richard T. *The Heart of the Storm: The Genesis of the Air Campaign against Iraq*. Maxwell Air Force Base, AL: Air University Press, 1995.

Rottman, Gordon L. *Armies of the Gulf War*. London: Osprey, 1993.

Sasson, Jean P. *The Rape of Kuwait: The True Story of Iraqi Atrocities against a Civilian Population*. New York: Knightsbridge, 1991.

Scales, Robert H., Jr., et al. *Certain Victory: The US Army in the Gulf War*. Washington, DC: Office of the Chief of Staff, US Army, 1993.

Schubert, Frank N., and Theresa L. Kraus, eds. *The Whirlwind War: The United States Army in Operations DESERT SHIELD and DESERT STORM*. Washington, DC: US Army Center of Military History, 1995.

Schwarzkopf, H. Norman, with Peter Petre. *It Doesn't Take a Hero*. New York: Bantam Books, 1992.

Shimko, Keith L. *The Iraq Wars and America's Military Revolution*. Cambridge: Cambridge University Press, 2010.

Sifry, Micah, and Christopher Cerf. *The Gulf War Reader: History, Documents, Opinion*. New York: Random House, 1991.

Simons, Geoff. *Iraq: From Sumer to Saddam*. New York: St. Martin's Press, 1994.

Simpson, John. *The Wars against Saddam: Taking the Hard Road to Baghdad.* Basingstoke: Palgrave Macmillan, 2004.

Smith, Jean Edward. *George Bush's War.* New York: Henry Holt, 1992.

Summers, Harry G. *On Strategy II: A Critical Analysis of the Gulf War.* New York: Dell, 1992.

Townshend, Charles. *When God Made Hell, the British Invasion of Mesopotamia and the Creation of Iraq, 1914–1921.* London: Faber and Faber, 2010.

Tripp, Charles. *A History of Iraq*, 3rd ed. Cambridge: Cambridge University Press, 2007.

United Nations, Department of Public Information. *The United Nations and the Iraq-Kuwait Conflict, 1990–1996.* New York: United Nations Department of Public Information, 1996.

United States Army Center of Military History. *War in the Persian Gulf: Operations DESERT SHIELD and DESERT STORM, August 1990–March 1991.* Washington, DC: US Army Center of Military History, 2010.

United States Department of Defense. *Conduct of the Persian Gulf War: Final Report to Congress.* Washington, DC: Department of Defense, 1992.

US News & World Report. *Triumph without Victory: The Unreported History of the Persian Gulf War.* New York: Times Books, 1992.

Warden, John A. *The Air Campaign: Planning for Combat.* San Jose: toExcel, 1998.

Watson, Bruce W., Bruce George, Peter Tsouras, and B.L. Cyr. *Military Lessons of the Gulf War.* London: Greenhill Books, 1993.

Woodward, Bob. *The Commanders.* New York: Simon and Schuster, 1991.

Yetiv, Steve A. *The Persian Gulf Crisis.* Westport, CT: Greenwood, 1997.

Index

Note: Arabic names beginning with the prefix 'al-' are alphabetised under the substantive part of the name and not the prefix. Locators in **bold** type indicate figures/illustrations.